Microsoft® Office

ILLUSTRATED

BRIEF

Jennifer A. Duffy

THOMSON
COURSE TECHNOLOGY

Australia • Canada • Mexico • Singapore • Spain • United Kingdom • United States

THOMSON

COURSE TECHNOLOGY

Microsoft® Office Word 2003 - Illustrated Brief

Jennifer A. Duffy

Executive Editor:
Nicole Jones Pinard

Product Manager:
Christina Kling Garrett

Associate Product Manager:
Emilie Perreault

Production Editor:
Melissa Panagos

Developmental Editor:
Pamela Conrad

Editorial Assistant:
Abbey Reider

QA Manuscript Reviewers:
John Freitas
Holly Schabowski

Text Designer:
Joseph Lee, Black Fish Design

Composition House:
GEX Publishing Services

Printed in the United States of America

1 2 3 4 5 6 7 8 9 BM 07 06 05 04 03

For more information, contact Course Technology, 25 Thomson Place, Boston, Massachusetts, 02210.

Or you can visit us on the World Wide Web at www.course.com

ISBN 0-619-18800-6

The Illustrated Series Vision

Teaching and writing about computer applications can be extremely rewarding and challenging. How do we engage students and keep their interest? How do we teach them skills that they can easily apply on the job? As we set out to write this book, our goals were to develop a textbook that

- works for a beginning student
- provides varied, flexible, and meaningful exercises and projects to reinforce skills
- serves as a reference tool
- makes your job as an educator easier, by providing resources above and beyond the textbook to help you teach your course

Our popular, streamlined format is based on advice from instructional designers and customers. This flexible design presents each lesson on a two-page spread, with step-by-step instructions on the left, and screen illustrations on the right. This signature style, coupled with high-caliber content, provides a comprehensive yet manageable introduction to Microsoft Office Word 2003—it is a teaching package for the instructor and a learning experience for the student.

Acknowledgments

Many talented people at Course Technology helped to shape this book — thank you all. I am especially indebted to Pam Conrad for her precision editing and endless good cheer throughout the many months of writing. On the home front, I am ever grateful to my family for their patience, and to Nancy Macalaster, who so lovingly cared for my babies when I needed to be at my desk.

Jennifer A. Duffy
and the Illustrated Team

Preface

Welcome to *Microsoft® Office Word 2003–Illustrated Brief*. Each lesson in this book contains elements pictured to the right.

How is the book organized?

The book is organized into four units on Word, covering creating, editing, and formatting text and documents.

What kinds of assignments are included in the book? At what level of difficulty?

The lessons use MediaLoft, a fictional chain of bookstores, as the case study. The assignments on the light purple pages at the end of each unit increase in difficulty. Data files and case studies, with many international examples, provide a great variety of interesting and relevant business applications. Assignments include:

- **Concepts Reviews** include multiple choice, matching, and screen identification questions.
- **Skills Reviews** provide additional hands-on, step-by-step reinforcement.
- **Independent Challenges** are case projects requiring critical thinking and application of the unit skills. The Independent Challenges increase in difficulty, with the first one in each unit being the easiest (most step-by-step with detailed instructions). Independent Challenges 2 and 3 become increasingly open-ended, requiring more independent problem solving.
- **E-Quest Independent Challenges** are case projects with a Web focus. E-Quests require the use of the World Wide Web to conduct research to complete the project.
- **Advanced Challenge Exercises** set within the Independent Challenges provide optional steps for more advanced students.
- **Visual Workshops** are practical, self-graded capstone projects that require independent problem solving.

Every lesson features large, full-color representations of what the screen should look like as students complete the numbered steps.

Brightly colored tabs indicate which section of the book you are in.

FIGURE A-7: Save As dialog box

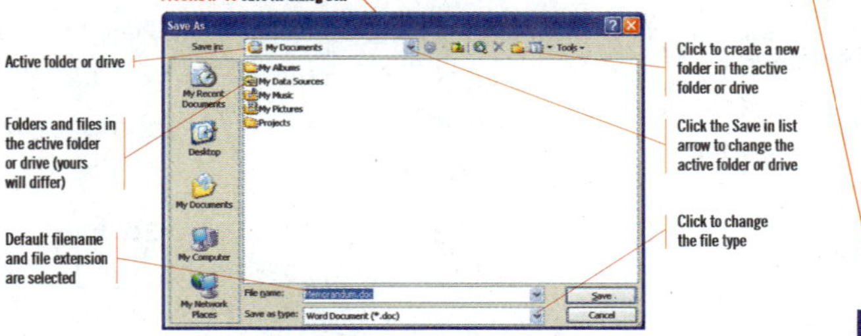

Word 2003

FIGURE A-8: File to be saved to the UnitA folder

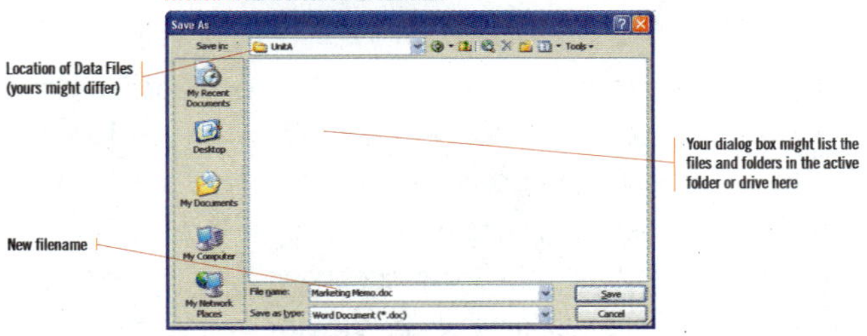

TABLE A-3: Save As dialog box buttons

button	use to
Back	Navigate to the drive or folder previously shown in the Save in list box; click the Back list arrow to navigate to a recently displayed drive or folder
Up One Level	Navigate to the next highest level in the folder hierarchy (to the drive or folder that contains the current folder)
Search the Web	Connect to the World Wide Web to locate a folder or file
Delete	Delete the selected folder or file
Create New Folder	Create a new folder in the current folder or drive
Views	Change the way folder and file information is shown in the Save As dialog box; click the Views list arrow to open a menu of options
Tools	Open a menu of commands related to the selected drive, folder, or file

OFFICE–103

GETTING STARTED WITH WORD 2003 WORD A-11

Tables provide quickly accessible summaries of key terms, toolbar buttons, or keyboard alternatives connected with the lesson material. Students can refer easily to this information when working on their own projects at a later time.

The pages are numbered according to section and unit. Word indicates the section, A indicates the unit, 11 indicates the page.

What online content solutions are available to accompany this book?

Visit www.course.com for more information on our online content for Illustrated titles. Options include:

MyCourse 2.0

Need a quick, simple tool to help you manage your course? Try MyCourse 2.0, the most flexible syllabus and content management tool available. MyCourse 2.0 offers you brand new content, including Topic Reviews, Extra Case Projects, and Quizzes, to accompany this book.

WebCT

Course Technology and WebCT have partnered to provide you with the highest quality online resources and Web-based tools for your class. Course Technology offers content for this book to help you create your WebCT class, such as a suggested Syllabus, Lecture Notes, Practice Test questions, and more.

Blackboard

Course Technology and Blackboard have also partnered to provide you with the highest quality online resources and Web-based tools for your class. Course Technology offers content for this book to help you create your Blackboard class, such as a suggested Syllabus, Lecture Notes, Practice Test questions, and more.

Instructor Resources

The Instructor Resources CD is Course Technology's way of putting the resources and information needed to teach and learn effectively into your hands. We believe that with an integrated array of teaching and learning tools that offers you and your students a broad range of technology-based instructional options, this CD represents the highest quality and most cutting edge resources available to instructors today. Many of these resources are available at www.course.com. The resources available with this book are:

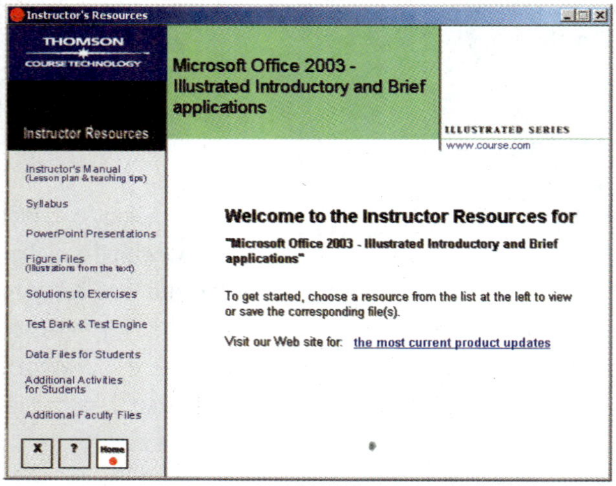

- **Data Files for Students**—To complete most of the units in this book, your students will need Data Files. Put them on a file server for students to copy. The Data Files are available on the Instructor Resources CD-ROM and the Review Pack, and can also be downloaded from www.course.com.

  Instruct students to use the **Data Files List** located on the Review Pack and the Instructor Resources CD. This list gives instructions on copying and organizing files.

- **Solutions to Exercises**—Solutions to Exercises contains every file students are asked to create or modify in the lessons and End-of-Unit material. A Help file on the Instructor Resource CD includes information for using the Solution Files. There is also a document outlining the solutions for the End-of-Unit Concepts Review, Skills Review, and Independent Challenges.
- **PowerPoint Presentations**—Each unit has a corresponding PowerPoint presentation that you can use in lecture, distribute to your students, or customize to suit your course.
- **Instructor's Manual**—Available as an electronic file, the Instructor's Manual is quality-assurance tested and includes unit overviews and detailed lecture topics with teaching tips for each unit.
- **Sample Syllabus**—Prepare and customize your course easily using this sample course outline.
- **Figure Files**—The figures in the text are provided on the Instructor Resources CD to help you illustrate key topics or concepts. You can create traditional overhead transparencies by printing the figure files. Or you can create electronic slide shows by using the figures in a presentation program such as PowerPoint.
- **ExamView**—ExamView is a powerful testing software package that allows you to create and administer printed, computer (LAN-based), and Internet exams. ExamView includes hundreds of questions that correspond to the topics covered in this text, enabling students to generate detailed study guides that include page references for further review. The computer-based and Internet testing components allow students to take exams at their computers, and also save you time by grading each exam automatically.

SAM 2003 Assessment & Training

SAM 2003 helps you energize your class exams and training assignments by allowing students to learn and test important computer skills in an active, hands-on environment.

With SAM 2003 Assessment, you create powerful interactive exams on critical applications such as Word, Outlook, PowerPoint, Windows, the Internet, and much more. The exams simulate the application environment, allowing your students to demonstrate their knowledge and think through the skill by performing real-world tasks.

Designed to be used with the Illustrated series, SAM 2003 Assessment & Training includes built-in page references so students can create study guides that match the Illustrated textbooks you use in class. Powerful administrative options allow you to schedule exams and assignments, secure your tests, and run reports with almost limitless flexibility.

Contents

Read This Before You Begin

Software Information and Required Installation

This book was written and tested using Microsoft Office 2003 - Professional Edition, with a typical installation on Microsoft Windows XP, including installation of the most recent Windows XP Service Pack, and with Internet Explorer 6.0 or higher. Some of the exercises in this book assume that your computer is connected to the Internet. If you are not connected to the Internet, see your instructor.

Tips for Students

What are Data Files?

To complete many of the units in this book, you need to use Data Files. A Data File contains a partially completed document, so that you don't have to type in all the information in the document yourself. Your instructor will either provide you with copies of the Data Files or ask you to make your own copies. Your instructor can also give you instructions on how to organize your files, as well as a complete file listing, or you can find the list and the instructions for organizing your files in the Review Pack. In addition, because Unit A does not have supplied Data Files, you will need to create a Unit A directory at the same level as all of the other unit directories in order to save the files you create in Unit A.

Why is my screen different from the book?

Your desktop components and some dialog box options might be different if you are using an operating system other than Windows XP.

Depending on your computer hardware and the Display settings on your computer, you may notice the following differences:

- Your screen may look larger or smaller because of your screen resolution (the height and width of your screen).
- Your title bars and dialog boxes may not display file extensions. To display file extensions, click Start on the taskbar, click Control Panel, click Appearance and Themes, then click Folder Options. Click the View tab if necessary, click Hide extensions for known file types to deselect it, then click OK. Your Office dialog boxes and title bars should now display file extensions.
- Depending on your Office settings, your toolbars may be displayed on a single row and your menus may display a shortened list of frequently used commands. Office menus and toolbars can modify themselves to your working style by displaying only the most frequently used buttons and menu commands.

Toolbars in one row

To view buttons not currently displayed, click a Toolbar Options button at the right end of either the Standard or Formatting toolbar. To view the full list of menu commands, click the double arrow at the bottom of the menu.

In order to have your toolbars displayed in two rows, showing all buttons, and to have the full menus displayed, you must turn off the personalized menus and toolbars feature. Click Tools on the menu bar, click Customize, select the show Standard and Formatting toolbars on two rows and Always show full menus check boxes on the Options tab, and then click Close. This book assumes you are displaying toolbars in two rows and displaying full menus.

Toolbars in two rows

UNIT
A
Word 2003

Getting Started with Word 2003

OBJECTIVES

- Understand word processing software
- Start Word 2003
- Explore the Word program window
- Start a document
- Save a document
- Print a document
- Use the Help system
- Close a document and exit Word

If you have a SAM user profile, you may have access to hands-on instruction, practice, and assessment of the skills covered in this unit. Log in to your SAM account and go to your assignments page to see what your instructor has assigned.

Microsoft Office Word 2003 is a word processing program that makes it easy to create a variety of professional-looking documents, from simple letters and memos to newsletters, research papers, Web pages, business cards, resumes, financial reports, and other documents that include multiple pages of text and sophisticated formatting. In this unit, you will explore the editing and formatting features available in Word, learn how to start Word, and create a document. You have just been hired to work in the Marketing Department at MediaLoft, a chain of bookstore cafés that sells books, music, and videos. Shortly after reporting to your new office, Alice Wegman, the marketing manager, asks you to familiarize yourself with Word and use it to create a memo to the marketing staff.

UNIT
A
Word 2003

Understanding Word Processing Software

A **word processing program** is a software program that includes tools for entering, editing, and formatting text and graphics. Microsoft Word is a powerful word processing program that allows you to create and enhance a wide range of documents quickly and easily. Figure A-1 shows the first page of a report created using Word and illustrates some of the Word features you can use to enhance your documents. The electronic files you create using Word are called **documents**. One of the benefits of using Word is that document files can be stored on a disk, making them easy to transport, exchange, and revise. You need to write a memo to the marketing staff to inform them of an upcoming meeting. Before beginning your memo, you explore the editing and formatting capabilities available in Word.

DETAILS

You can use Word to accomplish the following tasks:

- **Type and edit text**
  The Word editing tools make it simple to insert and delete text in a document. You can add text to the middle of an existing paragraph, replace text with other text, undo an editing change, and correct typing, spelling, and grammatical errors with ease.
- **Copy and move text from one location to another**
  Using the more advanced editing features of Word, you can copy or move text from one location and insert it in a different location in a document. You also can copy and move text between documents. Being able to copy and move text means you don't have to retype text that is already entered in a document.
- **Format text and paragraphs with fonts, colors, and other elements**
  The sophisticated formatting tools available in Word allow you to make the text in your documents come alive. You can change the size, style, and color of text, add lines and shading to paragraphs, and enhance lists with bullets and numbers. Formatting text creatively helps you highlight important ideas in your documents.
- **Format and design pages**
  The Word page-formatting features give you power to design attractive newsletters, create powerful resumes, and produce documents such as business cards, CD labels, and books. You can change the paper size and orientation of your documents, add headers and footers to pages, organize text in columns, and control the layout of text and graphics on each page of a document.
- **Enhance documents with tables, charts, diagrams, and graphics**
  Using the powerful graphic tools available in Word, you can spice up your documents with pictures, photographs, lines, shapes, and diagrams. You also can illustrate your documents with tables and charts to help convey your message in a visually interesting way.
- **Create Web pages**
  The Word Web page design tools allow you to create documents that others can read over the Internet or an intranet. You can enhance Web pages with themes and graphics, add hyperlinks, create online forms, and preview Web pages in your Web browser.
- **Use Mail Merge to create form letters and mailing labels**
  The Word Mail Merge feature allows you to easily send personalized form letters to many different people. You can also use Mail Merge to create mailing labels, directories, e-mail messages, and many other types of documents.

FIGURE A-1: A report created using Word

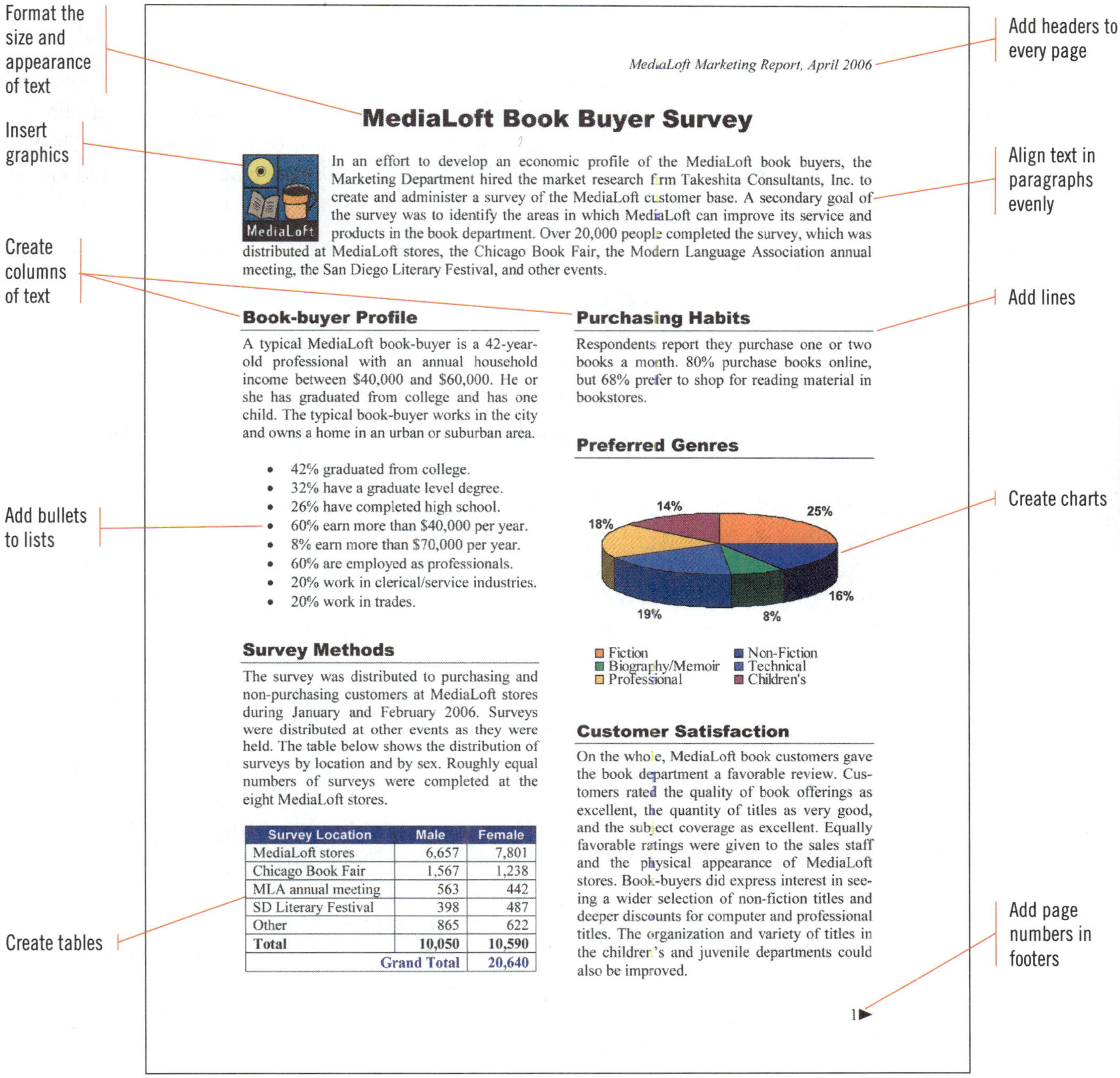

MediaLoft Marketing Report, April 2006

MediaLoft Book Buyer Survey

In an effort to develop an economic profile of the MediaLoft book buyers, the Marketing Department hired the market research firm Takeshita Consultants, Inc. to create and administer a survey of the MediaLoft customer base. A secondary goal of the survey was to identify the areas in which MediaLoft can improve its service and products in the book department. Over 20,000 people completed the survey, which was distributed at MediaLoft stores, the Chicago Book Fair, the Modern Language Association annual meeting, the San Diego Literary Festival, and other events.

Book-buyer Profile

A typical MediaLoft book-buyer is a 42-year-old professional with an annual household income between $40,000 and $60,000. He or she has graduated from college and has one child. The typical book-buyer works in the city and owns a home in an urban or suburban area.

- 42% graduated from college.
- 32% have a graduate level degree.
- 26% have completed high school.
- 60% earn more than $40,000 per year.
- 8% earn more than $70,000 per year.
- 60% are employed as professionals.
- 20% work in clerical/service industries.
- 20% work in trades.

Survey Methods

The survey was distributed to purchasing and non-purchasing customers at MediaLoft stores during January and February 2006. Surveys were distributed at other events as they were held. The table below shows the distribution of surveys by location and by sex. Roughly equal numbers of surveys were completed at the eight MediaLoft stores.

Survey Location	Male	Female
MediaLoft stores	6,657	7,801
Chicago Book Fair	1,567	1,238
MLA annual meeting	563	442
SD Literary Festival	398	487
Other	865	622
Total	**10,050**	**10,590**
	Grand Total	**20,640**

Purchasing Habits

Respondents report they purchase one or two books a month. 80% purchase books online, but 68% prefer to shop for reading material in bookstores.

Preferred Genres

Customer Satisfaction

On the whole, MediaLoft book customers gave the book department a favorable review. Customers rated the quality of book offerings as excellent, the quantity of titles as very good, and the subject coverage as excellent. Equally favorable ratings were given to the sales staff and the physical appearance of MediaLoft stores. Book-buyers did express interest in seeing a wider selection of non-fiction titles and deeper discounts for computer and professional titles. The organization and variety of titles in the children's and juvenile departments could also be improved.

1

Clues to Use

Planning a document

Before you create a new document, it's a good idea to spend time planning it. Identify the message you want to convey, the audience for your document, and the elements, such as tables or charts, you want to include. You should also think about the tone and look of your document—is it a business letter, which should be written in a pleasant, but serious tone and have a formal appearance, or are you creating a flyer that must be colorful, eye-catching, and fun to read?

The purpose and audience for your document determines the appropriate design. Planning the layout and design of a document involves deciding how to organize the text, selecting the fonts to use, identifying the graphics to include, and selecting the formatting elements that will enhance the document's message and appeal. For longer documents, such as newsletters, it can be useful to sketch the layout and design of each page before you begin.

UNIT A

Word 2003

Starting Word 2003

Before starting Word, you must start Windows by turning on your computer. Once Windows is running, you can start Word or any other application by using the Start button on the Windows taskbar. You can also start Word by clicking the Word icon on the Windows desktop or the Word icon on the Microsoft Office Shortcut bar, if those items are available on your computer. You use the Start button to start Word so you can familiarize yourself with its features.

STEPS

1. **Click the Start button on the Windows taskbar**
   The Start menu opens on the desktop. The left pane of the Start menu includes shortcuts to the most frequently used programs on the computer.
2. **Point to All Programs on the Start menu**
   The All Programs menu opens. The All Programs menu displays the list of programs installed on your computer.
3. **Point to Microsoft Office**
   A menu listing the Office programs installed on your computer opens, as shown in Figure A-2.
4. **Click Microsoft Office Word 2003 on the Microsoft Office menu**
   The **Word program window** opens and displays a blank document in the document window and the Getting Started task pane, as shown in Figure A-3. The blank document opens in the most recently used view. **Views** are different ways of displaying a document in the document window. Figure A-3 shows a blank document in Print Layout view. The lessons in this unit will use Print Layout view.
5. **Click the Print Layout View button as shown in Figure A-3**
   If your blank document opened in a different view, the view changes to Print Layout view.
6. **Click the Zoom list arrow on the Standard toolbar as shown in Figure A-3, then click Page Width**
   The blank document fills the document window. Your screen should now match Figure A-3. The blinking vertical line in the upper-left corner of the document window is the **insertion point**. It indicates where text appears as you type.
7. **Move the mouse pointer around in the Word program window**
   The mouse pointer changes shape depending on where it is in the Word program window. In the document window in Print Layout view, the mouse pointer changes to an **I-beam pointer** or a **click and type pointer**. You use these pointers to move the insertion point in the document or to select text to edit. Table A-1 describes common Word pointers.
8. **Place the mouse pointer over a toolbar button**
   When you place the pointer over a button or some other element of the Word program window, a ScreenTip appears. A **ScreenTip** is a label that identifies the name of the button or feature.

TROUBLE

If Microsoft Office is not on your All Programs menu, ask your technical support person for assistance.

TROUBLE

If your toolbars are on one row, click the Toolbar Options button at the end of the Formatting toolbar, then click Show Buttons on Two Rows.

TABLE A-1: Common Word pointers

pointer	use to
I-beam	Move the insertion point in a document or to select text
click and type pointers (or)	Move the insertion point in a blank area of a document in Print Layout or Web Layout view; automatically applies the paragraph formatting required to position text at that location in the document
arrow	Click a button, menu command, or other element of the Word program window; appears when you point to elements of the Word program window
right arrow	Select a line or lines of text; appears when you point to the left edge of a line of text in the document window
hand	Open a hyperlink; appears when you point to a hyperlink in the task pane or a document

FIGURE A-2: Starting Word from the All Programs menu

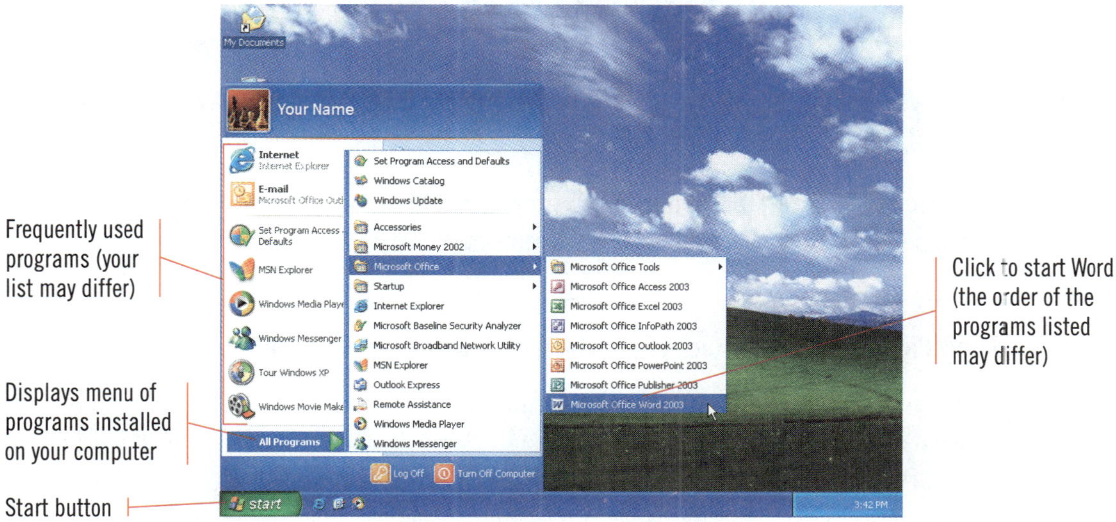

FIGURE A-3: Word program window in Print Layout view

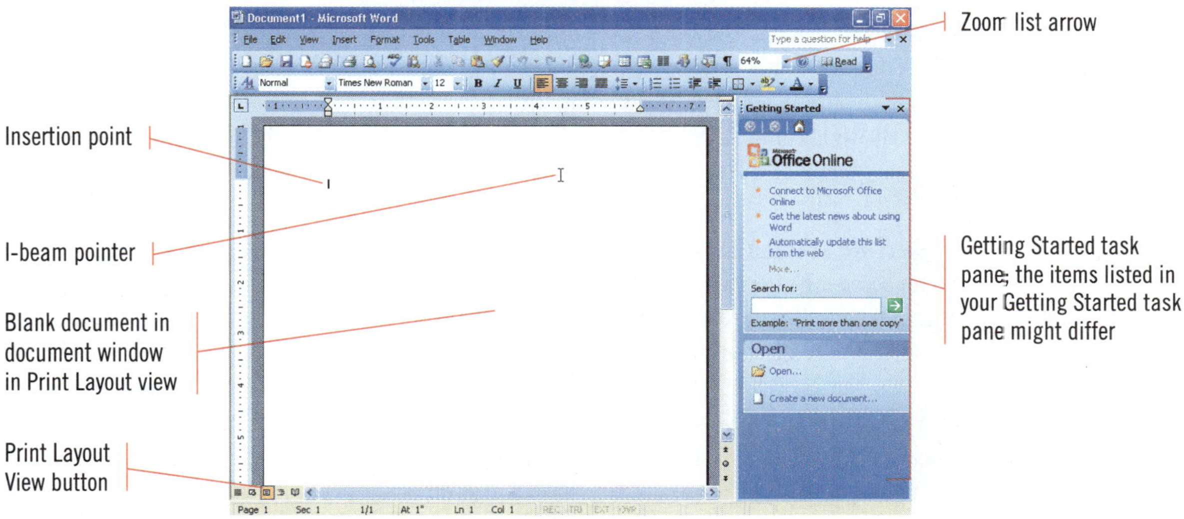

Clues to Use

Using Word document views

Each Word view provides features that are useful for working on different types of documents. The default view, **Print Layout view**, displays a document as it will look on a printed page. Print Layout view is helpful for formatting text and pages, including adjusting document margins, creating columns of text, inserting graphics, and formatting headers and footers. Also useful is **Normal view**, which shows a simplified layout of a document, without margins, headers and footers, or graphics. When you want to quickly type, edit, and format text, it's often easiest to work in Normal view. **Web Layout view** allows you to accurately format Web pages or documents that will be viewed on a computer screen. In Web Layout view, a document appears just as it will when viewed with a Web browser. **Outline view** is useful for editing and formatting longer documents that include multiple headings. Outline view allows you to reorganize text by moving the headings. You switch between these views by clicking the view buttons to the left of the horizontal scroll bar or by using the commands on the View menu.

Two additional views make it easier to read documents on the screen. **Reading Layout view** displays document text so that it is easy to read and annotate. When you are working with highlighting or comments in a document, it's useful to use Reading Layout view. You switch to Reading Layout view by clicking the Read button on the Standard toolbar or the Reading Layout button to the left of the horizontal scroll bar. You return to the previous view by clicking the Close button on the Reading Layout toolbar. **Full Screen view** displays only the document window on screen. You switch to Full Screen view by using the Full Screen command on the View menu; you return to the previous view by pressing [Esc].

Changing views does not affect how the printed document will appear. It simply changes the way you view the document in the document window.

UNIT

A

Word 2003

Exploring the Word Program Window

When you start Word, a blank document appears in the document window and the Getting Started task pane appears. You examine the elements of the Word program window.

DETAILS

Using Figure A-4 as a guide, find the elements described below in your program window.

- The **title bar** displays the name of the document and the name of the program. Until you give a new document a different name, its temporary name is Document1. The title bar also contains resizing buttons and the program Close button, buttons that are common to all Windows programs.
- The **menu bar** contains the names of the Word menus. Clicking a menu name opens a list of commands. The menu bar also contains the **Type a question for help box** and the Close Window button. You use the Type a question for help box to access the Word Help system.
- The **toolbars** contain buttons for the most commonly used commands. The **Standard toolbar** contains buttons for frequently used operating and editing commands, such as saving a document, printing a document, and cutting, copying, and pasting text. The **Formatting toolbar** contains buttons for commonly used formatting commands, such as changing font type and size, applying bold to text, and changing paragraph alignment. The Clues to Use in this lesson provides more information about working with toolbars and menus in Word.
- The **Getting Started task pane** contains shortcuts for opening a document, for creating new documents, and for accessing information on the Microsoft Web site. The blue words in the Open section of the task pane are **hyperlinks** that provide quick access to existing documents and the New Document task pane. If your computer is connected to the Internet, you can use the Microsoft Office Online section of the task pane to search the Microsoft Web site for information related to Office programs. As you learn more about Word, you will work with other task panes that provide shortcuts to Word formatting, editing, and research features. Clicking a hyperlink in a task pane can be quicker than using menu commands and toolbar buttons to accomplish a task.
- The **document window** displays the current document. You enter text and format your document in the document window.
- The horizontal and vertical rulers appear in the document window in Print Layout view. The **horizontal ruler** displays left and right document margins as well as the tab settings and paragraph indents, if any, for the paragraph in which the insertion point is located. The **vertical ruler** displays the top and bottom document margins.
- The **vertical and horizontal scroll bars** are used to display different parts of the document in the document window. The scroll bars include **scroll boxes** and **scroll arrows**, which you can use to easily move through a document.
- The **view buttons** to the left of the horizontal scroll bar allow you to display the document in Normal, Web Layout, Print Layout, Outline, or Reading Layout view.
- The **status bar** displays the page number and section number of the current page, the total number of pages in the document, and the position of the insertion point in inches, lines, and characters. The status bar also indicates the on/off status of several Word features, including tracking changes, overtype mode, and spelling and grammar checking.

FIGURE A-4: Elements of the Word program window

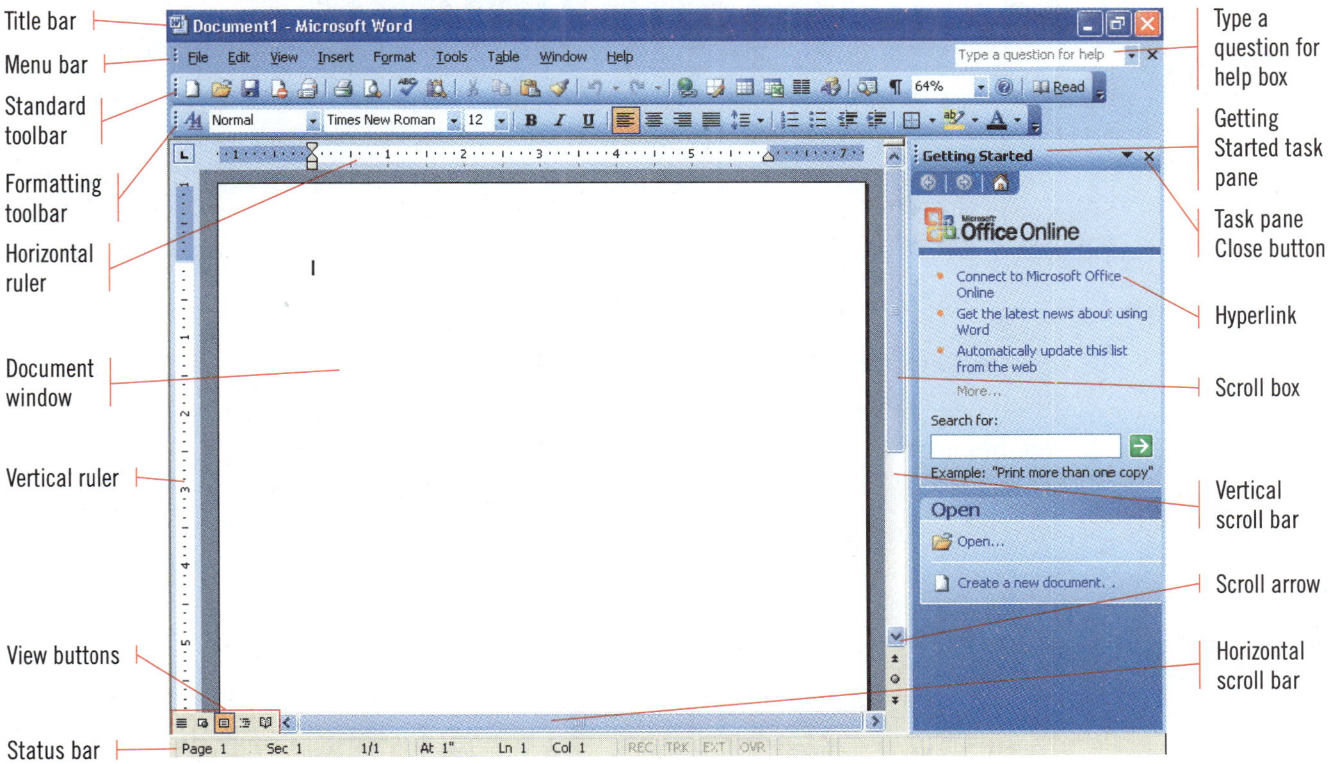

Word 2003

Clues to Use

Working with toolbars and menus in Word 2003

The lessons in this book assume you are working with full menus and toolbars visible, which means the Standard and Formatting toolbars appear on two rows and display all the buttons, and the menus display the complete list of menu commands.

You can also set Word to use personalized toolbars and menus that modify themselves to your working style. When you use personalized toolbars, the Standard and Formatting toolbars appear on the same row and display only the most frequently used buttons. To use a button that is not visible on a toolbar, click the Toolbar Options button at the end of the toolbar, and then click the button you want on the Toolbar Options list. As you work, Word adds the buttons you use to the visible toolbars, and moves the buttons you haven't used recently to the Toolbar Options list. Similarly, Word menus adjust to your work habits, so that the commands you use most often appear on shortened menus. You double-click the menu name or click the double arrow at the bottom of a menu to view additional menu commands.

To work with full toolbars and menus visible, you must turn off the personalized toolbars and menus features. To turn off personalized toolbars and menus, double-click Tools on the menu bar, click Customize, click the Options tab, select the Show Standard and Formatting toolbars on two rows and Always show full menus check boxes, and then click Close.

UNIT A

Word 2003

Starting a Document

You begin a new document by simply typing text in a blank document in the document window. Word includes a **word-wrap** feature, so that as you type Word automatically moves the insertion point to the next line of the document when you reach the right margin. You only press [Enter] when you want to start a new paragraph or insert a blank line. You can easily edit text in a document by inserting new text or by deleting existing text. You type a quick memo to the marketing staff to inform them of an upcoming meeting.

STEPS

1. **Click the Close button in the Getting Started task pane**
   The task pane closes and the blank document fills the screen.

QUICK TIP
If you press the wrong key, press [Backspace] to erase the mistake, then try again.

2. **Type Memorandum, then press [Enter] four times**
   Each time you press [Enter] the insertion point moves to the start of the next line.

3. **Type DATE:, then press [Tab] twice**
   Pressing [Tab] moves the insertion point several spaces to the right. You can use the [Tab] key to align the text in a memo header or to indent the first line of a paragraph.

QUICK TIP
Smart tags and other automatic feature markers appear on screen but do not print.

4. **Type April 21, 2006, then press [Enter]**
   When you press [Enter], a purple dotted line appears under the date. This dotted underline is a **smart tag**. It indicates that Word recognizes the text as a date. If you move the mouse pointer over the smart tag, a **Smart Tag Actions button** appears above the date. Smart tags are one of the many automatic features you will encounter as you type. Table A-2 describes other automatic features available in Word. You can ignore the smart tags in your memo.

5. **Type: TO: [Tab] [Tab] Marketing Staff [Enter]**
   FROM: [Tab] Your Name [Enter]
   RE: [Tab] [Tab] Marketing Meeting [Enter] [Enter]
   Red or green wavy lines may appear under the words you typed. A red wavy line means the word is not in the Word dictionary and might be misspelled. A green wavy line indicates a possible grammar error. You can correct any typing errors you make later.

QUICK TIP
To reverse an AutoCorrect adjustment, immediately click the Undo button on the Standard toolbar.

6. **Type The next marketing meeting will be held May 6th at 10 a.m. in the Bloomsbury room on the ground floor., then press [Spacebar]**
   As you type, notice that the insertion point moves automatically to the next line of the document. You also might notice that Word corrects typing errors or makes typographical adjustments as you type. This feature is called **AutoCorrect**. AutoCorrect automatically detects and adjusts typos, certain misspelled words (such as "taht" for "that"), and incorrect capitalization as you type. For example, Word automatically changed "6th" to "6th" in the memo.

QUICK TIP
Type just one space after a period at the end of a sentence when typing with a word processor.

7. **Type Heading the agenda will be a discussion of our new cafe music series, scheduled for August. Please bring ideas for promoting this exciting new series to the meeting.**
   When you type the first few characters of "August," the Word AutoComplete feature displays the complete word in a ScreenTip. **AutoComplete** suggests text to insert quickly into your documents. You can ignore AutoComplete for now. Your memo should resemble Figure A-5.

8. **Position the I pointer after for (but before the space) in the second sentence, then click**
   Clicking moves the insertion point after "for."

9. **Press [Backspace] three times, then type to debut in**
   Pressing [Backspace] removes the character before the insertion point.

10. **Move the insertion point before marketing in the first sentence, then press [Delete] ten times to remove the word marketing and the space after it**
    Pressing [Delete] removes the character after the insertion point. Figure A-6 shows the revised memo.

FIGURE A-5: Memo text in the document window

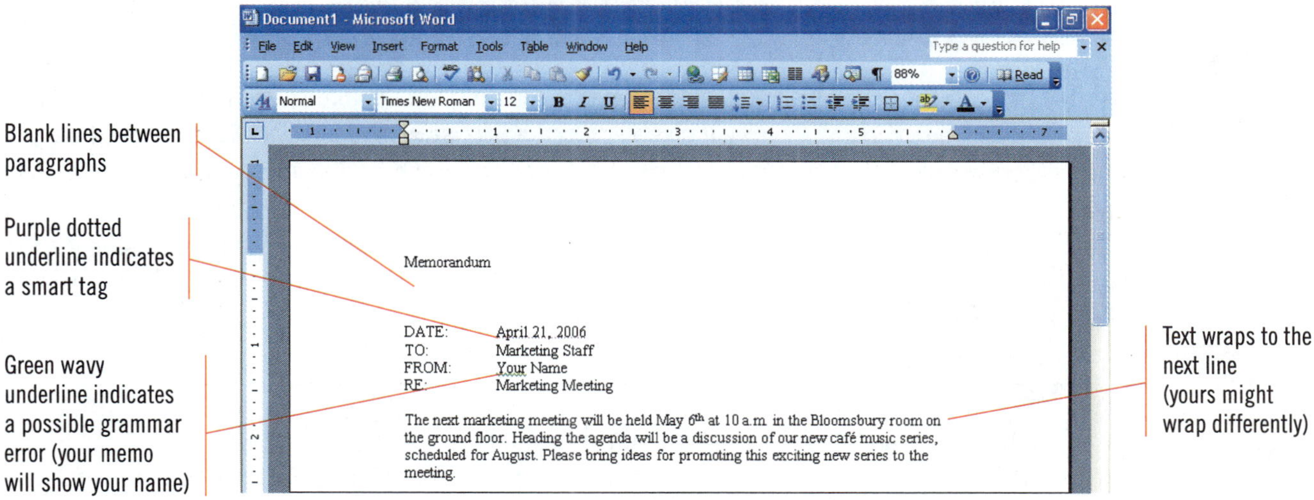

FIGURE A-6: Edited memo text

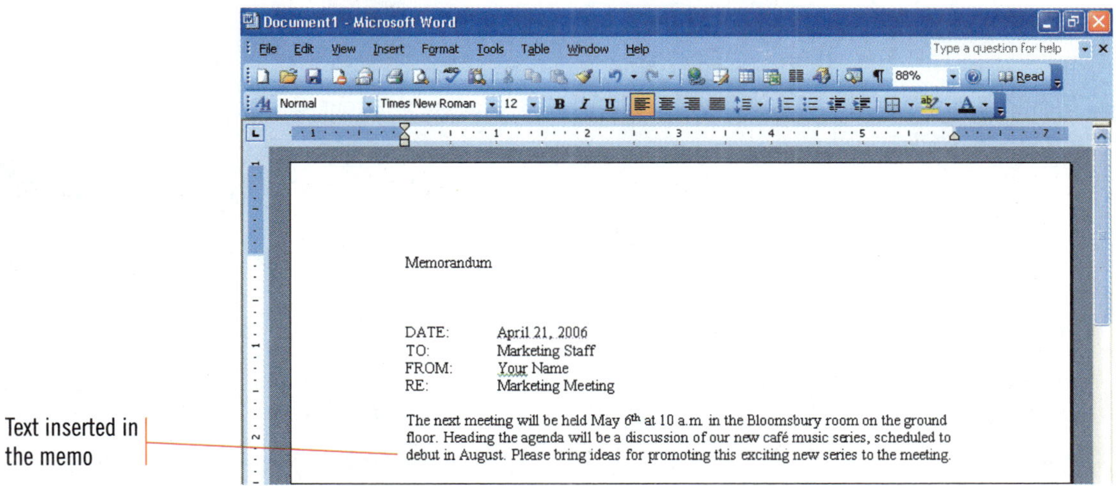

TABLE A-2: Automatic features in Word

feature	what appears	to use
AutoComplete	A ScreenTip suggesting text to insert appears	Press [Enter] to insert the text suggested by the ScreenTip; continue typing to reject the suggestion
Spelling and Grammar	A red wavy line under a word indicates a possible misspelling; a green wavy line under text indicates a possible grammar error	Right-click red- or green-underlined text to display a shortcut menu of correction options; click a correction to accept it and remove the wavy underline
AutoCorrect	A small blue box appears when you place the pointer under text corrected by AutoCorrect; an AutoCorrect Options button appears when you point to the corrected text	Word automatically corrects typos, minor spelling errors, and capitalization, and adds typographical symbols (such as © and ™) as you type; to reverse an AutoCorrect adjustment, click the AutoCorrect Options button, then click Undo or the option that will undo the action
Smart tag	A purple dotted line appears under text Word recognizes as a date, name, address, or place; a Smart Tag Actions button appears when you point to a smart tag	Click the Smart Tag Actions button to display a shortcut menu of options (such as adding a name to your address book in Outlook or opening your Outlook calendar); to remove a smart tag, click Remove this Smart Tag on the shortcut menu

UNIT A
Word 2003

Saving a Document

To store a document permanently so you can open it and edit it in the future, you must save it as a **file**. When you **save** a document you give it a name, called a **filename**, and indicate the location where you want to store the file. Files can be saved to your computer's internal hard disk, to a floppy disk, or to a variety of other locations. You can save a document using the Save button on the Standard toolbar or the Save command on the File menu. Once you have saved a document for the first time, you should save it again every few minutes and always before printing so that the saved file is updated to reflect your latest changes. You save your memo with the filename Marketing Memo.

STEPS

TROUBLE
If you don't see the extension .doc on the filename in the Save As dialog box, don't worry. Windows can be set to display or not to display the file extensions.

1. **Click the Save button on the Standard toolbar**
   The first time you save a document, the Save As dialog box opens, as shown in Figure A-7. The default filename, Memorandum, appears in the File name text box. The default filename is based on the first few words of the document. The .doc extension is assigned automatically to all Word documents to distinguish them from files created in other software programs. To save the document with a different filename, type a new filename in the File name text box, and use the Save in list arrow to select where you want to store the document file. You do not need to type .doc when you type a new filename. Table A-3 describes the functions of the buttons in the Save As dialog box.
2. **Type Marketing Memo in the File name text box**
   The new filename replaces the default filename. It's a good idea to give your documents brief filenames that describe the contents.

TROUBLE
This book assumes your Data Files for Unit A are stored in a folder titled UnitA. Substitute the correct drive or folder if this is not the case.

3. **Click the Save in list arrow, then navigate to the drive or folder where your Data Files are located**
   The drive or folder where your Data Files are located appears in the Save in list box. Your Save As dialog box should resemble Figure A-8.
4. **Click Save**
   The document is saved to the location you specified in the Save As dialog box, and the title bar displays the new filename, "Marketing Memo.doc."
5. **Place the insertion point before August in the second sentence, type early, then press [Spacebar]**
   You can continue to work on a document after you have saved it with a new filename.
6. **Click**
   Your change to the memo is saved. Saving a document after you give it a filename saves the changes you make to the document. You also can click File on the menu bar, and then click Save to save a document.

Clues to Use

Recovering lost document files

Sometimes while you are working on a document, Word might freeze, making it impossible to continue working, or you might experience a power failure that shuts down your computer. Should this occur, Word has a built-in recovery feature that allows you to open and save the files that were open at the time of the interruption. When you restart Word after an interruption, the Document Recovery task pane opens on the left side of your screen and lists both the original and the recovered versions of the Word files. If you're not sure which file to open (original or recovered), it's usually better to open the recovered file because it includes your latest changes to the document. You can, however, open and review all the versions of the file that were recovered and select the best one to save. Each file listed in the Document Recovery task pane has a list arrow with options that allow you to open the file, save the file, delete the file, or show repairs made to the file.

FIGURE A-7: Save As dialog box

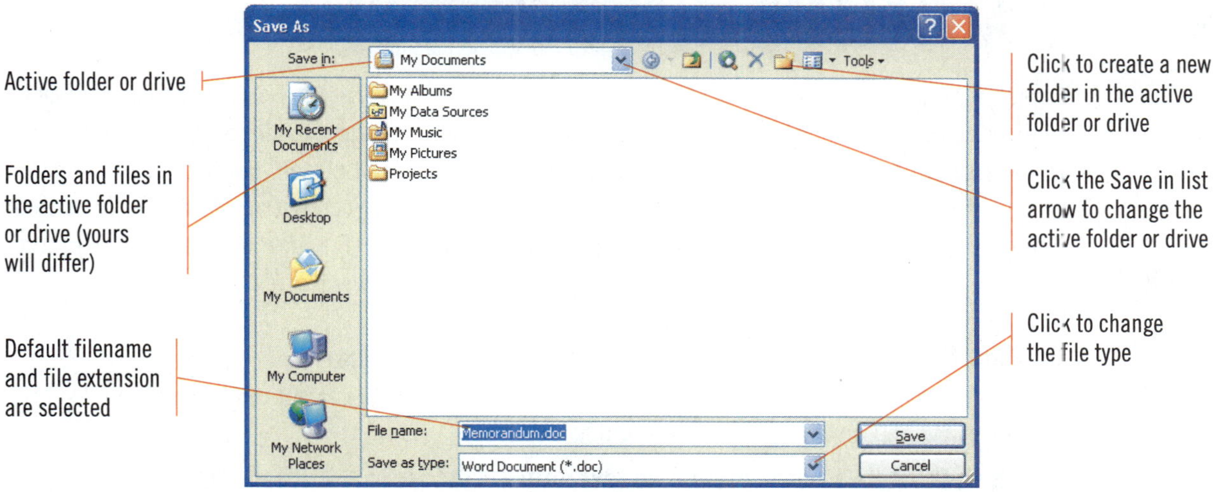

FIGURE A-8: File to be saved to the UnitA folder

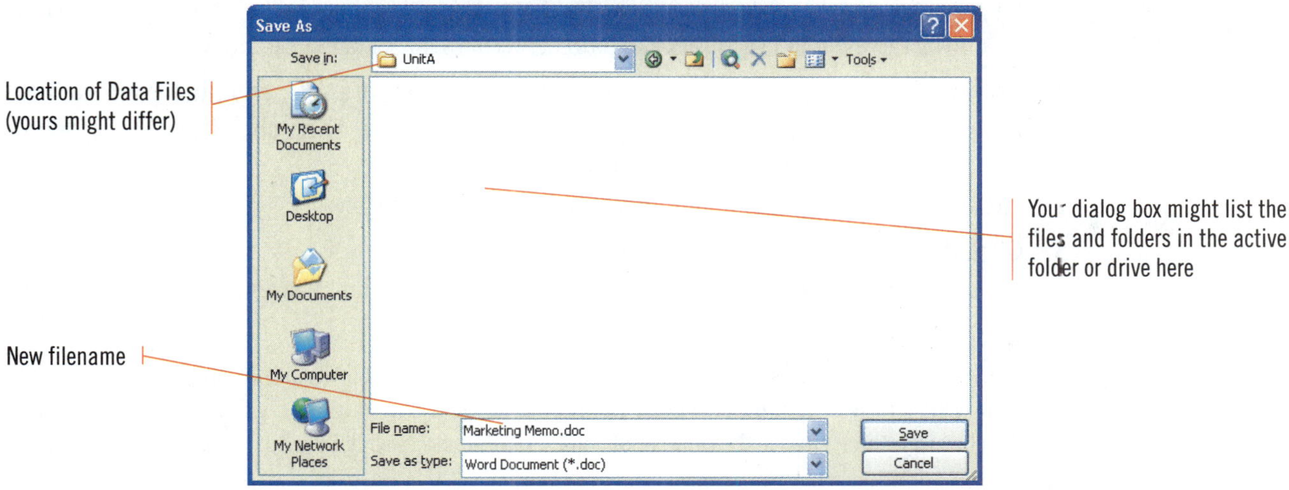

Word 2003

TABLE A-3: Save As dialog box buttons

button	use to
Back	Navigate to the drive or folder previously shown in the Save in list box; click the Back list arrow to navigate to a recently displayed drive or folder
Up One Level	Navigate to the next highest level in the folder hierarchy (to the drive or folder that contains the current folder)
Search the Web	Connect to the World Wide Web to locate a folder or file
Delete	Delete the selected folder or file
Create New Folder	Create a new folder in the current folder or drive
Views	Change the way folder and file information is shown in the Save As dialog box; click the Views list arrow to open a menu of options
Tools	Open a menu of commands related to the selected drive, folder, or file

UNIT

A

Word 2003

Printing a Document

Before you print a document, it's a good habit to examine it in **Print Preview** to see what it will look like when printed. When a document is ready to print, you can print it using the Print button on the Standard toolbar or the Print command on the File menu. When you use the Print button, the document prints using the default print settings. If you want to print more than one copy of a document or select other printing options, you must use the Print command. You display your memo in Print Preview and then print a copy.

STEPS

QUICK TIP

You can also use the Zoom list arrow on the Print Preview toolbar to change the magnification in the Print Preview window.

1. **Click the Print Preview button on the Standard toolbar**
   The document appears in Print Preview. It is useful to examine a document carefully in Print Preview so that you can correct any problems before printing it.
2. **Move the pointer over the memo text until it changes to, then click**
   Clicking with the pointer magnifies the document in the Print Preview window and changes the pointer to. The memo appears in the Print Preview window exactly as it will look when printed, as shown in Figure A-9. Clicking with the pointer reduces the size of the document in the Print Preview window.
3. **Click the Magnifier button on the Print Preview toolbar**
   Clicking the Magnifier button turns off the magnification feature and allows you to edit the document in Print Preview. In edit mode, the pointer changes to I. The Magnifier button is a **toggle button**, which means you can use it to switch back and forth between magnification mode and edit mode.
4. **Compare the text on your screen with the text in Figure A-9, examine your memo carefully for typing or spelling errors, correct any mistakes, then click the Close Preview button Close on the Print Preview toolbar**
   Print Preview closes and the memo appears in the document window.
5. **Click the Save button on the Standard toolbar**
   If you made any changes to the document since you last saved it, the changes are saved.
6. **Click File on the menu bar, then click Print**
   The Print dialog box opens, as shown in Figure A-10. Depending on the printer installed on your computer, your print settings might differ slightly from those in the figure. You can use the Print dialog box to change the current printer, change the number of copies to print, select what pages of a document to print, and modify other printing options.
7. **Click OK**
   The dialog box closes and a copy of the memo prints using the default print settings. You can also click the Print button on the Standard toolbar or the Print Preview toolbar to print a document using the default print settings.

FIGURE A-9: Memo in the Print Preview window

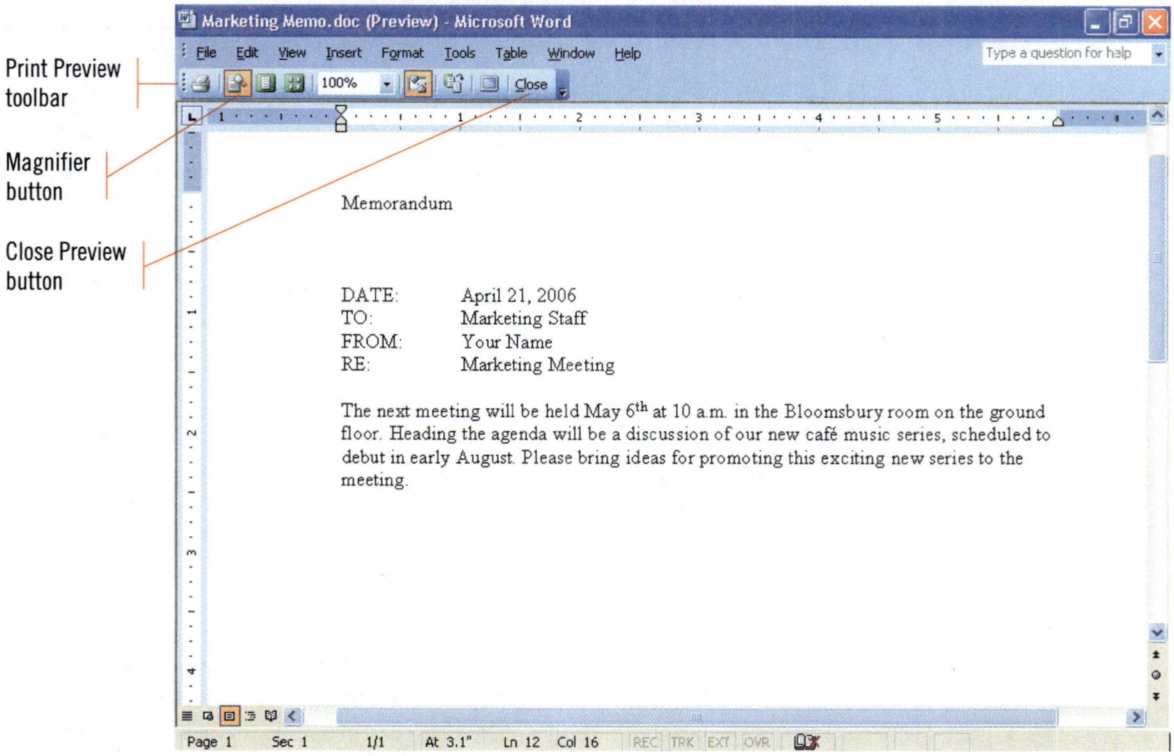

FIGURE A-10: Print dialog box

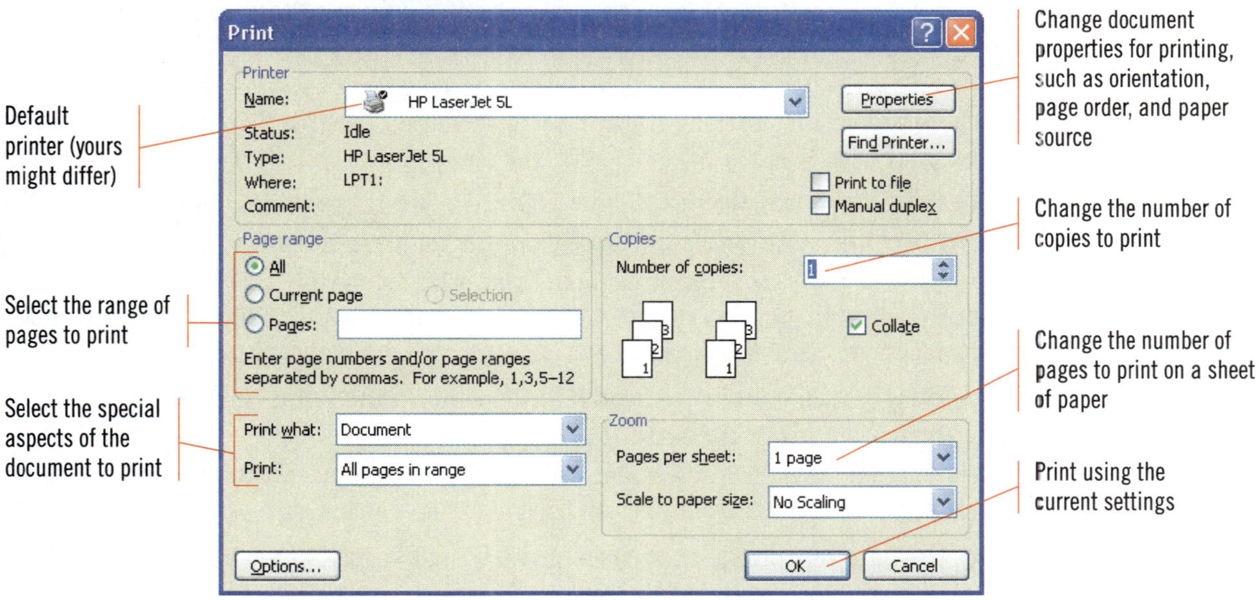

Word 2003

UNIT A
Word 2003

Using the Help System

Word includes an extensive Help system that provides immediate access to definitions, instructions, and useful tips for working with Word. You can quickly access the Help system by typing a question in the Type a question for help box on the menu bar, by clicking the Microsoft Office Word Help button on the Standard toolbar, or by selecting an option from the Help menu. If you are working with an active Internet connection, your queries to the Help system will also return information from the Microsoft Office Online Web site. Table A-4 describes the many ways to get help while using Word. You are curious to learn more about typing with AutoCorrect and viewing and printing documents. You search the Word Help system to discover more about these features.

STEPS

TROUBLE
The figures in this lesson reflect an active Internet connection. If you are not connected to the Internet, then connect if possible.

1. **Type AutoCorrect in the Type a question for help box on the menu bar, then press [Enter]**
   The Search Results task pane opens. Help topics related to AutoCorrect are listed in blue in the task pane. Notice that the pointer changes to when you move it over the blue hyperlink text. If you are working online, it may take a few seconds for information to appear in the task pane.
2. **Click About automatic corrections in the Search Results task pane**
   The Microsoft Office Word Help window opens, as shown in Figure A-11. The Help window displays the "About automatic corrections" Help topic you selected. The colored text in the Help window indicates a link to a definition or to more information about the topic. Like all windows, you can maximize the Help window by clicking the Maximize button on its title bar, or you can resize the window by dragging a top, bottom, or side edge.

TROUBLE
If the hyperlink is not visible in your Help window, click the down scroll arrow until it appears.

3. **Read the information in the Help window, then click the colored text hyperlinks**
   Clicking the link expands the Help topic to display more detailed information. A definition of the word "hyperlink" appears in colored text in the Help window.
4. **Read the definition, then click hyperlinks again to close the definition**
5. **Click Using AutoCorrect to correct errors as you type in the Help window, then read the expanded information, clicking the down scroll arrow as necessary to read the entire Help topic**
   Clicking the up or down scroll arrow allows you to navigate through the Help topic when all the text does not fit in the Help window. You can also **scroll** by clicking the scroll bar above and below the scroll box, or by dragging the scroll box up or down in the scroll bar.
6. **Click the Close button in the Microsoft Office Word Help window title bar, then click the Microsoft Office Word Help button on the Standard toolbar**
   The Word Help task pane opens, as shown in Figure A-12. You use this task pane to search for Help topics related to a keyword or phrase, to browse the Table of Contents for the Help system, or to connect to the Microsoft Office Online Web site, where you can search for more information on a topic.
7. **Type print a document in the Search for text box in the Word Help task pane, then click the green Start searching button**
   When you click the green Start searching button, a list of Help topics related to your query appears in the Search Results task pane. You can also press [Enter] to return a list of Help topics.
8. **Click the Back button at the top of the Search Results task pane, then click Table of Contents in the Word Help task pane**
   The table of contents for the Help system appears in the Word Help task pane. To peruse the table of contents, you simply click a category in the list to expand it and see a list of subcategories and Help topics. Categories are listed in black text in the task pane and are preceded by a book icon. Help topics are listed in blue text and are preceded by a question mark icon.

QUICK TIP
Click the Back and Forward buttons on the Word Help window toolbar to navigate between the Help topics you have viewed.

9. **Click Viewing and Navigating Documents, click a blue Help topic, read the information in the Microsoft Office Word Help window, then click the Close button in the Help window**

FIGURE A-11: Microsoft Office Word Help window

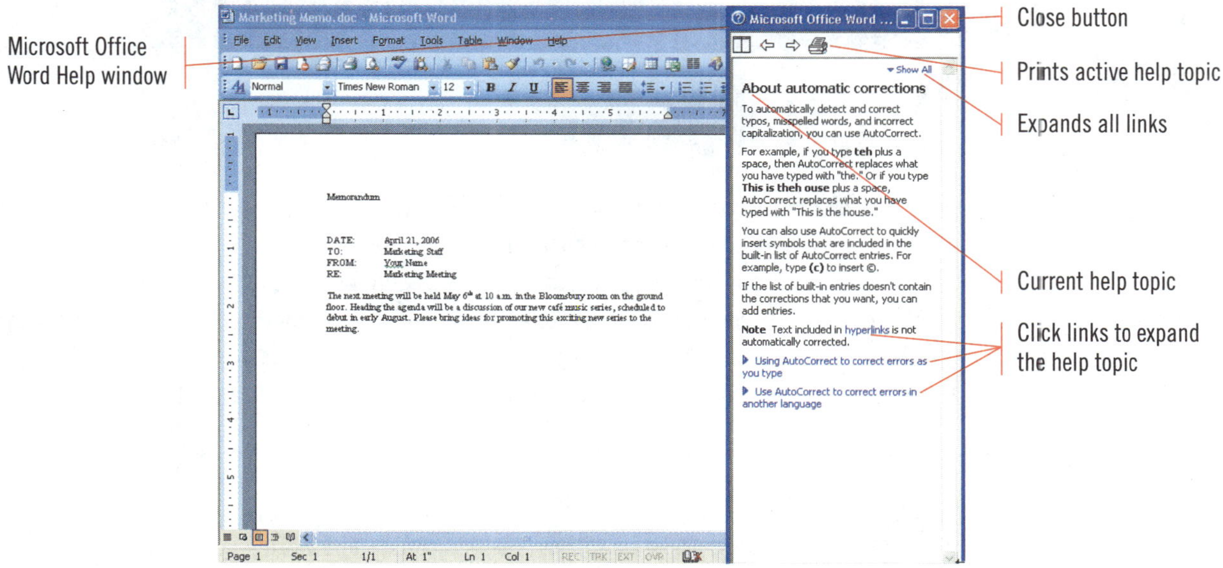

FIGURE A-12: Word Help task pane

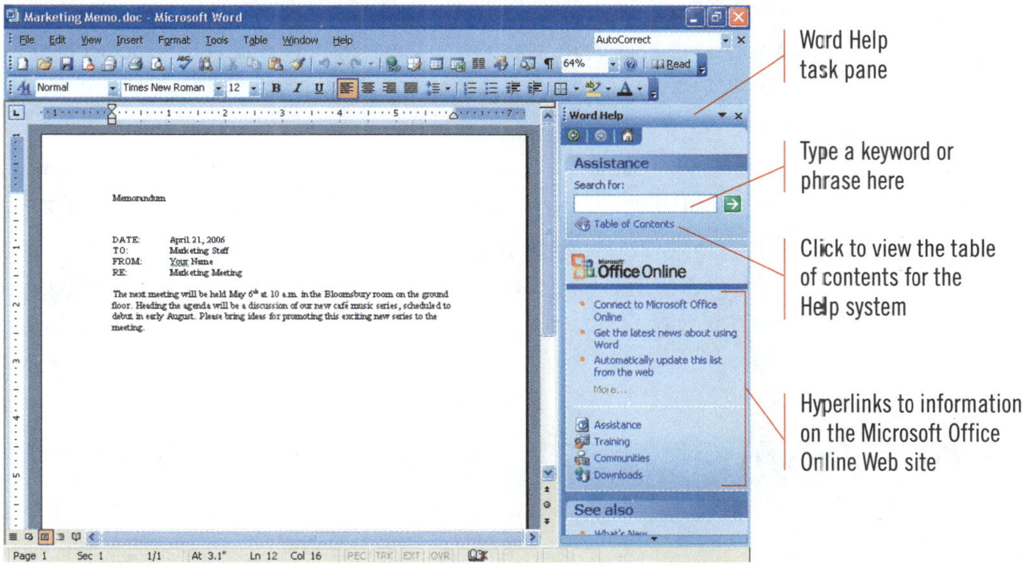

TABLE A-4: Word resources for getting Help

resource	function	to use
Type a question for help box	Provides quick access to the Help system	Type a word or question in the Type a question for help box, then press [Enter]
Word Help task pane	Displays the table of contents for the Help system, provides access to a search function, and includes hyperlinks to Help information on the Microsoft Office Online Web site	Press [F1] or click the Microsoft Office Word Help button on the Standard toolbar; in the Word Help task pane, type a word or phrase in the Search for text box to return a list of possible Help topics, click Table of Contents to browse the complete list of Help topics, or click a link to access information on the Microsoft Office Online Web site
Microsoft Office Online Web site	Connects to the Microsoft Office Online Web site, where you can search for information on a topic	Click the Microsoft Office Online command on the Help menu, or click a link in the Word Help task pane
Office Assistant	Displays tips related to your current task and provides access to the Help system	Click Show the Office Assistant on the Help menu to display the Office Assistant; click Hide the Office Assistant on the Help menu to hide the Office Assistant

UNIT A

Word 2003

Closing a Document and Exiting Word

When you have finished working on a document and have saved your changes, you can close the document using the Close Window button on the menu bar or the Close command on the File menu. Closing a document closes the document only, it does not close the Word program window. To close the Word program window and exit Word, you can use the Close button on the title bar or the Exit command on the File menu. Using the Exit command closes all open documents. It's good practice to save and close your documents before exiting Word. Figure A-13 shows the Close buttons on the title bar and menu bar. You close the memo and exit Word.

STEPS

1. **Click the Close button on the Word Help task pane**

   The task pane closes. It is not necessary to close the task pane before closing a file or the program, but it can be helpful to reduce the amount of information displayed on the screen. Table A-5 describes the functions of the Word task panes.

2. **Click File on the menu bar, then click Close**

   If you saved your changes to the document before closing it, the document closes. If you did not save your changes, an alert box opens asking if you want to save the changes.

3. **Click Yes if the alert box opens**

   The document closes, but the Word program window remains open, as shown in Figure A-14. You can create or open another document, access Help, or close the Word program window.

4. **Click File on the menu bar, then click Exit**

   The Word program window closes. If any Word documents were still open when you exited Word, Word closes all open documents, prompting you to save changes to those documents if necessary.

QUICK TIP

To create a new blank document, click the New Blank Document button on the Standard toolbar.

TABLE A-5: Word task panes

task pane	use to
Getting Started	Open a document, create a new blank document, or search for information on the Microsoft Office Online Web site
Word Help	Access Help topics and connect to Help on the Microsoft Office Online Web site
Search Results	View the results of a search for Help topics and perform a new search
Clip Art	Search for clip art and insert clip art in a document
Research	Search reference books and other sources for information related to a word, such as for synonyms
Clipboard	Cut, copy, and paste items within and between documents
New Document	Create a new blank document, XML document, Web page, or e-mail message, or create a new document using a template
Shared Workspace	Create a Web site (called a document workspace) that allows a group of people to share files, participate in discussions, and work together on a document
Document Updates	View information on a document that is available in a document workspace
Protect Document	Apply formatting and editing restrictions to a shared document
Styles and Formatting	Apply styles to text
Reveal Formatting	Display the formatting applied to text
Mail Merge	Perform a mail merge
XML Structure	Apply XML elements to a Word XML document

FIGURE A-13: Close and Close Window buttons

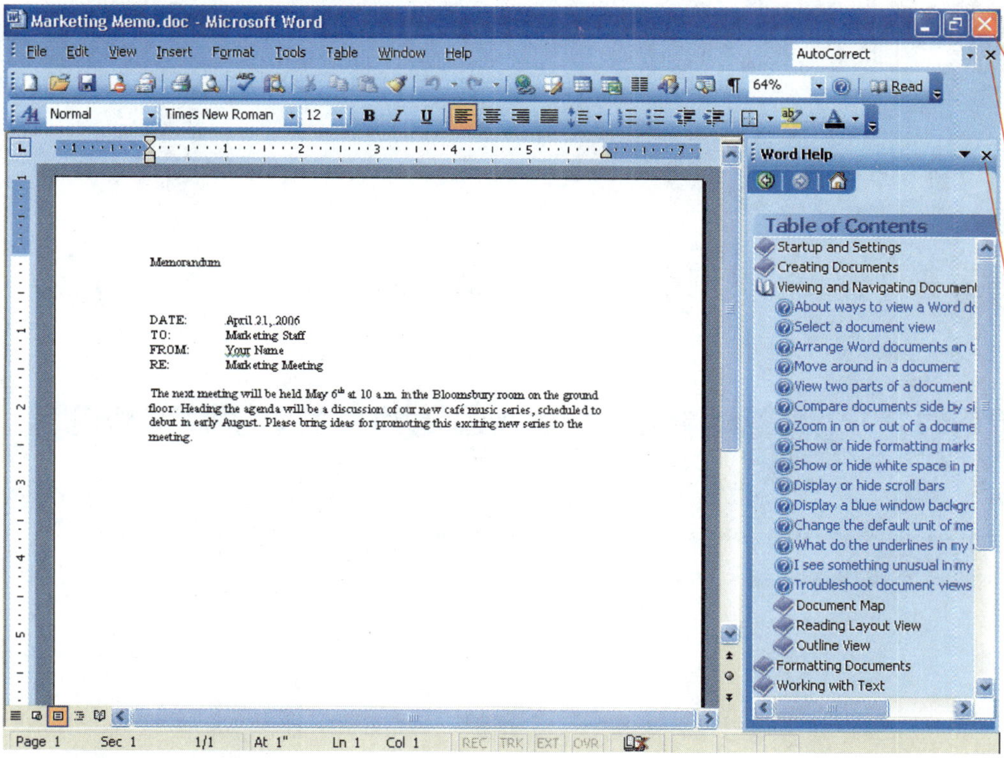

FIGURE A-14: Word program window with no documents open

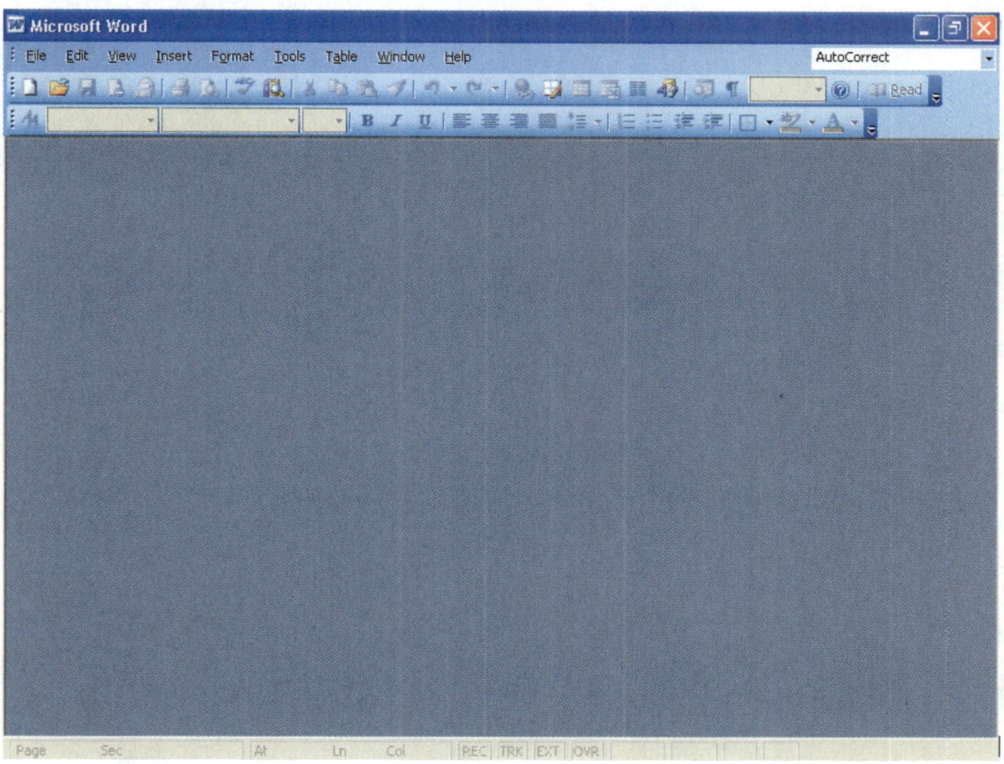

Word 2003

Practice

▼ CONCEPTS REVIEW

Label the elements of the Word program window shown in Figure A-15.

FIGURE A-15

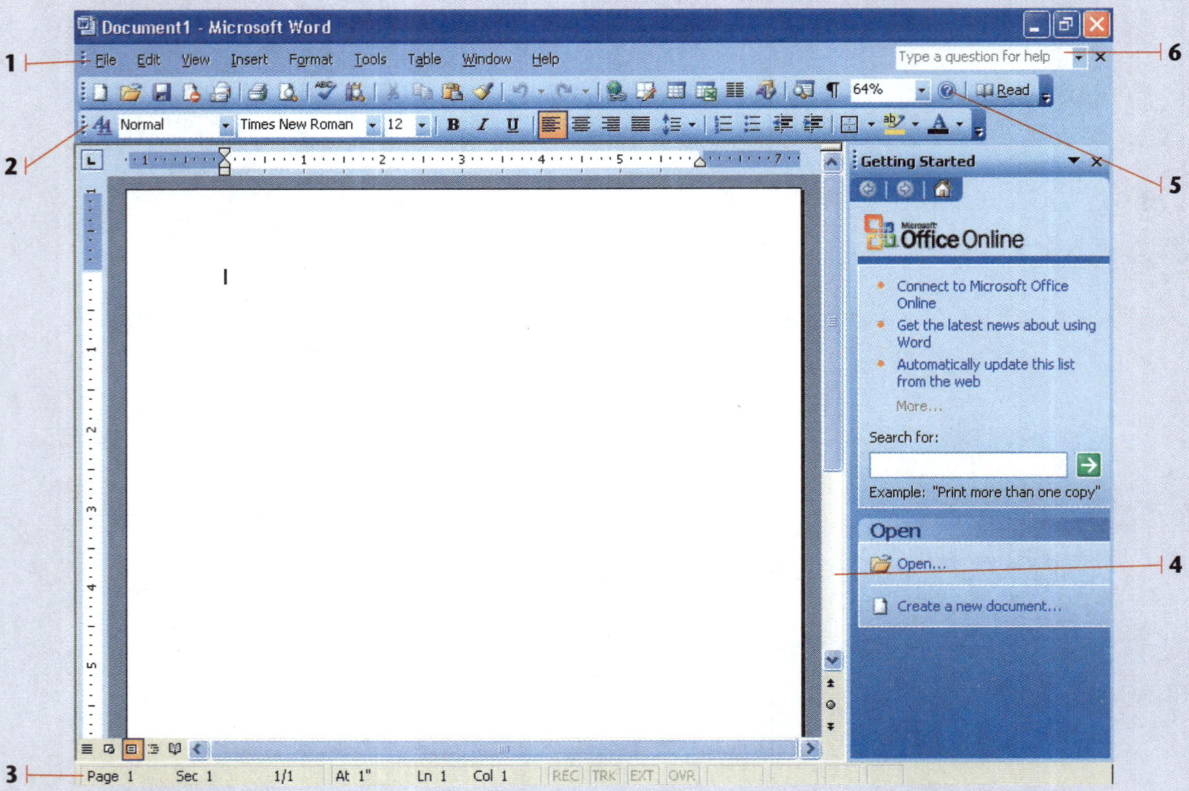

Match each term with the statement that best describes it.

7. **Print Preview**
8. **Office Assistant**
9. **Status bar**
10. **Menu bar**
11. **AutoComplete**
12. **Horizontal ruler**
13. **AutoCorrect**
14. **Normal view**

a. Displays a simple layout view of a document
b. Displays tips on using Word
c. Displays the document exactly as it will look when printed
d. Suggests text to insert into a document
e. Fixes certain errors as you type
f. Displays the number of pages in the current document
g. Displays tab settings and document margins
h. Provides access to Word commands

Select the best answer from the list of choices.

15. Which task pane opens automatically when you start Word?
- **a.** Document Updates
- **b.** Getting Started
- **c.** Word Help
- **d.** New Document

16. Which element of the Word program window shows the settings for the left and right document margins?
- **a.** Formatting toolbar
- **b.** Status bar
- **c.** Horizontal ruler
- **d.** Getting Started task pane

17. What is the function of the Exit command on the File menu?
- **a.** To close the current document without saving changes
- **b.** To close all open documents and the Word program window
- **c.** To save changes to and close the current document
- **d.** To close all open programs

18. Which view do you use when you want to adjust the margins in a document?
- **a.** Outline view
- **b.** Web Layout view
- **c.** Normal view
- **d.** Print Layout view

19. Which of the following does not appear on the status bar?
- **a.** The current page number
- **b.** The current tab settings
- **c.** The Overtype mode status
- **d.** The current line number

20. Which of the following is not used to access the Help system?
- **a.** Type a question for help box
- **b.** The Office Assistant
- **c.** Microsoft Office Online
- **d.** The Research task pane

▼ SKILLS REVIEW

1. Start Word 2003.
- **a.** Start Word.
- **b.** Switch to Print Layout view if your blank document opened in a different view.
- **c.** Change the zoom level to Page Width.

2. Explore the Word program window.
- **a.** Identify as many elements of the Word program window as you can without referring to the unit material.
- **b.** Click each menu name on the menu bar and drag the pointer through the menu commands.
- **c.** Point to each button on the Standard and Formatting toolbars and read the ScreenTips.
- **d.** Point to each hyperlink in the Getting Started task pane.

▼ SKILLS REVIEW (CONTINUED)

e. Click the view buttons to view the blank document in Normal, Web Layout, Print Layout, Outline, and Reading Layout view.
f. Click the Close button in Reading Layout view, then return to Print Layout view.

3. Start a document.

a. Close the Getting Started task pane.
b. In a new blank document, type **FAX** at the top of the page, then press [Enter] four times.
c. Type the following, pressing [Tab] as indicated and pressing [Enter] at the end of each line:
To: [Tab] **Dr. Beatrice Turcotte**
From: [Tab] **Your Name**
Date: [Tab] **Today's date**
Re: [Tab] **Travel arrangements**
Pages: [Tab] **1**
Fax: [Tab] **(514) 555-3948**
d. Press [Enter], then type **I have reserved a space for you on the March 4-18 Costa Rica Explorer tour. You are scheduled to depart Montreal's Dorval Airport on Plateau Tours and Travel charter flight 234 at 7:45 a.m. on March 4th, arriving in San Jose at 4:30 p.m. local time.**
e. Press [Enter] twice, then type **Please call me at (514) 555-4983 or stop by our offices on rue St-Denis.**
f. Insert this sentence at the beginning of the second paragraph: **I must receive full payment within 48 hours to hold your reservation.**
g. Using the [Backspace] key, delete **Travel** in the Re: line, then type **Costa Rica tour.**
h. Using the [Delete] key, delete **48** in the last paragraph, then type **72**.

4. Save a document.

a. Click File on the menu bar, then click Save.
b. Save the document as **Turcotte Fax** to the drive and folder where your Data Files are located.
c. After your name, type a comma, press [Spacebar], then type **Plateau Tours and Travel**.
d. Click the Save button to save your changes to the document.

5. Print a document.

a. Click the Print Preview button to view the document in Print Preview.
b. Click the word FAX to zoom in on the document, then proofread the fax.
c. Click the Magnifier button to switch to edit mode, then correct any typing errors in your document.
d. Close Print Preview, then save your changes to the document.
e. Print the fax using the default print settings.

6. Use the Help system.

a. Click the Microsoft Office Word Help button to open the Word Help task pane.
b. Type **open a document** in the Search text box, then press [Enter].
c. Click the topic Open a file.
d. Read about saving documents in Word by clicking the links to expand the Help topic.
e. Close the Help window, type **viewing documents** in the Type a question for help box, then press [Enter].
f. Click the link Zoom in on or out of a document in the Search Results task pane, then read the Help topic.
g. Close the Help window, then close the Search Results task pane.

7. Close a document and exit Word.

a. Close the Turcotte Fax document, saving your changes if necessary.
b. Exit Word.

▼ INDEPENDENT CHALLENGE 1

You are a performance artist, well known for your innovative work with computers. The Missoula Arts Council president, Sam McCrum, has asked you to be the keynote speaker at an upcoming conference in Missoula, Montana, on the role of technology in the arts. You are pleased at the invitation, and write a letter to Mr. McCrum accepting the invitation and confirming the details. Your letter to Mr. McCrum should reference the following information:

- The conference will be held October 10–12, 2006, at the civic center in Missoula.
- You have been asked to speak for one hour on Saturday, October 11, followed by a half hour for questions.
- Mr. McCrum suggested the lecture topic "Technology's Effect on Art and Culture."
- Your talk will include a 20-minute slide presentation.
- The Missoula Arts Council will make your travel arrangements.
- Your preference is to arrive in Missoula on Friday, October 10, and depart on Sunday, October 12.
- You want to fly in and out of the airport closest to your home.

a. Start Word.

b. Save a new blank document as **McCrum Letter** to the drive and folder where your Data Files are located.

c. Model your letter to Mr. McCrum after the sample business letter shown in Figure A-16. Use the following formatting guidelines: 3 blank lines after the date, 1 blank line after the inside address, 1 blank line after the salutation, 1 blank line after each body paragraph, and 3 blank lines between the closing and your typed name.

d. Begin the letter by typing today's date.

e. Type the inside address. Be sure to include Mr. McCrum's title and the name of the organization. Make up a street address and zip code.

f. Type a salutation.

g. Using the information listed above, type the body of the letter:
- In the first paragraph, accept the invitation to speak and confirm the important conference details.
- In the second paragraph, confirm your lecture topic and provide any relevant details.
- In the third paragraph, state your travel preferences.
- Type a short final paragraph.

h. Type a closing, then include your name in the signature block.

Advanced Challenge Exercise

- View the letter in Normal view, then correct your spelling and grammar errors, if any, by right-clicking any red- or green-underlined text and then choosing from the options on the shortcut menu.
- View the letter in Print Layout view, then remove any smart tags.
- View the letter in Reading Layout view, then click the Close button on the Reading Layout toolbar to close Reading Layout view.

i. Proofread your letter, make corrections as needed, then save your changes.

j. Preview the letter, print the letter, close the document, then exit Word.

FIGURE A-16

June 12, 2006

Dr. Leslie Morris
Professor of American Literature
Department of Literature
Manchester State College
Manchester, NH 03258

Dear Dr. Morris:

Thank you very much for your kind invitation to speak at your upcoming conference on the literature of place. I will be happy to oblige. I understand the conference will be held September 16 and 17 in the Sanders Auditorium.

I will address my remarks to the topic you suggested, "Writers of the Monadnock region." I understand you would like me to speak at 2:30 p.m. on September 16 for forty minutes, with twenty minutes of questions to follow. My talk will include a slide show. I presume you will have the necessary equipment—a slide projector and viewing screen—on hand.

My preference is to arrive in Manchester on the morning of September 16, and to depart that evening. It is easiest for me to use New York's LaGuardia Airport. I am grateful that your office will be taking care of my travel arrangements.

I look forward to meeting you in September.

Sincerely,

Jessica Grange

▼ INDEPENDENT CHALLENGE 2

Your company has recently installed Word 2003 on its company network. As the training manager, it's your responsibility to teach employees how to use the new software productively. Now that they have begun working with Word 2003, several employees have asked you about smart tags. In response to their queries, you decide to write a memo to all employees explaining how to use the smart tag feature. You know that smart tags are designed to help users perform tasks in Word that normally would require opening a different program, such as Microsoft Outlook (a desktop information-management program that includes e-mail, calendar, and address book features). Before writing your memo, you'll learn more about smart tags by searching the Word Help system.

a. Start Word and save a new blank document as **Smart Tags Memo** to the drive and folder where your Data Files are located.

b. Type **WORD TRAINING MEMORANDUM** at the top of the document, press [Enter] four times, then type the memo heading information shown in Figure A-17. Make sure to include your name in the From line and the current date in the Date line.

c. Press [Enter] twice to place the insertion point where you will begin typing the body of your memo.

d. Search the Word Help system for information on working with smart tags.

e. Type your memo after completing your research. In your memo, define smart tags, then explain what they look like, how to use smart tags, and how to remove smart tags from a document.

FIGURE A-17

WORD TRAINING MEMORANDUM

To: All employees
From: Your Name, Training Manager
Date: Today's date
Re: Smart tags in Microsoft Word

Advanced Challenge Exercise

ACE

- Search the Help system for information on how to check for new smart tags developed by Microsoft and third-party vendors.
- Print the information you find.
- Add a short paragraph to your memo explaining how to find new smart tags.

f. Save your changes, preview and print the memo, then close the document and exit Word.

▼ INDEPENDENT CHALLENGE 3

Yesterday you interviewed for a job as marketing director at Komata Web Designs. You spoke with several people at Komata, including Shige Murata, Director of Operations, whose business card is shown in Figure A-18. You need to write a follow-up letter to Mr. Murata, thanking him for the interview and expressing your interest in the company and the position. He also asked you to send him some samples of your marketing work, which you will enclose with the letter.

a. Start Word and save a new blank document as **Komata Letter** to the drive and folder where your Data Files are located.

b. Begin the letter by typing today's date.

c. Four lines below the date, type the inside address, referring to Figure A-18 for the address information. Be sure to include the recipient's title, company name, and full mailing address in the inside address. (*Hint*: When typing a foreign address, type the name of the country in capital letters by itself on the last line.)

d. Two lines below the inside address, type the salutation.

FIGURE A-18

▼ INDEPENDENT CHALLENGE 3 (CONTINUED)

e. Two lines below the salutation, type the body of the letter according to the following guidelines:
- In the first paragraph, thank him for the interview. Then restate your interest in the position and express your desire to work for the company. Add any specific details you think will enhance the power of your letter.
- In the second paragraph, note that you are enclosing three samples of your work and explain something about the samples you are enclosing.
- Type a short final paragraph.

f. Two lines below the last body paragraph, type a closing, then four lines below the closing, type the signature block. Be sure to include your name in the signature block.

g. Two lines below the signature block, type an enclosure notation. (*Hint*: An enclosure notation usually includes the word "Enclosures" or the abbreviation "Enc." followed by the number of enclosures in parentheses.)

h. Save your changes.

i. Preview and print the letter, then close the document and exit Word.

E-QUEST

▼ INDEPENDENT CHALLENGE 4

Unlike personal letters or many e-mail messages, business letters are formal in tone and format. The World Wide Web is one source for information on writing styles, proper document formatting, and other business etiquette issues. In this independent challenge, you will research guidelines and tips for writing effective and professional business letters. Your online research should seek answers to the following questions: What is important to keep in mind when writing a business letter? What are the parts of a business letter? What are some examples of business letter types? What are some useful tips for writing business letters?

a. Use your favorite search engine to search the Web for information on writing and formatting business letters. Use the keywords **business letters** to conduct your search.

b. Review the Web sites you find. Print at least two Web pages that offer useful guidelines for writing business letters.

c. Start Word and save a new blank document as **Business Letters** to the drive and folder where your Data Files are located.

d. Type your name at the top of the document, then press [Enter] twice.

e. Type a brief report on the results of your research. Your report should answer the following questions:
- What are the URLs of the Web sites you visited to research guidelines for writing a business letter? (*Hint*: A URL is a Web page's address. An example of a URL is www.eHow.com.)
- What is important to keep in mind when writing a business letter?
- What are the parts of a business letter?
- In what situations do people write business letters? Provide at least five examples.

f. Save your changes to the document, preview and print it, then close the document and exit Word

▼ VISUAL WORKSHOP

Create the cover letter shown in Figure A-19. Save the document with the name **Publishing Cover Letter** to the drive and folder where your Data Files are stored, print a copy of the letter, then close the document and exit Word.

FIGURE A-19

July 17, 2006

Ms. Charlotte Janoch
Managing Editor
Sunrise Press
6354 Baker Street
Townsend, MA 02181

Dear Ms. Janoch:

I read of the opening for an editorial assistant on the July 15 edition of Boston.com, and I would like to be considered for the position. A recent graduate of Merrimack College, I am interested in pursuing a career in publishing.

My desire for a publishing career springs from my interest in writing and editing. At Merrimack College, I was a frequent contributor to the student newspaper and was involved in creating a Web site for student poetry and short fiction.

I have a wealth of experience using Microsoft Word in professional settings. For the past several summers I worked as an office assistant for Packer Investment Consultants, where I used Word to create newsletters and financial reports for clients. During the school year, I also worked part-time in the Merrimack College admissions office. Here I used Word's mail merge feature to create form letters and mailing labels.

My enclosed resume details my talents and experience. I would welcome the opportunity to discuss the position and my qualifications with you. I can be reached at 617-555-3849.

Sincerely,

Your Name

Enc.

UNIT B

Word 2003

Editing Documents

OBJECTIVES

- Open a document
- Select text
- Cut and paste text
- Copy and paste text
- Use the Office Clipboard
- Find and replace text
- Check spelling and grammar
- Use the Thesaurus
- Use wizards and templates

If you have a SAM user profile, you may have access to hands-on instruction, practice, and assessment of the skills covered in this unit. Log in to your SAM account and go to your assignments page to see what your instructor has assigned.

The sophisticated editing features in Word make it easy to revise and polish your documents. In this unit, you learn how to open an existing file, revise it by replacing, copying, and moving text, and then save the document as a new file. You also learn how to perfect your documents using proofing tools and how to quickly create attractive, professionally designed documents using wizards and templates. You have been asked to create a press release about a new MediaLoft lecture series in New York. The press release should provide information about the series so that newspapers, radio stations, and other media outlets can announce it to the public. MediaLoft press releases are disseminated by fax, so you also need to create a fax coversheet to use when you fax the press release to your list of press contacts.

UNIT B
Word 2003

Opening a Document

Sometimes the easiest way to create a document is to edit an existing document and save it with a new filename. To modify a document, you must first **open** it so that it displays in the document window. Word offers several methods for opening documents, described in Table B-1. Once you have opened a file, you can use the Save As command to create a new file that is a copy of the original. You can then edit the new file without making changes to the original. Rather than write your press release from scratch, you decide to modify a press release written for a similar event. You begin by opening the press release document and saving it with a new filename.

STEPS

TROUBLE

If the task pane is not open, click View on the menu bar, then click Task Pane.

1. **Start Word**

   Word opens and a blank document and the Getting Started task pane appear in the program window, as shown in Figure B-1. The Getting Started task pane contains links for opening existing documents and for creating new documents.

2. **Click the Open or More hyperlink at the bottom of the Getting Started task pane**

   The Open dialog box opens. You use the Open dialog box to locate and select the file you want to open. The Look in list box displays the current drive or folder. You also can use the Open button on the Standard toolbar or the Open command on the File menu to open the Open dialog box.

3. **Click the Look in list arrow, click the drive containing your Data Files, then double-click the folder containing your Data Files**

   A list of the Data Files for this unit appears in the Open dialog box, as shown in Figure B-2.

QUICK TIP

You also can double-click a filename in the Open dialog box to open the file.

4. **Click the filename WD B-1.doc in the Open dialog box to select it, then click Open**

   The document opens. Notice that the filename WD B-1.doc appears in the title bar. Once you have opened a file, you can edit it and use the Save or the Save As command to save your changes. You use the **Save** command when you want to save the changes you make to a file, overwriting the file that is stored on a disk. You use the **Save As** command when you want to create a new file with a different filename, leaving the original file intact.

5. **Click File on the menu bar, then click Save As**

   The Save As dialog box opens. By saving a file with a new filename, you create a document that is identical to the original document. The original filename is selected (highlighted) in the File name text box. Any text you type replaces the selected text.

6. **Type NY Press Release in the File name text box, then click Save**

   The original file closes and the NY Press Release file is displayed in the document window. Notice the new filename in the title bar. You can now make changes to the press release file without affecting the original file.

Clues to Use

Managing files and folders

The Open and Save As dialog boxes include powerful tools for navigating, creating, deleting, and renaming files and folders on your computer, a network, or the Web. By selecting a file or folder and clicking the Delete button, you can delete the item and send it to the Recycle Bin. You can also create a new folder for storing files by clicking the Create New Folder button and typing a name for the folder. The new folder is created in the current folder. To rename a file or folder, simply right-click it in the dialog box, click Rename, type a new name, and then press [Enter].

Using the Save As dialog box, you can create new files that are based on existing files. To create a new file, you can save an existing file with a different filename or save it in a different location on your system. You also can save a file in a different file format so that it can be opened in a different software program. To save a file in a different format, click the Save as type list arrow, then click the type of file you want to create. For example, you can save a Word document (which has a .doc file extension) as a plain text file (.txt), as a Web page file (.htm), or in a variety of other file formats.

FIGURE B-1: Getting Started task pane

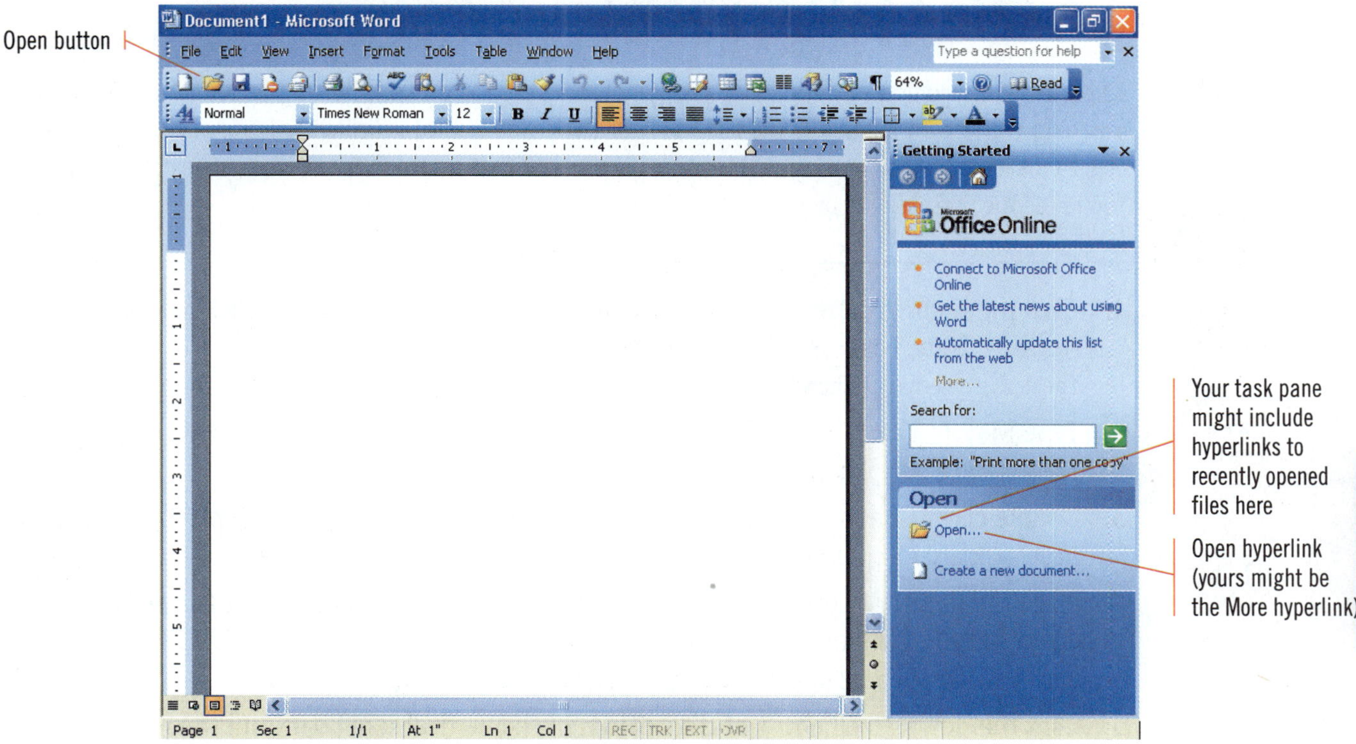

FIGURE B-2: Open dialog box

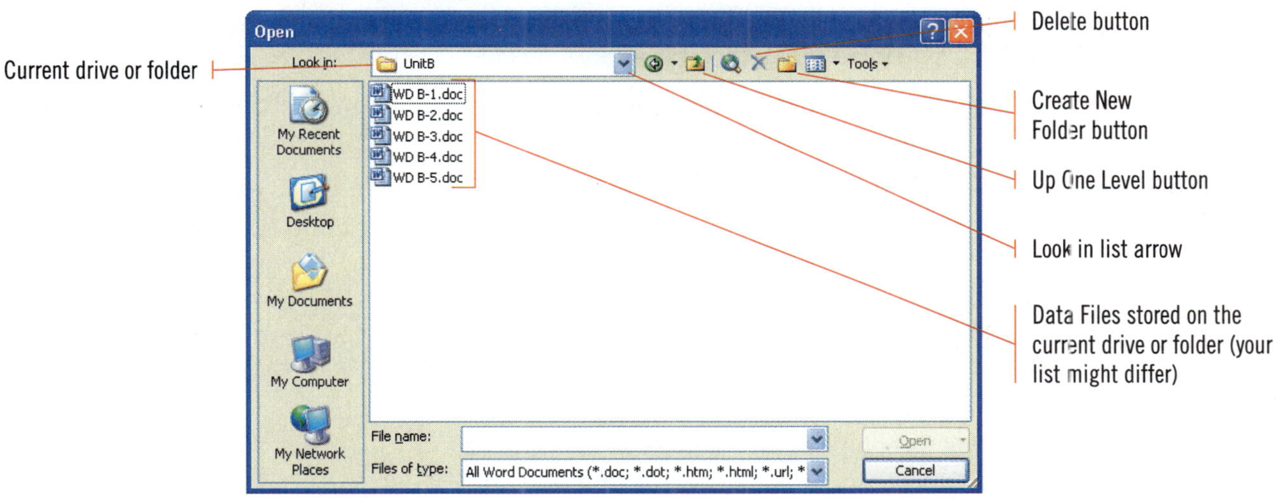

TABLE B-1: Methods for opening documents

use	to	if you want to
The Open button on the Standard toolbar, the Open command on the File menu, the Open or More hyperlink in the Getting Started task pane, or [Ctrl][O]	Open the Open dialog box	Open an existing file
A filename hyperlink in the Getting Started task pane	Open the file in the document window	Open the file; a fast way to open a file that was recently opened on your computer
The From existing document hyperlink in the New Document task pane	Open the New from Existing Document dialog box	Create a copy of an existing file; a fast way to open a document you intend to save with a new filename

UNIT B
Word 2003

Selecting Text

Before deleting, editing, or formatting text, you must **select** the text. Selecting text involves clicking and dragging the I-beam pointer across text to highlight it. You also can click with the pointer in the blank area to the left of text to select lines or paragraphs. Table B-2 describes the many ways to select text. You revise the press release by selecting text and replacing it with new text.

STEPS

TROUBLE

If you make a mistake, you can deselect the text by clicking anywhere in the document window.

1. **Click the Zoom list arrow on the Standard toolbar, click Page Width, click before April 14, 2006, then drag the I pointer over the text to select it**
   The date is selected, as shown in Figure B-3.
2. **Type May 1, 2006**
   The text you type replaces the selected text.
3. **Double-click James, type your first name, double-click Callaghan, then type your last name**
   Double-clicking a word selects the entire word.
4. **Place the pointer in the margin to the left of the phone number so that the pointer changes to , click to select the phone number, then type (415) 555-8293**
   Clicking to the left of a line of text with the pointer selects the entire line.
5. **Click the down scroll arrow at the bottom of the vertical scroll bar until the headline Alex Fogg to Speak... is at the top of your document window**
   The scroll arrows or scroll bars allow you to scroll through a document. You scroll through a document when you want to display different parts of the document in the document window.
6. **Select SAN FRANCISCO, then type NEW YORK**
7. **In the fourth body paragraph, select the sentence All events will be held at the St. James Hotel., then press [Delete]**
   Selecting text and pressing [Delete] removes the text from the document.
8. **Select and replace text in the second and last paragraphs using the following table:**

select	type
May 12	June 14
St. James Hotel in downtown San Francisco	Waldorf-Astoria Hotel
National Public Radio's Helen DeSaint	New York Times literary editor Janet Richard

   The edited press release is shown in Figure B-4.
9. **Click the Save button on the Standard toolbar**
   Your changes to the press release are saved. Always save before and after editing text.

QUICK TIP

If you delete text by mistake, immediately click the Undo button on the Standard toolbar to restore the deleted text to the document.

TABLE B-2: Methods for selecting text

to select	use the mouse pointer to
Any amount of text	Drag over the text
A word	Double-click the word
A line of text	Click with the pointer to the left of the line
A sentence	Press and hold [Ctrl], then click the sentence
A paragraph	Triple-click the paragraph or double-click with the pointer to the left of the paragraph
A large block of text	Click at the beginning of the selection, press and hold [Shift], then click at the end of the selection
Multiple nonconsecutive selections	Select the first selection, then press and hold [Ctrl] as you select each additional selection
An entire document	Triple-click with the pointer to the left of any text, click Select All on the Edit menu, or press [Ctrl][A]

FIGURE B-3: Date selected in the press release

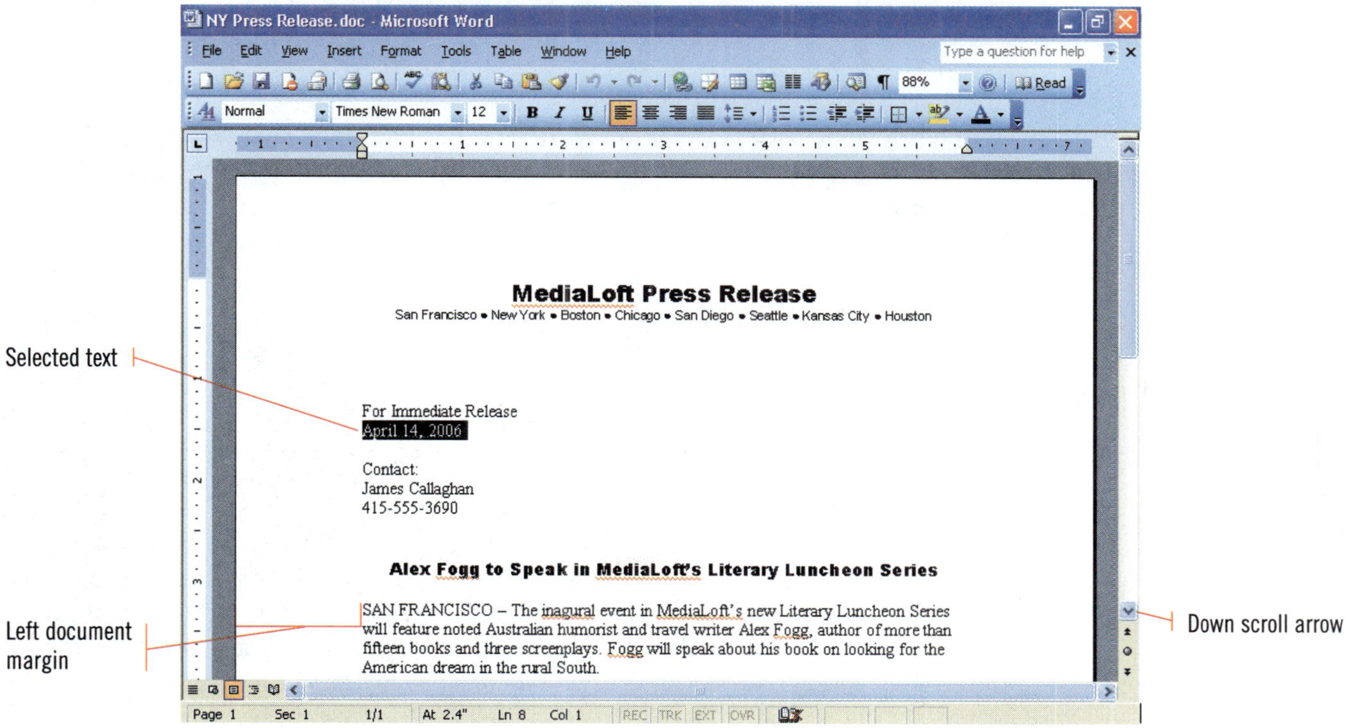

FIGURE B-4: Edited press release

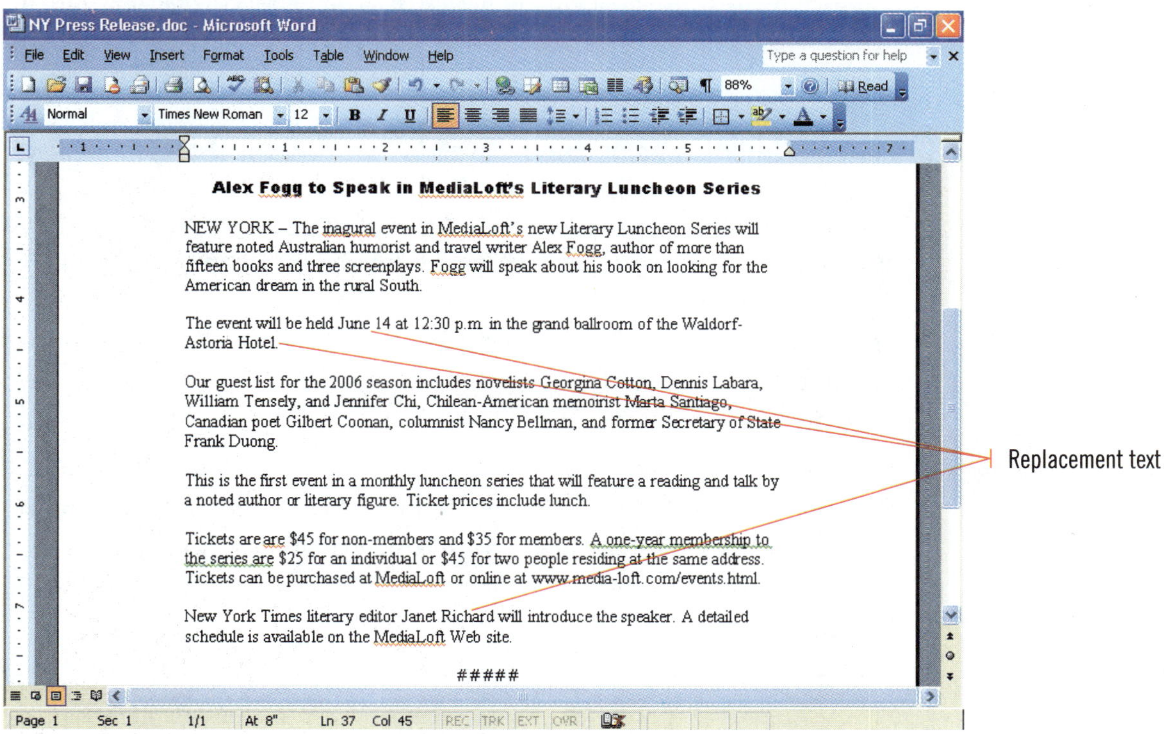

Clues to Use

Replacing text in Overtype mode

Normally you must select text before typing to replace the existing characters, but by turning on **Overtype mode** you can type over existing characters without selecting them first. To turn Overtype mode on and off on your computer, double-click OVR in the status bar. On some computers you also can turn Overtype mode on and off by pressing [Insert]. When Overtype mode is on, OVR appears in black in the status bar. When Overtype mode is off, OVR is dimmed.

UNIT
B
Word 2003

Cutting and Pasting Text

The editing features in Word allow you to move text from one location to another in a document. The operation of moving text is often called **cut and paste**. When you cut text from a document, you remove it from the document and add it to the **Clipboard**, a temporary storage area for text and graphics that you cut or copy from a document. You cut text by selecting it and using the Cut command on the Edit menu or the Cut button. To insert the text from the Clipboard into the document, you place the insertion point where you want to insert the text, and then use the Paste command on the Edit menu or the Paste button to paste the text at that location. You also can move text by dragging it to a new location using the mouse. This operation is called **drag and drop**. You reorganize the information in the press release using the cut-and-paste and drag-and-drop methods.

STEPS

1. **Click the Show/Hide ¶ button on the Standard toolbar**
   Formatting marks appear in the document window. **Formatting marks** are special characters that appear on your screen and do not print. Common formatting marks include the paragraph symbol (¶), which shows the end of a paragraph—wherever you press [Enter]; the dot symbol (•), which represents a space—wherever you press [Spacebar]; and the arrow symbol (→), which shows the location of a tab stop—wherever you press [Tab]. Working with formatting marks turned on can help you to select, edit, and format text with precision.

> **TROUBLE**
> If the Clipboard task pane opens, close it.

2. **In the third paragraph, select Canadian poet Gilbert Coonan, (including the comma and the space after it), then click the Cut button on the Standard toolbar**
   The text is removed from the document and placed on the Clipboard. Word uses two different clipboards: the **system Clipboard** (the Clipboard), which holds just one item, and the **Office Clipboard**, which holds up to 24 items. The last item you cut or copy is always added to both clipboards. You'll learn more about the Office Clipboard in a later lesson.
3. **Place the insertion point before novelists (but after the space) in the first line of the third paragraph, then click the Paste button on the Standard toolbar**
   The text is pasted at the location of the insertion point, as shown in Figure B-5. The Paste Options button appears below text when you first paste it in a document. You'll learn more about the Paste Options button in the next lesson. For now, you can ignore it.
4. **Press and hold [Ctrl], click the sentence Ticket prices include lunch. in the fourth paragraph, then release [Ctrl]**
   The entire sentence is selected.

> **TROUBLE**
> If you make a mistake, click the Undo button on the Standard toolbar, then try again.

5. **Press and hold the mouse button over the selected text until the pointer changes to , then drag the pointer's vertical line to the end of the fifth paragraph (between the period and the paragraph mark) as shown in Figure B-6**
   The pointer's vertical line indicates the location the text will be inserted when you release the mouse button.
6. **Release the mouse button**
   The selected text is moved to the location of the insertion point. It's convenient to move text using the drag-and-drop method when the locations of origin and destination are both visible on the screen. Text is not removed to the Clipboard when you move it using drag-and-drop.
7. **Deselect the text, then click the Save button on the Standard toolbar**
   Your changes to the press release are saved.

FIGURE B-5: Moved text with Paste Options button

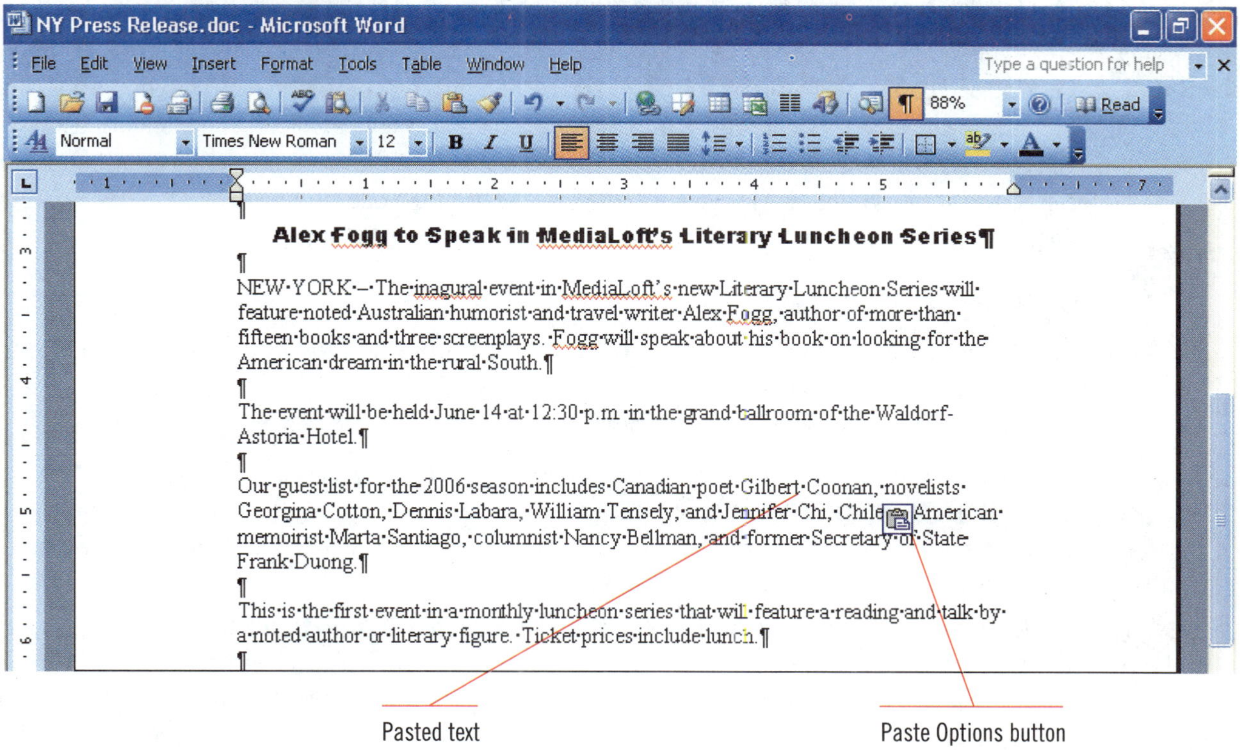

FIGURE B-6: Text being dragged to a new location

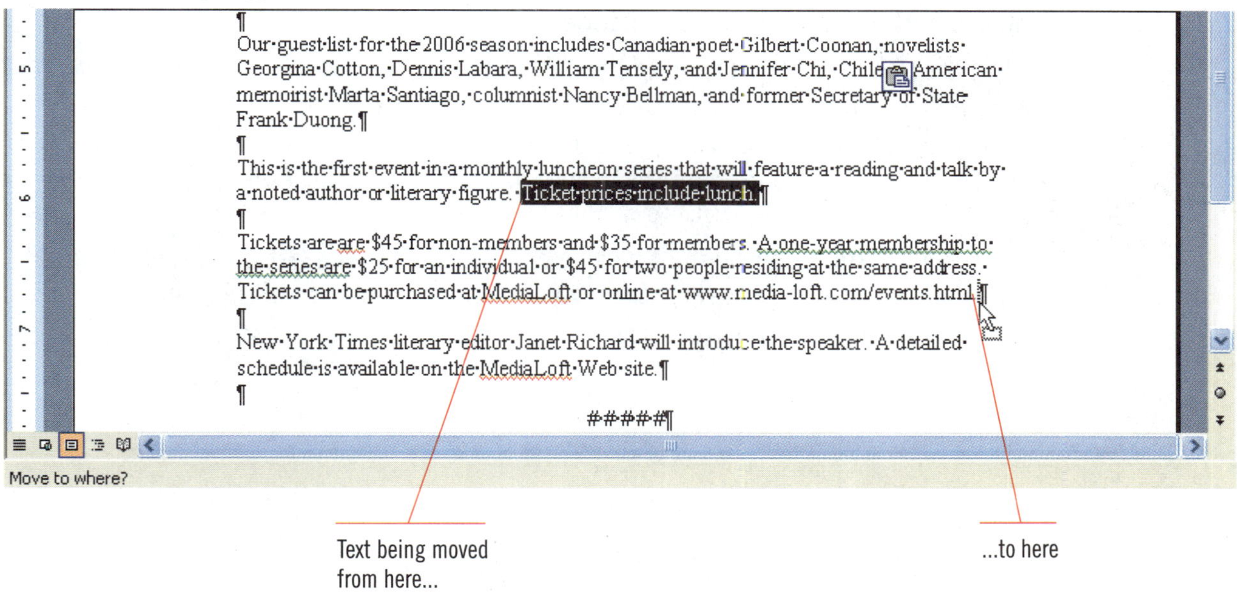

Clues to Use

Using keyboard shortcuts

Instead of using the Cut, Copy, and Paste commands to edit text in Word, you can use the **keyboard shortcuts** [Ctrl][X] to cut text, [Ctrl][C] to copy text, and [Ctrl][V] to paste text. A **shortcut key** is a function key, such as [F1], or a combination of keys, such as [Ctrl][S], that you press to perform a command. For example, pressing [Ctrl][S] saves changes to a document just as clicking the Save button or using the Save command on the File menu saves a document. Becoming skilled at using keyboard shortcuts can help you to quickly accomplish many of the tasks you perform frequently in Word. If a keyboard shortcut is available for a menu command, then it is listed next to the command on the menu.

Word 2003

UNIT
B
Word 2003

Copying and Pasting Text

Copying and pasting text is similar to cutting and pasting text, except that the text you copy is not removed from the document. Rather, a copy of the text is placed on the Clipboard, leaving the original text in place. You can copy text to the Clipboard using the Copy command on the Edit menu or the Copy button, or you can copy text by pressing [Ctrl] as you drag the selected text from one location to another. You continue to edit the press release by copying text from one location to another.

STEPS

TROUBLE

If the Clipboard task pane opens, close it.

QUICK TIP

If you don't like the result of a paste option, try another option or click the Undo button and then paste the text again.

1. **In the headline, select Literary Luncheon, then click the Copy button on the Standard toolbar**

   A copy of the text is placed on the Clipboard, leaving the text you copied in place.

2. **Place the insertion point before season in the third body paragraph, then click the Paste button on the Standard toolbar**

   "Literary Luncheon" is inserted before "season," as shown in Figure B-7. Notice that the pasted text is formatted differently than the paragraph in which it was inserted.

3. **Click the Paste Options button, then click Match Destination Formatting**

   The Paste Options button allows you to change the formatting of pasted text. The formatting of "Literary Luncheon" is changed to match the rest of the paragraph. The options available on the Paste Options menu depend on the format of the text you are pasting and the format of the surrounding text.

4. **Scroll down if necessary so that the last two paragraphs are visible on your screen**

5. **In the fifth paragraph, select www.media-loft.com, press and hold [Ctrl], then press the mouse button until the pointer changes to**

6. **Drag the pointer's vertical line to the end of the last paragraph, placing it between site and the period, release the mouse button, then release [Ctrl]**

   The text is copied to the last paragraph. Since the formatting of the text you copied is the same as the formatting of the paragraph in which you inserted it, you can ignore the Paste Options button. Text is not copied to the Clipboard when you copy it using the drag-and-drop method.

7. **Place the insertion point before www.media-loft.com in the last paragraph, type at followed by a space, then click the Save button on the Standard toolbar**

   Compare your document with Figure B-8.

Clues to Use

Copying and moving items in a long document

If you want to copy or move items between parts of a long document, it can be useful to split the document window into two panes so that the item you want to copy or move is displayed in one pane and the destination for the item is displayed in the other pane. To split a window, click the Split command on the Window menu, drag the horizontal split bar that appears to the location you want to split the window, and then click. Once the document window is split into two panes, you can drag the split bar to resize the panes and use the scroll bars in each pane to display different parts of the document. To copy or move an item from one pane to another, you can use the Cut, Copy, and Paste commands, or you can drag the item between the panes. When you are finished editing the document, double-click the split bar to restore the window to a single pane.

FIGURE B-7: Text pasted in document

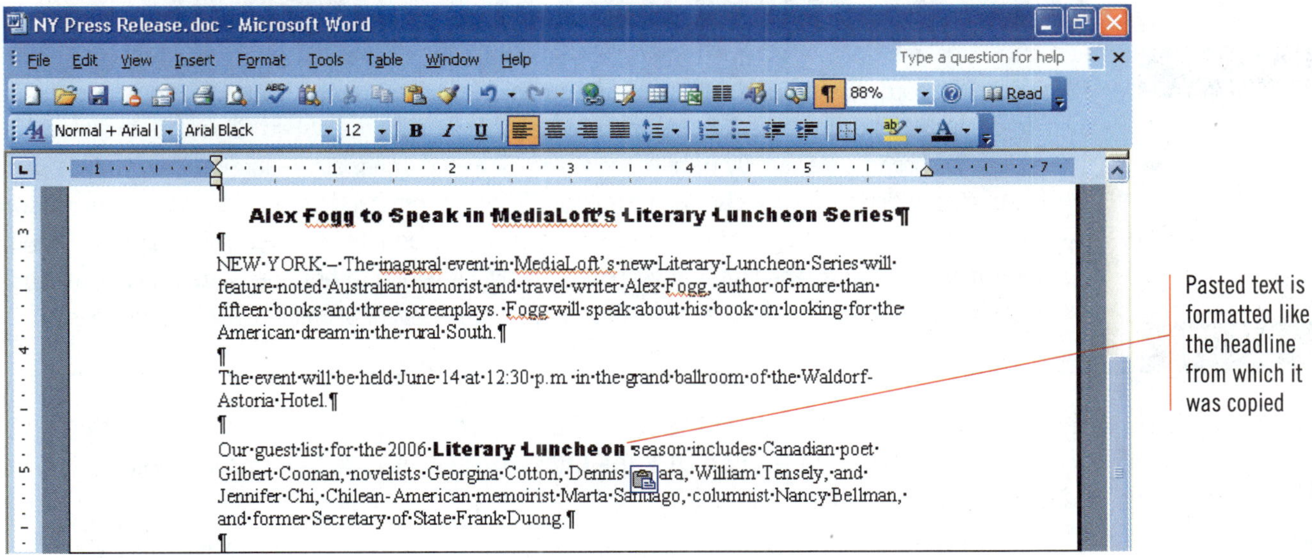

FIGURE B-8: Copied text in press release

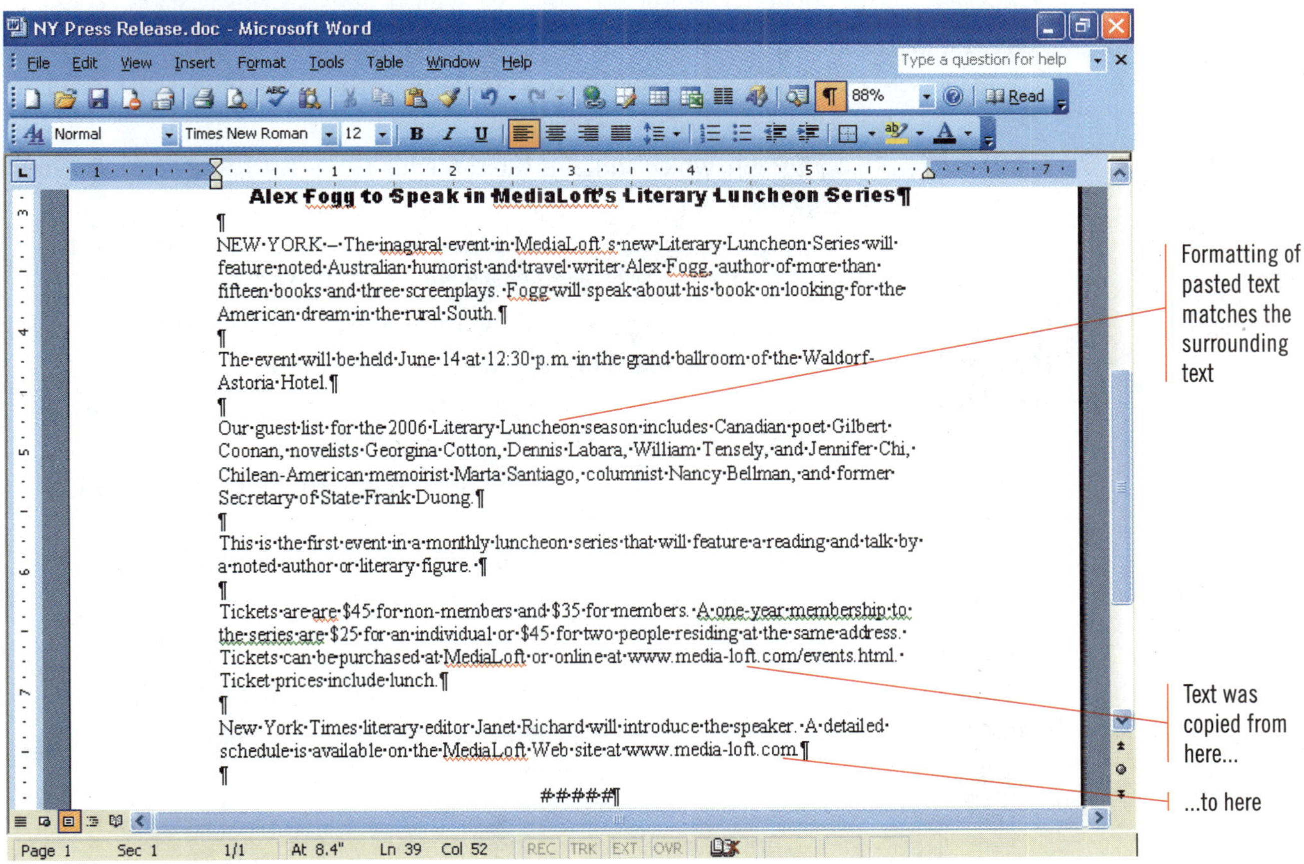

UNIT
B
Word 2003

Using the Office Clipboard

The Office Clipboard allows you to collect text and graphics from files created in any Office program and insert them into your Word documents. It holds up to 24 items and, unlike the system Clipboard, the items on the Office Clipboard can be viewed. By default, the Office Clipboard opens automatically when you cut or copy two items consecutively. You can also use the Office Clipboard command on the Edit menu to manually display the Office Clipboard if you prefer to work with it open. You add items to the Office Clipboard using the Cut and Copy commands. The last item you collect is always added to both the system Clipboard and the Office Clipboard. You use the Office Clipboard to move several sentences in your press release.

STEPS

TROUBLE

If the Office Clipboard does not open, click Office Clipboard on the Edit menu, click the Undo button on the Standard toolbar two times, click Clear All on the Clipboard task pane, then repeat Steps 1 and 2. To restore the default, click Options on the Clipboard task pane, click Show Office Clipboard Automatically to select it, then click outside the menu.

QUICK TIP

To delete an individual item from the Office Clipboard, click the list arrow next to the item, then click Delete.

QUICK TIP

Many Word users prefer to work with formatting marks turned on at all times. Experiment for yourself and see which method you prefer.

1. **In the last paragraph, select the sentence New York Times literary editor... (including the space after the period), then click the Cut button on the Standard toolbar**
   The sentence is cut to the Clipboard.
2. **Select the sentence A detailed schedule is... (including the ¶ mark), then click**
   The Office Clipboard opens in the Clipboard task pane, as shown in Figure B-9. It displays the items you cut from the press release. The icon next to each item indicates the items are from a Word document.
3. **Place the insertion point at the end of the second paragraph (after Hotel. but before the ¶ mark), then click the New York Times literary editor... item on the Office Clipboard**
   Clicking an item on the Office Clipboard pastes the item in the document at the location of the insertion point. Notice that the item remains on the Office Clipboard even after you pasted it. Items remain on the Office Clipboard until you delete them or close all open Office programs. Also, if you add a 25th item to the Office Clipboard, the first item is deleted.
4. **Place the insertion point at the end of the third paragraph (after Duong.), then click the A detailed schedule is... item on the Office Clipboard**
   The sentence is pasted in the document.
5. **Select the fourth paragraph, which contains the sentence This is the first event... (including the ¶ mark), then click**
   The sentence is cut to the Office Clipboard. Notice that the last item collected displays at the top of the Clipboard task pane. The last item collected is also stored on the system Clipboard.
6. **Place the insertion point at the beginning of the third paragraph (before Our...), click the Paste button on the Standard toolbar, then press [Backspace]**
   The "This is the first..." sentence is pasted at the beginning of the "Our guest list..." paragraph. You can paste the last item collected using either the Paste command or the Office Clipboard.
7. **Place the insertion point at the end of the third paragraph (after www.media-loft.com and before the ¶ mark), then press [Delete] twice**
   The ¶ symbols and the blank line between the third and fourth paragraphs are deleted.
8. **Click the Show/Hide ¶ button on the Standard toolbar**
   Compare your press release with Figure B-10.
9. **Click the Clear All button on the Office Clipboard to remove the items from it, close the Clipboard task pane, press [Ctrl][Home], then click the Save button**
   Pressing [Ctrl][Home] moves the insertion point to the top of the document.

FIGURE B-9: Office Clipboard in Clipboard task pane

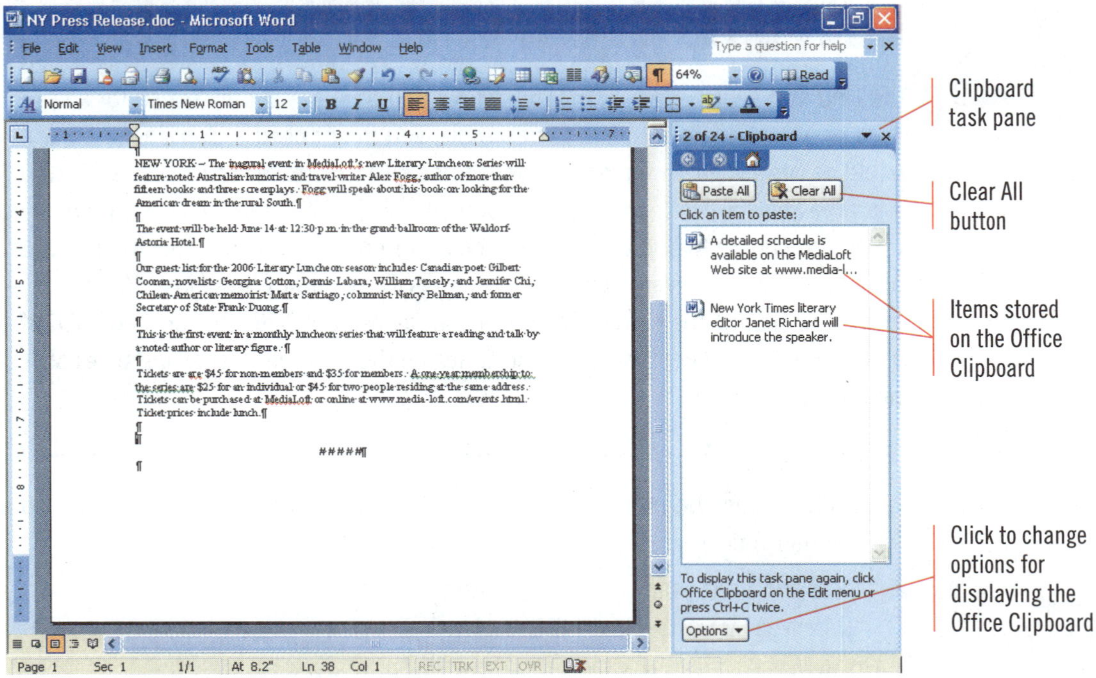

FIGURE B-10: Revised press release

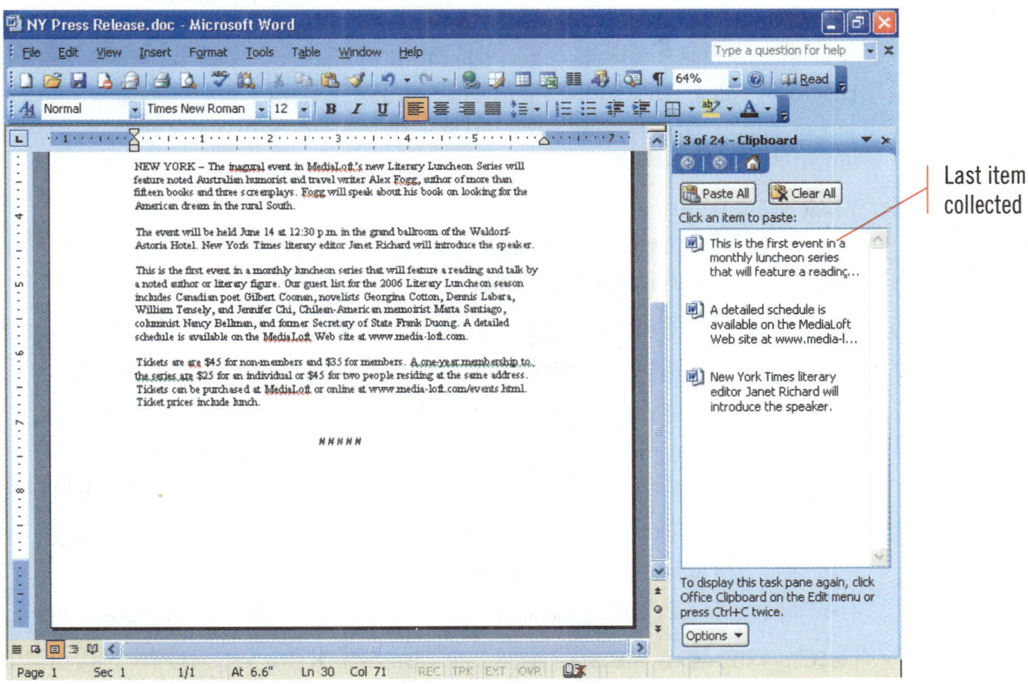

Clues to Use

Copying and moving items between documents

The system and Office Clipboards also can be used to copy and move items between Word documents. To copy or cut items from one Word document and paste them into another, first open both documents and the Clipboard task pane in the program window. With multiple documents open, you can copy and move items between documents by copying or cutting the item(s) from one document and then switching to another document and pasting the item(s). To switch between open documents, click the button on the taskbar for the document you want to appear in the document window. You can also display both documents at the same time by clicking the Arrange All command on the Window menu. The Office Clipboard stores all the items collected from all documents, regardless of which document is displayed in the document window. The system Clipboard stores the last item collected from any document.

Finding and Replacing Text

The Find and Replace feature in Word allows you to automatically search for and replace all instances of a word or phrase in a document. For example, you might need to substitute "bookstore" for "store," and it would be very time-consuming to manually locate and replace each instance of "store" in a long document. Using the Replace command you can automatically find and replace all occurrences of specific text at once, or you can choose to find and review each occurrence individually. You also can use the Find command to locate and highlight every occurrence of a specific word or phrase in a document. MediaLoft has decided to change the name of the New York series from "Literary Luncheon Series" to "Literary Limelight Series." You use the Replace command to search the document for all instances of "Luncheon" and replace them with "Limelight."

STEPS

1. **Click Edit on the menu bar, click Replace, then click More in the Find and Replace dialog box**
   The Find and Replace dialog box opens, as shown in Figure B-11.
2. **Click the Find what text box, then type Luncheon**
   "Luncheon" is the text that will be replaced.
3. **Press [Tab], then type Limelight in the Replace with text box**
   "Limelight" is the text that will replace "Luncheon."
4. **Click the Match case check box in the Search Options section to select it**
   Selecting the Match case check box tells Word to find only exact matches for the uppercase and lowercase characters you entered in the Find what text box. You want to replace all instances of "Luncheon" in the proper name "Literary Luncheon Series." You do not want to replace "luncheon" when it refers to a lunchtime event.
5. **Click Replace All**
   Clicking Replace All changes all occurrences of "Luncheon" to "Limelight" in the press release. A message box reports three replacements were made.
6. **Click OK to close the message box, then click Close to close the Find and Replace dialog box**
   Word replaced "Luncheon" with "Limelight" in three locations, but did not replace "luncheon."
7. **Click Edit on the menu bar, then click Find**
   The Find and Replace dialog box opens with the Find tab displayed. The Find command allows you to quickly locate all instances of text in a document. You can use it to verify that Word did not replace "luncheon."
8. **Type luncheon in the Find what text box, click the Highlight all items found in check box to select it, click Find All, then click Close**
   The Find and Replace dialog box closes and "luncheon" is selected in the document, as shown in Figure B-12.
9. **Deselect the text, press [Ctrl][Home], then click the Save button on the Standard toolbar**

QUICK TIP

Click Find Next to find, review, and replace each occurrence individually.

Clues to Use

Inserting text with AutoCorrect

As you type, AutoCorrect automatically corrects many commonly misspelled words. By creating your own AutoCorrect entries, you also can set Word to quickly insert text that you type often, such as your name or contact information, or to correct words you frequently misspell. For example, you could create an AutoCorrect entry so that the name "Alice Wegman" is automatically inserted whenever you type "aw" followed by a space. To create an AutoCorrect entry, click AutoCorrect Options on the Tools menu. On the AutoCorrect tab in the AutoCorrect dialog box, type the text you want to be automatically corrected in the Replace text box (such as "aw"), type the text you want to be automatically inserted in its place in the With text box (such as "Alice Wegman"), then click Add. The AutoCorrect entry is added to the list. Note that Word inserts an AutoCorrect entry in a document only when you press [Spacebar] after typing the text you want Word to correct. For example, Word will insert "Alice Wegman" when you type "aw" followed by a space, but not when you type "awful."

FIGURE B-11: Find and Replace dialog box

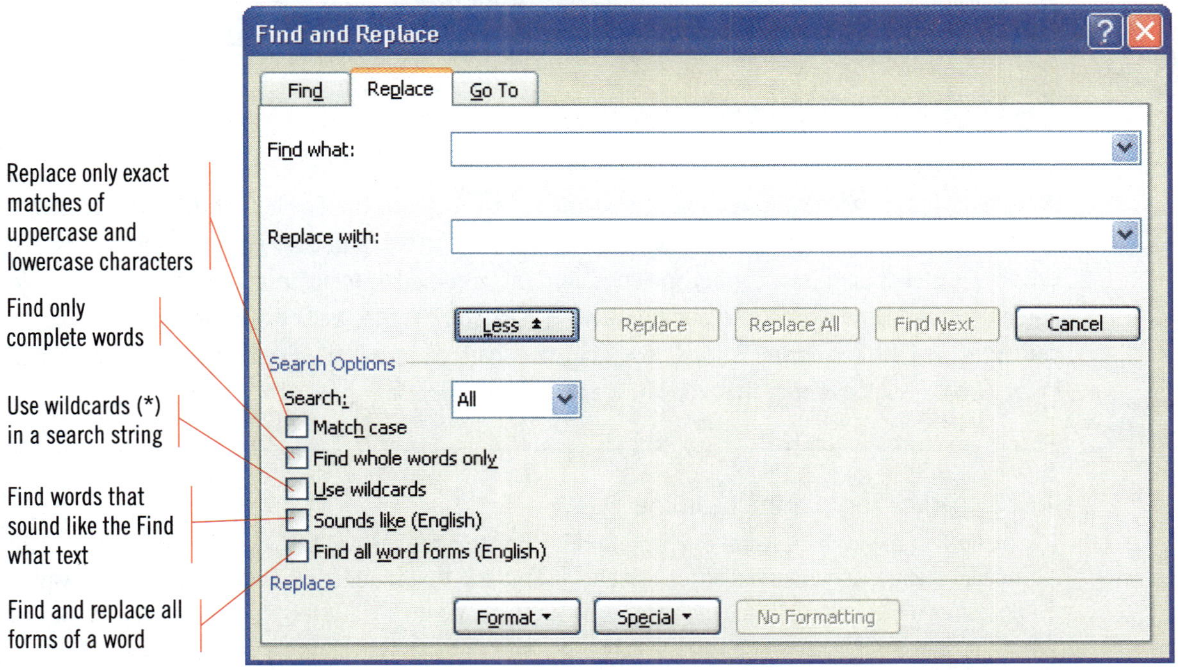

FIGURE B-12: Found text highlighted in document

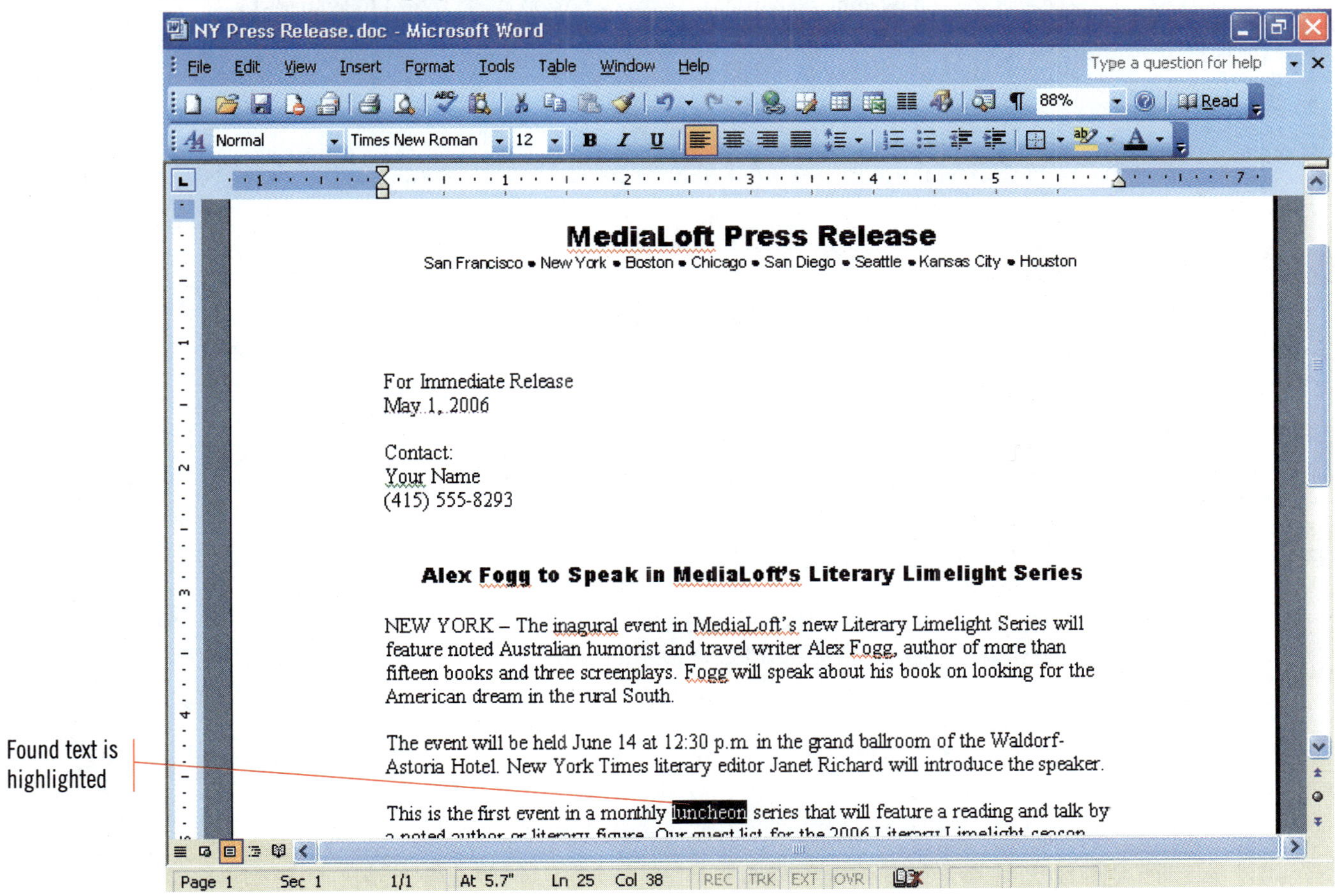

UNIT B
Word 2003

Checking Spelling and Grammar

When you finish typing and revising a document, you can use the Spelling and Grammar command to search the document for misspelled words and grammar errors. The Spelling and Grammar checker flags possible mistakes, suggests correct spellings, and offers remedies for grammar errors such as subject-verb agreement, repeated words, and punctuation. You use the Spelling and Grammar checker to search your press release for errors. Before beginning the search, you set the Spelling and Grammar checker to ignore words, such as Fogg, that you know are spelled correctly.

STEPS

TROUBLE
If Word flags your name as misspelled, right-click it, then click Ignore All.

1. **Right-click Fogg in the headline**
   A shortcut menu that includes suggestions for correcting the spelling of "Fogg" opens. You can correct individual spelling and grammar errors by right-clicking text that is underlined with a red or green wavy line and selecting a correction. Although "Fogg" is not in the Word dictionary, it is spelled correctly in the document.

2. **Click Ignore All**
   Clicking Ignore All tells Word not to flag "Fogg" as misspelled.

TROUBLE
If "MediaLoft" and "MediaLoft's" are not flagged as misspelled, skip this step.

3. **Right-click MediaLoft at the top of the document, click Ignore All, right-click MediaLoft's in the headline, then click Ignore All**
   The red wavy underline is removed from all instances of "MediaLoft" and "MediaLoft's."

QUICK TIP
To change the language used by the Word proofing tools, click Tools on the menu bar, point to Language, then click Set Language.

4. **Press [Ctrl][Home], then click the Spelling and Grammar button on the Standard toolbar**
   The Spelling and Grammar: English (U.S.) dialog box opens, as shown in Figure B-13. The dialog box identifies "inagural" as misspelled and suggests possible corrections for the error. The word selected in the Suggestions box is the correct spelling.

5. **Click Change**
   Word replaces the misspelled word with the correctly spelled word. Next, the dialog box indicates "are" is repeated in a sentence.

TROUBLE
You might need to correct other spelling and grammar errors.

6. **Click Delete**
   Word deletes the second occurrence of the repeated word. Next, the dialog box flags a subject-verb agreement error and suggests using "is" instead of "are," as shown in Figure B-14. The phrase selected in the Suggestions box is correct.

QUICK TIP
If Word does not offer a valid correction, correct the error yourself.

7. **Click Change**
   The word "is" replaces the word "are" in the sentence and the Spelling and Grammar dialog box closes. Keep in mind that the Spelling and Grammar checker identifies many common errors, but you cannot rely on it to find and correct all spelling and grammar errors in your documents. Always proofread your documents carefully.

8. **Click OK to complete the spelling and grammar check, press [Ctrl][Home], then click the Save button on the Standard toolbar**

FIGURE B-13: Spelling and Grammar: English (U.S.) dialog box

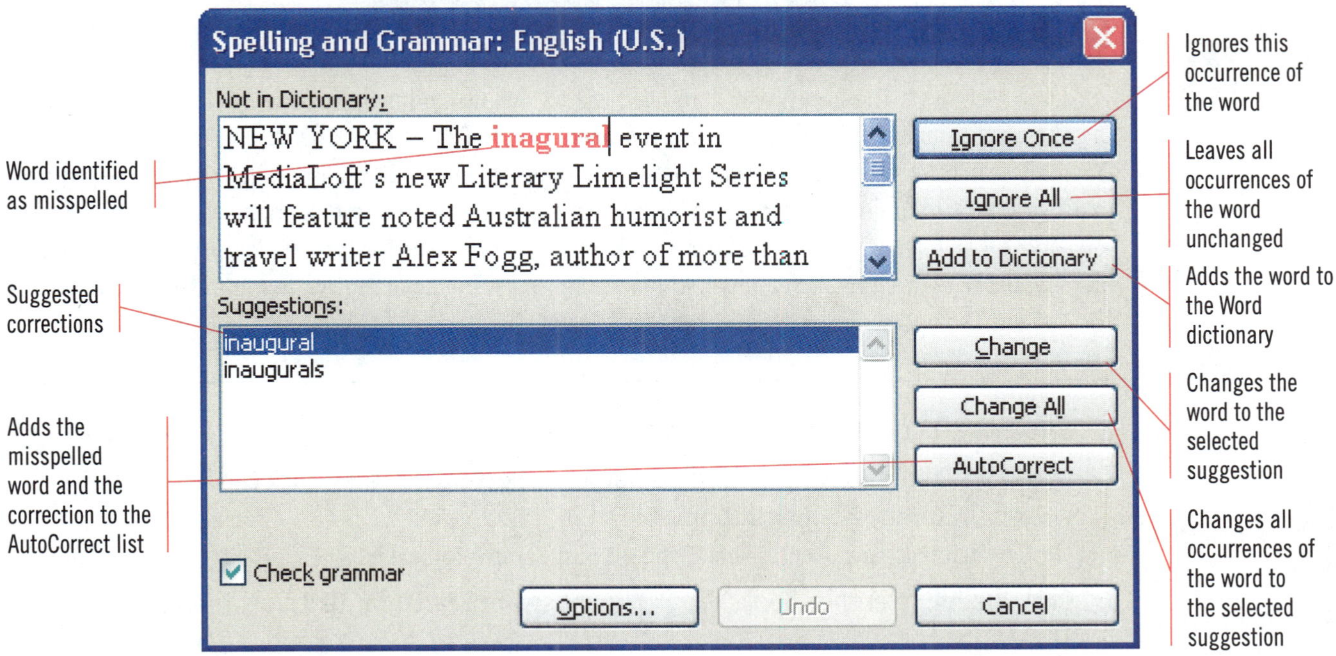

FIGURE B-14: Grammar error identified in Spelling and Grammar dialog box

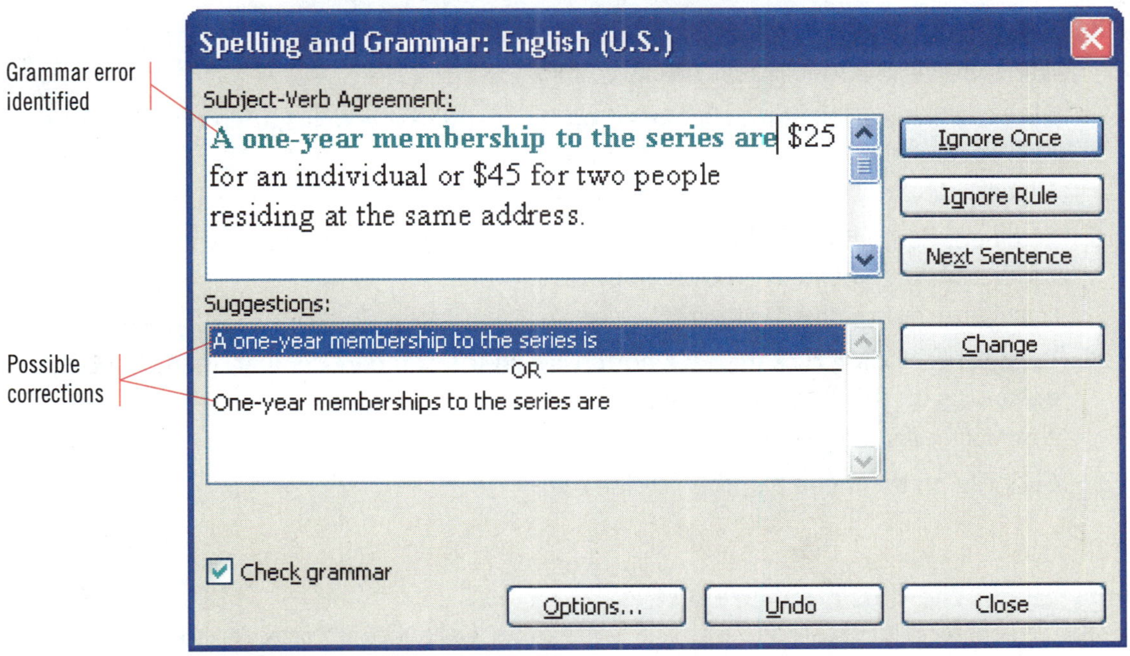

Clues to Use

Using the Undo, Redo, and Repeat commands

Word remembers the editing and formatting changes you make so that you can easily reverse or repeat them. You can reverse the last action you took by clicking the Undo button on the Standard toolbar, or you can undo a series of actions by clicking the Undo list arrow and selecting the action you want to reverse. When you undo an action using the Undo list arrow, you also undo all the actions above it in the list; that is, all actions that were performed after the action you selected. Similarly, you can keep the changes you just reversed by using the Redo button and the Redo list arrow.

If you want to repeat a change you just made, use the Repeat command on the Edit menu. The name of the Repeat command changes depending on the last action you took. For example, if you just typed "thank you," the name of the command is Repeat Typing. Clicking the Repeat Typing command inserts "thank you" at the location of the insertion point. You also can repeat the last action you took by pressing [F4].

UNIT B

Word 2003

Using the Thesaurus

Word also includes a Thesaurus, which you can use to look up synonyms for awkward or repetitive words. The Thesaurus is one of the reference sources available in the Research task pane. This task pane allows you to quickly search reference sources for information related to a word or phrase. When you are working with an active Internet connection, the Research task pane provides access to dictionary, encyclopedia, translation, and other reference sources and research services. After proofreading your document for errors, you decide the press release would read better if several adjectives were more descriptive. You use the Thesaurus to find synonyms for "noted" and "new".

STEPS

1. **Scroll down until the headline is displayed at the top of your screen**
2. **In the first sentence of the third paragraph, select noted, then click the Research button on the Standard toolbar**

   The Research task pane opens. "Noted" appears in the Search for text box.

3. **Click the All Reference Books list arrow under the Search for text box, then click Thesaurus: English (U.S.)**

   Possible synonyms for "noted" are listed under the Thesaurus: English (U.S.) heading in the task pane, as shown in Figure B-15.

4. **Point to distinguished in the list of synonyms**

   A box containing an arrow appears around the word.

5. **Click the arrow in the box, click Insert on the menu that appears, then close the Research task pane**

   "Distinguished" replaces "noted" in the press release.

6. **Scroll up, right-click new in the first sentence of the first paragraph, point to Synonyms on the shortcut menu, then click innovative**

   "Innovative" replaces "new" in the press release.

7. **Press [Ctrl][Home], click the Save button on the Standard toolbar, then click the Print button on the Standard toolbar**

   A copy of the finished press release prints. Compare your document to Figure B-16.

8. **Click File on the menu bar, then click Close**

QUICK TIP

You can also select a word, click Tools on the menu bar, point to Language, and then click Thesaurus to open the Research task pane and display a list of synonyms for the word.

QUICK TIP

Right-click a word, then click Look up to open the Research task pane.

Clues to Use

Viewing and modifying the document properties

Document properties are details about a file that can help you to organize and search your files. The author name, the date the file was created, the title, and keywords that describe the contents of the file are examples of document property information. You can view and modify the properties of an open document by clicking Properties on the File menu to open the Properties dialog box. The General, Statistics, and Contents tabs of the Properties dialog box display information about the file that is automatically created and updated by Word. The General tab shows the file type, location, size, and date and time the file was created and last modified; the Statistics tab displays information about revisions to the document along with the number of pages, words, lines, paragraphs, and characters in the file; and the Contents tab shows the title of the document.

You can define other document properties using the Summary and Custom tabs of the Properties dialog box. The Summary tab includes identifying information about the document such as the title, subject, author, and keywords. Some of this information is entered by Word when the document is first saved, but you can modify or add to the summary details by typing new information in the text boxes on the Summary tab. The Custom tab allows you to create new document properties, such as client, project, or date completed. To create a custom property, select a property name in the Name list box on the Custom tab, use the Type list arrow to select the type of data you want for the property, and then type the identifying detail (such as a project name) in the Value text box. When you are finished viewing or modifying the document properties, click OK to close the Properties dialog box.

FIGURE B-15: Research task pane

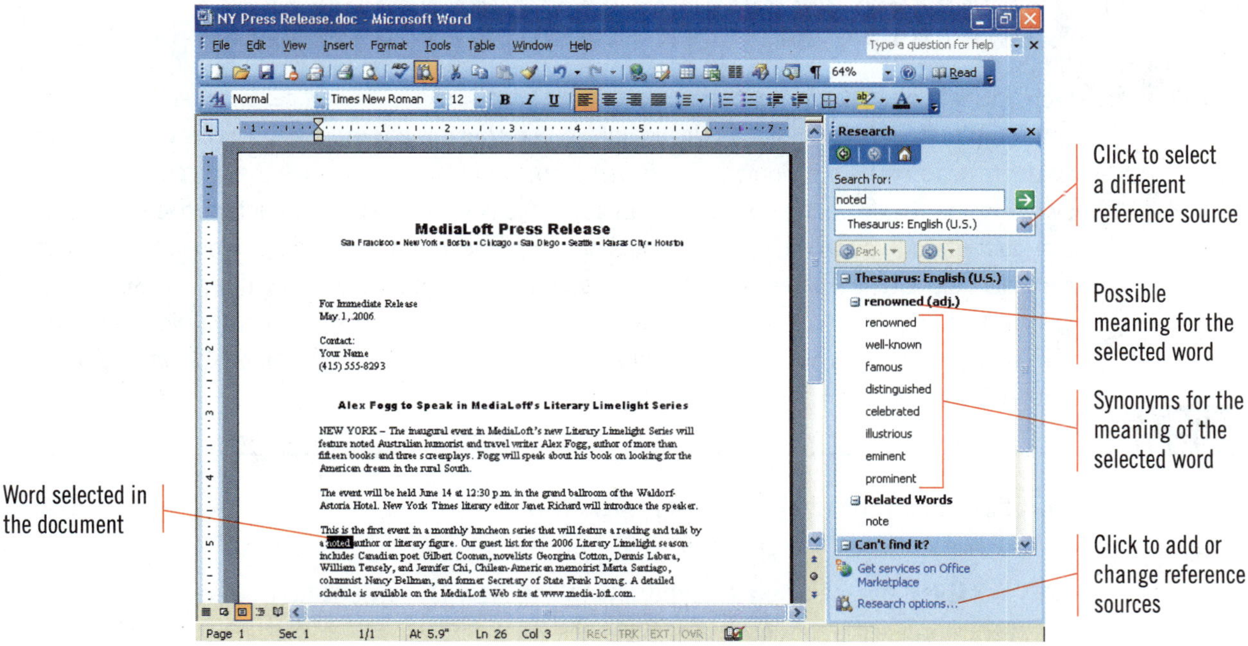

FIGURE B-16: Completed press release

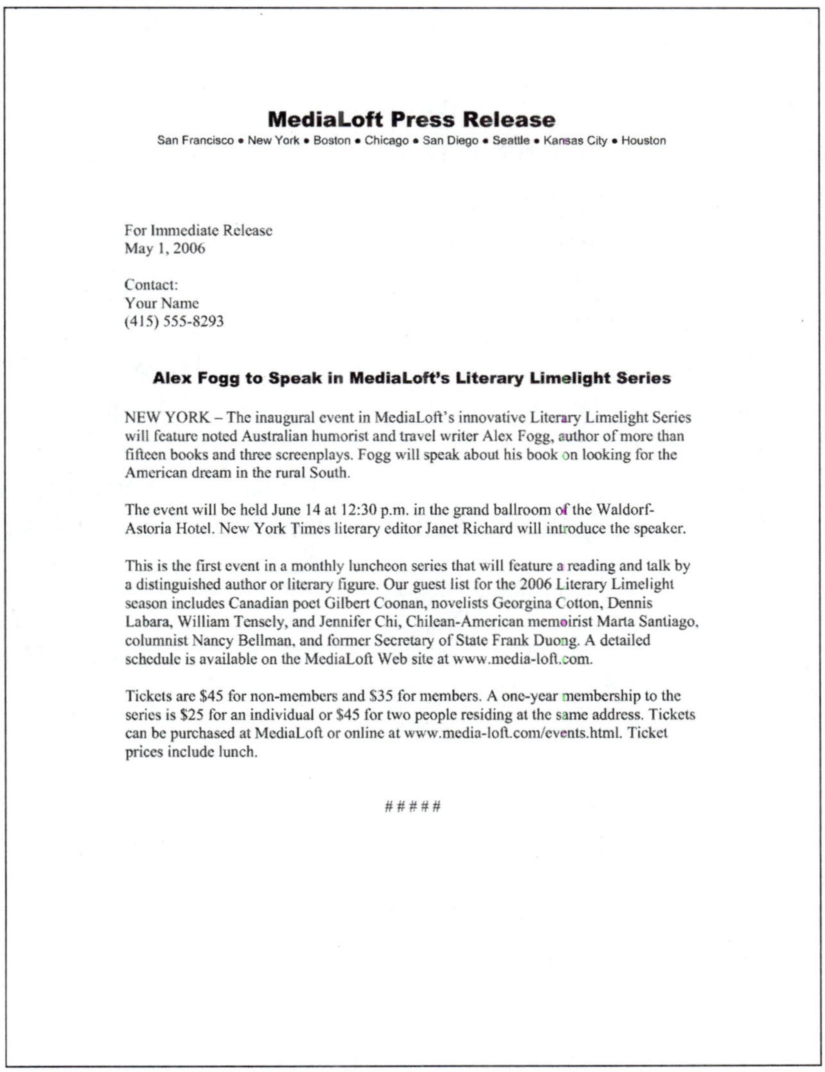

MediaLoft Press Release

San Francisco • New York • Boston • Chicago • San Diego • Seattle • Kansas City • Houston

For Immediate Release
May 1, 2006

Contact:
Your Name
(415) 555-8293

Alex Fogg to Speak in MediaLoft's Literary Limelight Series

NEW YORK – The inaugural event in MediaLoft's innovative Literary Limelight Series will feature noted Australian humorist and travel writer Alex Fogg, author of more than fifteen books and three screenplays. Fogg will speak about his book on looking for the American dream in the rural South.

The event will be held June 14 at 12:30 p.m. in the grand ballroom of the Waldorf-Astoria Hotel. New York Times literary editor Janet Richard will introduce the speaker.

This is the first event in a monthly luncheon series that will feature a reading and talk by a distinguished author or literary figure. Our guest list for the 2006 Literary Limelight season includes Canadian poet Gilbert Coonan, novelists Georgina Cotton, Dennis Labara, William Tensely, and Jennifer Chi, Chilean-American memoirist Marta Santiago, columnist Nancy Bellman, and former Secretary of State Frank Duong. A detailed schedule is available on the MediaLoft Web site at www.media-loft.com.

Tickets are $45 for non-members and $35 for members. A one-year membership to the series is $25 for an individual or $45 for two people residing at the same address. Tickets can be purchased at MediaLoft or online at www.media-loft.com/events.html. Ticket prices include lunch.

# # # # #

UNIT
B
Word 2003

Using Wizards and Templates

Word includes many templates that you can use to quickly create memos, faxes, letters, reports, brochures, and other professionally designed documents. A **template** is a formatted document that contains placeholder text. To create a document that is based on a template, you replace the placeholder text with your own text and then save the document with a new filename. A **wizard** is an interactive set of dialog boxes that guides you through the process of creating a document. A wizard prompts you to provide information and select formatting options, and then it creates the document for you based on your specifications. You can create a document with a wizard or template using the New command on the File menu. You will fax the press release to your list of press contacts, beginning with the *New York Times*. You use a template to create a fax coversheet for the press release.

STEPS

1. **Click File on the menu bar, then click New**
   The New Document task pane opens.
2. **Click the On my computer hyperlink in the New Document task pane**
   The Templates dialog box opens. The tabs in the dialog box contain icons for the Word templates and wizards.
3. **Click the Letters & Faxes tab, then click the Professional Fax icon**
   A preview of the Professional Fax template appears in the Templates dialog box, as shown in Figure B-17.
4. **Click OK**
   The Professional Fax template opens as a new document in the document window. It contains placeholder text, which you can replace with your own information.
5. **Drag to select Company Name Here, then type MediaLoft**
6. **Click the Click here and type return address and phone and fax numbers placeholder**
   Clicking the placeholder selects it. When a placeholder says Click here... you do not need to drag to select it.
7. **Type MediaLoft San Francisco, press [Enter], then type Tel: (415) 555-8293**
   The text you type replaces the placeholder text.
8. **Replace the remaining placeholder text with the text shown in Figure B-18**
   Word automatically inserted the current date in the document. You do not need to replace the current date with the date shown in the figure.
9. **Click File on the menu bar, click Save As, use the Save in list arrow to navigate to the drive or folder where your Data Files are located, type NYT Fax in the File name text box, then click Save**
   The document is saved with the filename NYT Fax.
10. **Click the Print button on the Standard toolbar, click File on the menu bar, then click Exit**
    A copy of the fax coversheet prints and the document and Word close.

QUICK TIP
Double-clicking an icon in the Templates dialog box also opens a new document based on the template.

QUICK TIP
Delete any placeholder text you do not want to replace.

FIGURE B-17: Letters & Faxes tab in Templates dialog box

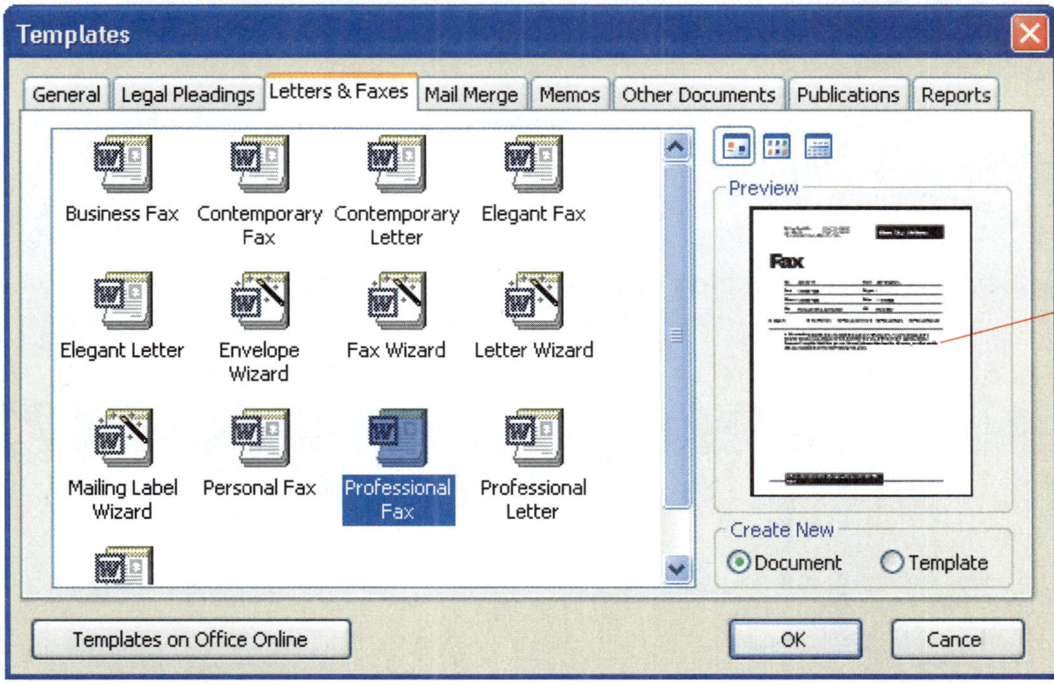

Preview of selected template

FIGURE B-18: Completed fax coversheet

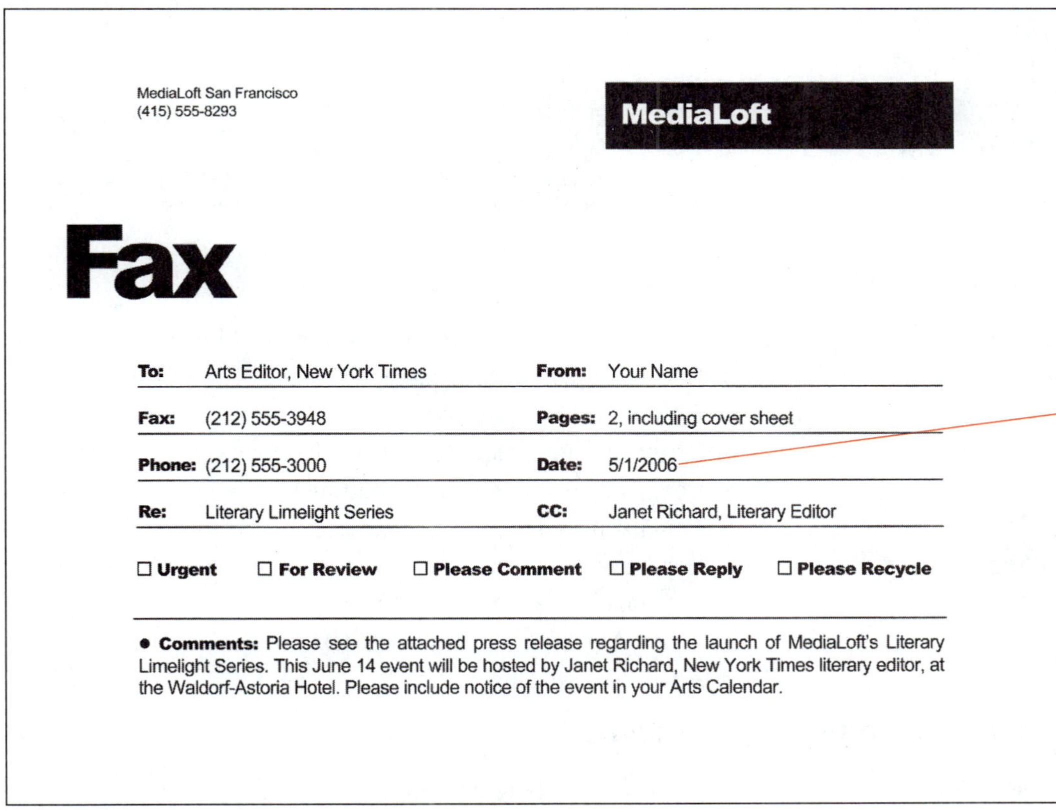

MediaLoft San Francisco
(415) 555-8293

MediaLoft

Fax

To:	Arts Editor, New York Times	**From:**	Your Name
Fax:	(212) 555-3948	**Pages:**	2, including cover sheet
Phone:	(212) 555-3000	**Date:**	5/1/2006
Re:	Literary Limelight Series	**CC:**	Janet Richard, Literary Editor

☐ **Urgent** ☐ **For Review** ☐ **Please Comment** ☐ **Please Reply** ☐ **Please Recycle**

● **Comments:** Please see the attached press release regarding the launch of MediaLoft's Literary Limelight Series. This June 14 event will be hosted by Janet Richard, New York Times literary editor, at the Waldorf-Astoria Hotel. Please include notice of the event in your Arts Calendar.

Your document will show the current date

Practice

▼ CONCEPTS REVIEW

Label the elements of the Open dialog box shown in Figure B-19.

FIGURE B-19

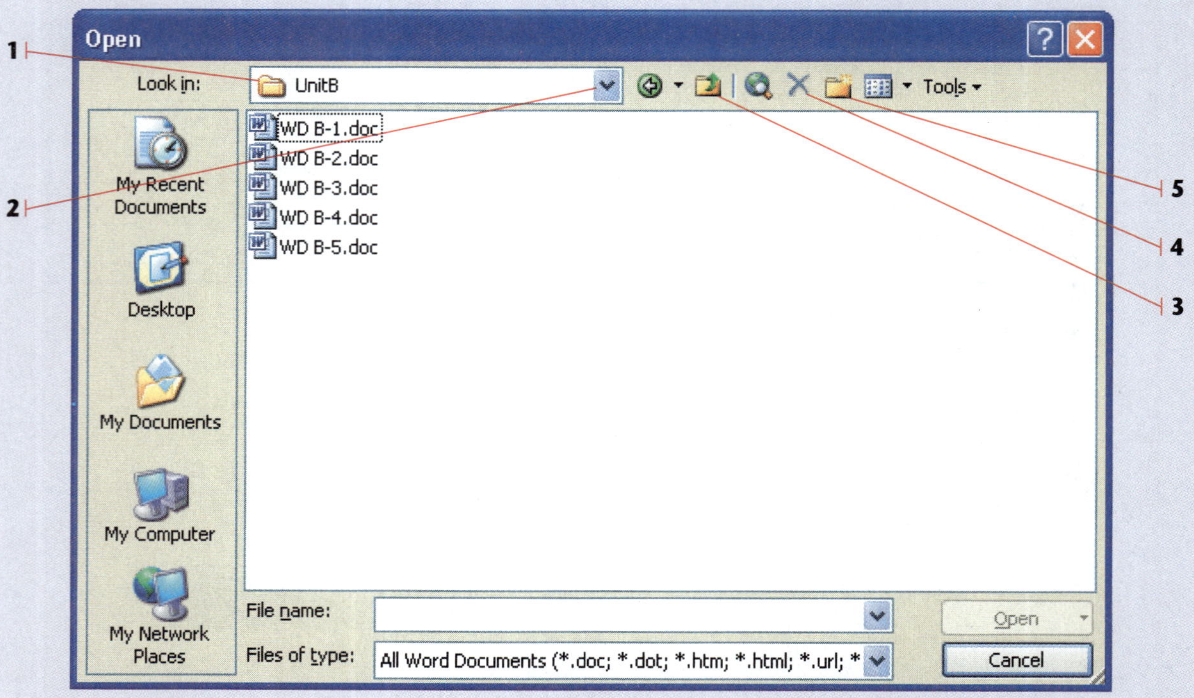

Match each term with the statement that best describes it.

6. **System Clipboard**
7. **Show/Hide**
8. **Select**
9. **Thesaurus**
10. **Undo**
11. **Template**
12. **Office Clipboard**
13. **Paste**
14. **Replace**

a. Command used to insert text stored on the Clipboard into a document
b. Document that contains placeholder text
c. Feature used to suggest synonyms for words
d. Temporary storage area for only the last item cut or copied from a document
e. Command used to display formatting marks in a document
f. Command used to locate and replace occurrences of specific text in a document
g. Command used to reverse the last action you took in a document
h. Temporary storage area for up to 24 items collected from any Office file
i. Action that must be taken before text can be cut, copied, or deleted

Select the best answer from the list of choices.

15. Which of the following is *not* used to open an existing document?

a. Blank document hyperlink in the New Document task pane
b. Open button on the Standard toolbar
c. Open or More hyperlink in the Getting Started task pane
d. Open command on the Edit menu

16. To locate and change all instances of a word in a document, which menu command do you use?

- **a.** Find
- **b.** Search
- **c.** Paste
- **d.** Replace

17. Which of the following statements is *not* true?

- **a.** The last item cut or copied from a document is stored on the system Clipboard.
- **b.** You can view the contents of the Office Clipboard.
- **c.** When you move text by dragging it, a copy of the text you move is stored on the system Clipboard.
- **d.** The Office Clipboard can hold more than one item.

18. Which Word feature corrects errors as you type?

- **a.** Thesaurus
- **b.** AutoCorrect
- **c.** Spelling and Grammar
- **d.** Undo and Redo

19. Which command is used to display a document in two panes in the document window?

- **a.** Split
- **b.** New Window
- **c.** Arrange All
- **d.** Compare Side by Side with...

20. What does the symbol ¶ represent when it is displayed in the document window?

- **a.** Hidden text
- **b.** A space
- **c.** A tab stop
- **d.** The end of a paragraph

▼ SKILLS REVIEW

1. Open a document.

- **a.** Start Word, click the Open button, then open the file WD B-2.doc from the drive and folder where your Data Files are located.
- **b.** Save the document with the filename **CAOS Press Release**.

2. Select text.

- **a.** Select **Today's Date** and replace it with the current date.
- **b.** Select **Your Name** and **Your Phone Number** and replace them with the relevant information.
- **c.** Scroll down, then select and replace text in the body of the press release using the following table as a guide:

in paragraph	select	replace with
1	13 and 14	**16 and 17**
1	eighth	**eleventh**
4	open his renovated Pearl St studio for the first time this year	**offer a sneak-preview of his Peace sculpture commissioned by the city of Prague**

- **d.** In the fourth paragraph, delete the sentence **Exhibiting with him will be sculptor Francis Pilo**.
- **e.** Save your changes to the press release.

3. Cut and paste text.

- **a.** Display paragraph and other formatting marks in your document if they are not already displayed.
- **b.** Use the Cut and Paste buttons to switch the order of the two sentences in the fourth paragraph (which begins New group shows...).
- **c.** Use the drag-and-drop method to switch the order of the second and third paragraphs.
- **d.** Adjust the spacing if necessary so that there is one blank line between paragraphs, then save your changes.

4. Copy and paste text.

- **a.** Use the Copy and Paste buttons to copy **CAOS 2003** from the headline and paste it before the word **map** in the third paragraph.
- **b.** Change the formatting of the pasted text to match the formatting of the third paragraph, then insert a space between **2003** and **map** if necessary.
- **c.** Use the drag-and-drop method to copy **CAOS** from the third paragraph and paste it before the word **group** in the second sentence of the fourth paragraph, then save your changes.

▼ SKILLS REVIEW (CONTINUED)

5. **Use the Office Clipboard.**
   - **a.** Use the Office Clipboard command on the Edit menu to open the Clipboard task pane.
   - **b.** Scroll so that the first body paragraph is displayed at the top of the document window.
   - **c.** Select the fifth paragraph (which begins Studio location maps…) and cut it to the Office Clipboard.
   - **d.** Select the third paragraph (which begins Cambridgeport is easily accessible…) and cut it to the Office Clipboard.
   - **e.** Use the Office Clipboard to paste the Studio location maps… item as the new fourth paragraph.
   - **f.** Use the Office Clipboard to paste the Cambridgeport is easily accessible… item as the new fifth paragraph.
   - **g.** Use any method to switch the order of the two sentences in the fourth paragraph (which begins Studio location maps…).
   - **h.** Adjust the spacing if necessary so that there is one blank line between each of the six body paragraphs.
   - **i.** Turn off the display of formatting marks, clear and close the Office Clipboard, then save your changes.
6. **Find and replace text.**
   - **a.** Using the Replace command, replace all instances of **2003** with **2006**.
   - **b.** Replace all instances of the abbreviation **st** with **street**, taking care to replace whole words only when you perform the replace. (*Hint*: Click More to expand the Find and Replace dialog box, and then deselect Match case if it is selected.)
   - **c.** Use the Find command to find all instances of **st** in the document, and make sure no errors occurred when you replaced st with street. (*Hint*: Deselect the Find whole words only check box.)
   - **d.** Save your changes to the press release.
7. **Check Spelling and Grammar and use the Thesaurus.**
   - **a.** Set Word to ignore the spelling of Cambridgeport, if it is marked as misspelled. (*Hint*: Right-click Cambridgeport.)
   - **b.** Move the insertion point to the top of the document, then use the Spelling and Grammar command to search for and correct any spelling and grammar errors in the press release.
   - **c.** Use the Thesaurus to replace **thriving** in the second paragraph with a different suitable word.
   - **d.** Proofread your press release, correct any errors, save your changes, print a copy, then close the document.
8. **Use wizards and templates.**
   - **a.** Use the New command to open the New Document task pane.
   - **b.** Use the On my computer hyperlink to open the Templates dialog box.
   - **c.** Create a new document using the Business Fax template.
   - **d.** Replace the placeholder text in the document using Figure B-20 as a guide. Delete any placeholders that do not apply to your fax. The date in your fax will be the current date.
   - **e.** Save the document as **CAOS Fax**, print a copy, close the document, then exit Word.

FIGURE B-20

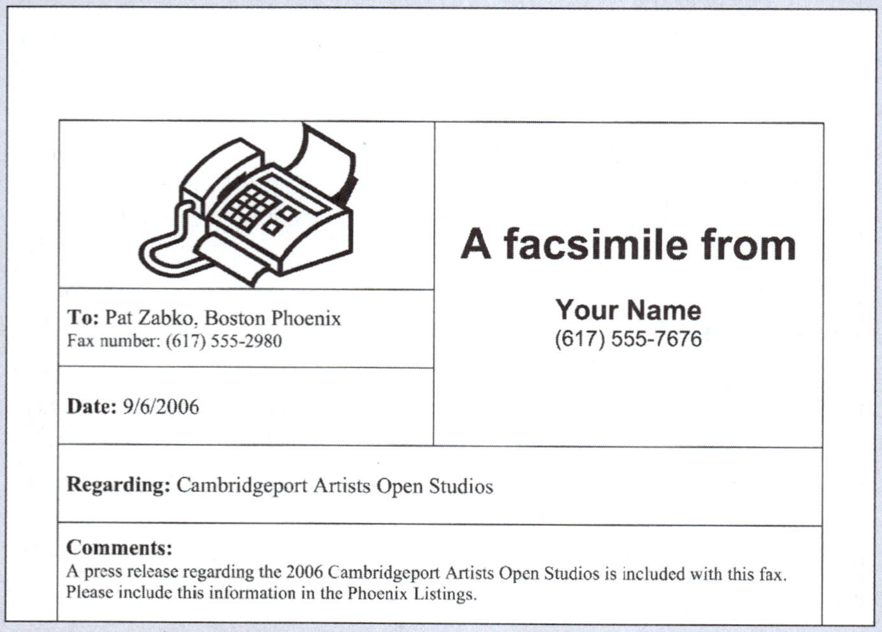

A facsimile from

Your Name
(617) 555-7676

To: Pat Zabko, Boston Phoenix
Fax number: (617) 555-2980

Date: 9/6/2006

Regarding: Cambridgeport Artists Open Studios

Comments:
A press release regarding the 2006 Cambridgeport Artists Open Studios is included with this fax. Please include this information in the Phoenix Listings.

▼ INDEPENDENT CHALLENGE 1

Because of your success in revitalizing an historic theatre in Hobart, Tasmania, you were hired as the director of The Auckland Lyric Theatre in Auckland, New Zealand, to breathe life into its theatre revitalization efforts. After a year on the job, you are launching your first major fund-raising drive. You'll create a fund-raising letter for the Lyric Theatre by modifying a letter you wrote for the theatre in Hobart.

a. Start Word, open the file WD B-3.doc from the drive and folder where your Data Files are located, then save it as **Lyric Theatre Letter**.

b. Replace the theatre name and address, the date, the inside address, and the salutation with the text shown in Figure B-21.

c. Use the Replace command to replace all instances of **Hobart** with **Auckland**.

d. Use the Replace command to replace all instances of **Tasmanians** with **New Zealanders**.

e. Use the Find command to locate the word **considerable**, then use the Thesaurus to replace the word with a synonym.

f. Create an AutoCorrect entry that inserts **Auckland Lyric Theatre** whenever you type **alt**.

g. Select each XXXXX, then type **alt** followed by a space.

h. Move the fourth body paragraph so that it becomes the second body paragraph.

i. Replace Your Name with your name in the signature block.

j. Use the Spelling and Grammar command to check for and correct spelling and grammar errors.

FIGURE B-21

The Auckland Lyric Theatre
64-70 Queen Street, Auckland, New Zealand

September 24, 2006

Ms. Keri Marshall
718 Elliott Street
Auckland

Dear Ms. Marshall,

Advanced Challenge Exercise

- Open the Properties dialog box, then review the paragraph, line, word, and character count on the Statistics tab.
- On the Summary tab, change the title to **Auckland Lyric Theatre** and add the keyword **fund-raising**.
- On the Custom tab, add a property named Project with the value **Capital Campaign**, then close the dialog box.

k. Proofread the letter, correct any errors, save your changes, print a copy, close the document, then exit Word.

▼ INDEPENDENT CHALLENGE 2

An advertisement for job openings in London caught your eye and you have decided to apply. The ad, shown in Figure B-22, was printed in last weekend's edition of your local newspaper. You'll use the Letter Wizard to create a cover letter to send with your resume.

a. Read the ad shown in Figure B-22 and decide which position to apply for. Choose the position that most closely matches your qualifications.

b. Start Word and open the Templates dialog box.

c. Double-click Letter Wizard on the Letters & Faxes tab, then select Send one letter in the Letter Wizard dialog box.

d. In the Letter Wizard—Step 1 of 4 dialog box, choose to include a date on your letter, select Elegant Letter for the page design, select Modified block for the letter style, include a header and footer with the page design, then click Next.

e. In the Letter Wizard—Step 2 of 4 dialog box, enter the recipient's name (Ms. Katherine Winn) and the delivery address, referring to the ad for the address information. Also enter the salutation **Dear Ms. Winn** using the business style, then click Next.

f. In the Letter Wizard—Step 3 of 4 dialog box, include a reference line in the letter, enter the appropriate position code (see Figure B-22) in the Reference line text box, then click Next.

g. In the Letter Wizard—Step 4 of 4 dialog box, enter your name as the sender, enter your return address (including your country), and select an appropriate complimentary closing. Then, because you will be including your resume with the letter, include one enclosure. Click Finish when you are done.

h. Save the letter with the filename **Global Dynamics Letter** to the drive and folder where your Data Files are located.

i. Replace the placeholder text in the body of the letter with three paragraphs that address your qualifications for the job:

- In the first paragraph, specify the job you are applying for, indicate where you saw the position advertised, and briefly state your qualifications and interest in the position.
- In the second paragraph, describe your work experience and skills. Be sure to relate your experience and qualifications to the position requirements listed in the ad.
- In the third paragraph, politely request an interview for the position and provide your phone number and e-mail address.

j. When you are finished typing the letter, check it for spelling and grammar errors and correct any mistakes.

k. Save your changes to the letter, print a copy, close the document, then exit Word.

FIGURE B-22

***Global*Dynamics**

Career Opportunities in London

Global Dynamics, an established software development firm with offices in North America, Asia, and Europe, is seeking candidates for the following positions in its London facility:

Instructor

Responsible for delivering software training to our expanding European customer base. Duties include delivering hands-on training, keeping up-to-date with product development, and working with the Director of Training to ensure the high quality of course materials. Successful candidate will have excellent presentation skills and be proficient in Microsoft PowerPoint and Microsoft Word. **Position B12C6**

Administrative Assistant

Proficiency with Microsoft Word a must! Administrative office duties include making travel arrangements, scheduling meetings, taking notes and publishing meeting minutes, handling correspondence, and ordering office supplies. Must have superb multi-tasking abilities, excellent communication, organizational, and interpersonal skills, and be comfortable working with e-mail and the Internet. **Position B16F5**

Copywriter

The ideal candidate will have marketing or advertising writing experience in a high tech environment, including collateral, newsletters, and direct mail. Experience writing for the Web, broadcast, and multimedia is a plus. Fluency with Microsoft Word required. **Position C13D4**

Positions offer salary, excellent benefits, moving expenses, and career growth opportunities.

Send resume and cover letter referencing position code to:

Katherine Winn
Director of Recruiting
Global Dynamics
483 Briar Terrace
London LH3 9JH
United Kingdom

▼ INDEPENDENT CHALLENGE 3

As administrative director of continuing education, you drafted a memo to instructors asking them to help you finalize the course schedule for next semester. Today you'll examine the draft and make revisions before printing it.

a. Start Word and open the file WD B-4.doc from the drive and folder where your Data Files are located.
b. Open the Save As dialog box, navigate to the drive and folder where your Data Files are located, then use the Create New Folder button to create a new folder called **Memos.**
c. Click the Up One Level button in the dialog box, rename the Memos folder **Spring Memos**, then save the document as **Instructor Memo** in the Spring Memos folder.
d. Replace Your Name with your name in the From line, then scroll down until the first body paragraph is at the top of the screen.

Advanced Challenge Exercise

- Use the Split command on the Window menu to split the window under the first body paragraph, then scroll until the last paragraph of the memo is displayed in the bottom pane.
- Use the Cut and Paste buttons to move the sentence **If you are planning to teach...** from the first body paragraph to become the first sentence in the last paragraph of the memo.
- Double-click the split bar to restore the window to a single pane.

e. Use the [Delete] key to merge the first two paragraphs into one paragraph.
f. Use the Office Clipboard to reorganize the list of twelve-week courses so that the courses are listed in alphabetical order. (*Hint*: Use the Zoom list arrow to enlarge the document as needed.)
g. Use the drag-and-drop method to reorganize the list of one-day seminars so that the seminars are listed in alphabetical order.
h. Use the Spelling and Grammar command to check for and correct spelling and grammar errors.
i. Clear and close the Office Clipboard, save your changes, print a copy, close the document, then exit Word.

E-QUEST

▼ INDEPENDENT CHALLENGE 4

Reference sources—dictionaries, thesauri, style and grammar guides, and guides to business etiquette and procedure—are essential for day-to-day use in the workplace. Much of this reference information is available on the World Wide Web. In this independent challenge, you will locate reference sources on the Web and use some of them to look up definitions, synonyms, and antonyms for words. Your goal is to familiarize yourself with online reference sources so you can use them later in your work.

a. Start Word, open the file WD B-5.doc from the drive and folder where your Data Files are located, and save it as **Web References**. This document contains the questions you will answer about the Web reference sources you find. You will type your answers to the questions in the document.
b. Replace the placeholder text at the top of the Web References document with your name and the date.
c. Use your favorite search engine to search the Web for grammar and style guides, dictionaries, and thesauri. Use the keywords **grammar**, **usage**, **dictionary**, **glossary**, and **thesaurus** to conduct your search.
d. Complete the Web References document, then proofread it and correct any mistakes.
e. Save the document, print a copy, close the document, then exit Word.

▼ VISUAL WORKSHOP

Using the Elegant Letter template, create the letter shown in Figure B-23. Save the document as **Visa Letter**. Check the letter for spelling and grammar errors, then print a copy.

FIGURE B-23

YOUR NAME

March 17, 2006

Embassy of Australia
Suite 710
50 O'Connor Street
Ottawa, Ontario K1P 6L2

Dear Sir or Madam:

I am applying for a long-stay (six-month) tourist visa to Australia, valid for four years. I am scheduled to depart for Sydney on July 1, 2006, returning to Vancouver on December 23, 2006.

While in Australia, I plan to conduct research for a book I am writing on coral reefs. I am interested in a multiple entry visa valid for four years so that I can return to Australia after this trip to follow-up on my initial research. I will be based in Cairns, but will be traveling frequently to other parts of Australia to meet with scientists, policy-makers, and environmentalists.

Enclosed please find my completed visa application form, my passport, a passport photo, a copy of my return air ticket, and the visa fee. Please let me know if I can provide further information.

Sincerely,

Your Name

35 HARDY STREET • VANCOUVER, BC • V6C 3K4
PHONE: (604) 555-8989 • FAX: (604) 555-8981

UNIT C

Word 2003

Formatting Text and Paragraphs

OBJECTIVES

- Format with fonts
- Change font styles and effects
- Change line and paragraph spacing
- Align paragraphs
- Work with tabs
- Work with indents
- Add bullets and numbering
- Add borders and shading

If you have a SAM user profile, you may have access to hands-on instruction, practice, and assessment of the skills covered in this unit. Log in to your SAM account and go to your assignments page to see what your instructor has assigned.

Formatting can enhance the appearance of a document, create visual impact, and help illustrate a document's structure. The formatting of a document can also add personality to it and lend it a degree of professionalism. In this unit you learn how to format text using different fonts and font-formatting options. You also learn how to change the alignment, indentation, and spacing of paragraphs, and how to spruce up documents with borders, shading, bullets, and other paragraph-formatting effects. You have finished drafting the quarterly marketing report for the MediaLoft Chicago store. You now need to format the report so it is attractive and highlights the significant information.

UNIT
C
Word 2003

Formatting with Fonts

Formatting text with different fonts is a quick and powerful way to enhance the appearance of a document. A **font** is a complete set of characters with the same typeface or design. Arial, Times New Roman, Comic Sans, Courier, and Tahoma are some of the more common fonts, but there are hundreds of others, each with a specific design and feel. Another way to alter the impact of text is to increase or decrease its **font size**, which is measured in points. A **point** is 1/72 of an inch. When formatting a document with fonts, it's important to pick fonts and font sizes that augment the document's purpose. You apply fonts and font sizes to text using the Font and Font Size list arrows on the Formatting toolbar. You change the font and font size of the title and headings in the report, selecting a font that enhances the business tone of the document. By formatting the title and headings in a font different from the body text, you help to visually structure the report for readers.

STEPS

1. **Start Word, open the file WD C-1.doc from the drive and folder where your Data Files are located, then save it as Chicago Marketing Report**
   The file opens in Print Layout view.
2. **Click the Normal View button on the horizontal scroll bar, click the Zoom list arrow on the Standard toolbar, then click 100% if necessary**
   The document switches to Normal view, a view useful for simple text formatting. The name of the font used in the document, Times New Roman, is displayed in the Font list box on the Formatting toolbar. The font size, 12, appears next to it in the Font Size list box.

> **QUICK TIP**
> There are two types of fonts: serif fonts have a small stroke, called a serif, at the ends of characters; sans serif fonts do not have a serif. Times New Roman is a serif font. Arial is a sans serif font.

3. **Select the title MediaLoft Chicago Quarterly Marketing Report, then click the Font list arrow on the Formatting toolbar**
   The Font list, which shows the fonts available on your computer, opens as shown in Figure C-1. Fonts you have used recently appear above the double line. All the fonts on your computer are listed in alphabetical order below the double line. You can click the font name in either location on the Font list to apply the font to the selected text.
4. **Click Arial**
   The font of the report title changes to Arial.
5. **Click the Font Size list arrow on the Formatting toolbar, then click 20**
   The font size of the title increases to 20 points.
6. **Click the Font Color list arrow on the Formatting toolbar**
   A palette of colors opens.
7. **Click Plum on the Font Color palette as shown in Figure C-2, then deselect the text**
   The color of the report title text changes to plum. The active color on the Font Color button also changes to plum.
8. **Scroll down until the heading Advertising is at the top of your screen, select Advertising, press and hold [Ctrl], select the heading Events, then release [Ctrl]**
   The Advertising and Events headings are selected. Selecting multiple items allows you to format several items at once.

> **QUICK TIP**
> For a clean look, limit the number of fonts you use in a document to two or three.

9. **Click the Font list arrow, click Arial, click the Font Size list arrow, click 14, click the Font Color button, then deselect the text**
   The headings are formatted in 14-point Arial with a plum color.
10. **Press [Ctrl][Home], then click the Save button on the Standard toolbar**
    Pressing [Ctrl][Home] moves the insertion point to the beginning of the document. Compare your document to Figure C-3.

FIGURE C-1: Font list

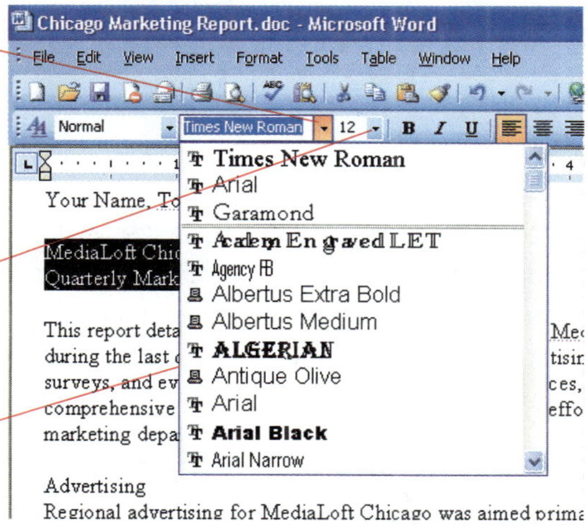

FIGURE C-2: Font Color palette

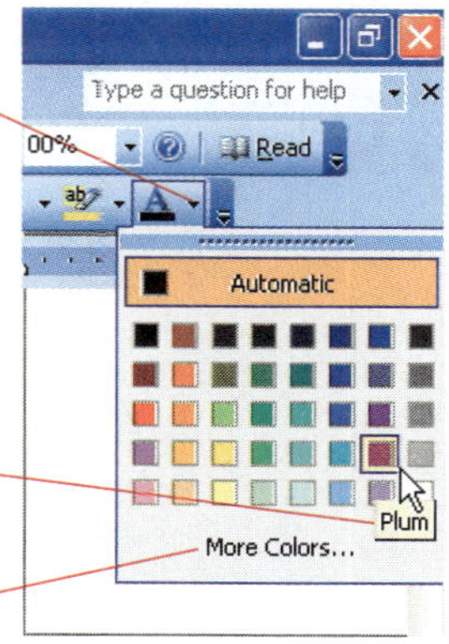

FIGURE C-3: Document formatted with fonts

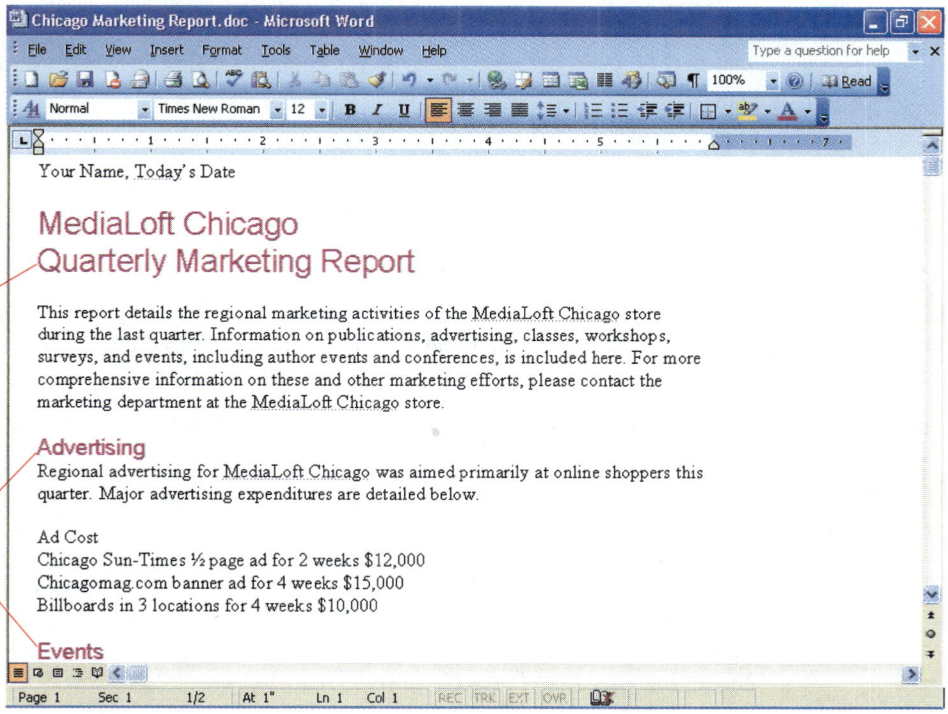

Clues to Use

Adding a drop cap

A fun way to illustrate a document with fonts is to add a drop cap to a paragraph. A **drop cap** is a large initial capital letter, often used to set off the first paragraph of an article. To create a drop cap, place the insertion point in the paragraph you want to format, and then click Drop Cap on the Format menu to open the Drop Cap dialog box. In the Drop Cap dialog box, shown in Figure C-4, select the position, font, number of lines to drop, and the distance you want the drop cap to be from the paragraph text, and then click OK to create the drop cap. The drop cap is added to the paragraph as a graphic object.

Once a drop cap is inserted in a paragraph, you can modify it by selecting it and then changing the settings in the Drop Cap dialog box. For even more interesting effects, try enhancing a drop cap with font color, font styles, or font effects, or try filling the graphic object with shading or adding a border around it. To enhance a drop cap, first select it, and then experiment with the formatting options available in the Font dialog box and in the Borders and Shading dialog box.

FIGURE C-4: Drop Cap dialog box

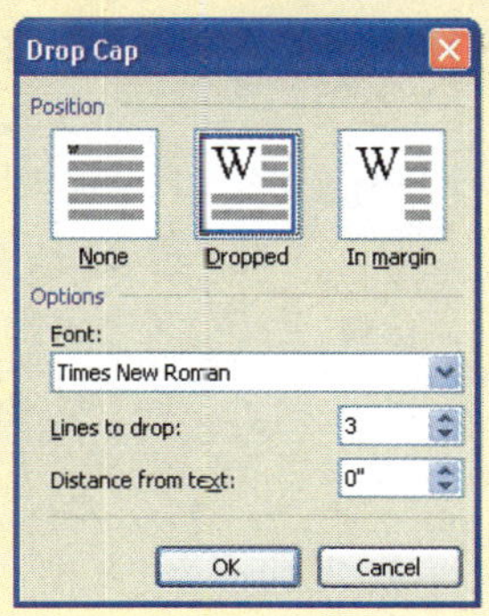

UNIT C

Word 2003

Changing Font Styles and Effects

You can dramatically change the appearance of text by applying different font styles, font effects, and character-spacing effects. For example, you can use the buttons on the Formatting toolbar to make text darker by applying **bold**, or to slant text by applying **italic**. You can also use the Font command on the Format menu to apply font effects and character-spacing effects to text. You spice up the appearance of the text in the document by applying different font styles and effects.

STEPS

QUICK TIP

Click the Underline button on the Formatting toolbar to underline text.

1. **Select MediaLoft Chicago Quarterly Marketing Report, then click the Bold button on the Formatting toolbar**

   Applying bold makes the characters in the title darker and thicker.

2. **Select Advertising, click , select Events, then press [F4]**

   Pressing [F4] repeats the last action you took, in this case applying bold. The Advertising and Events headings are both formatted in bold.

3. **Select the paragraph under the title, then click the Italic button on the Formatting toolbar**

   The paragraph is formatted in italic.

4. **Scroll down until the subheading Author Events is at the top of your screen, select Author Events, click Format on the menu bar, then click Font**

   The Font dialog box opens, as shown in Figure C-5. You can use options on the Font tab to change the font, font style, size, and color of text, and to add an underline and apply font effects to text.

QUICK TIP

To hide the selected text, click the Hidden check box on the Font tab. Hidden text is displayed when formatting marks are turned on.

5. **Scroll up the Font list, click Arial, click Bold Italic in the Font style list box, select the Small caps check box, then click OK**

   The subheading is formatted in Arial, bold, italic, and small caps. When you change text to small caps, the lowercase letters are changed to uppercase letters in a smaller font size.

6. **Select the subheading Travel Writers & Photographers Conference, then press [F4]**

   Because you formatted the previous subheading in one action (using the Font dialog box), the Travel Writers subheading is formatted in Arial, bold, italic, and small caps. If you apply formats one by one, then pressing [F4] repeats only the last format you applied.

7. **Under Author Events, select the book title Just H2O Please: Tales of True Adventure on the Environmental Frontline, click , select 2 in the book title, click Format on the menu bar, click Font, click the Subscript check box, click OK, then deselect the text**

   The book title is formatted in italic and the character 2 is subscript, as shown in Figure C-6.

QUICK TIP

To animate the selected text, click the Text Effects tab in the Font dialog box, then select an animation style. The animation appears only when a document is viewed in Word; animation effects do not print.

8. **Press [Ctrl][Home], select the report title, click Format on the menu bar, click Font, then click the Character Spacing tab in the Font dialog box**

   You use the Character Spacing tab to change the scale, or width, of the selected characters, to alter the spacing between characters, or to raise or lower the position of the characters.

9. **Click the Scale list arrow, click 150%, click OK, deselect the text, then click the Save button on the Standard toolbar**

   Increasing the scale of the characters makes them wider and gives the text a short, squat appearance, as shown in Figure C-7.

FIGURE C-5: Font tab in Font dialog box

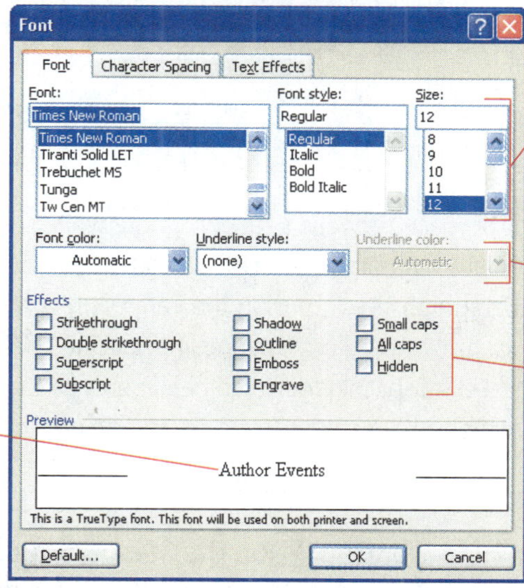

Select font, font style, and font size

Select font color and underline style and color

Select font effects

Preview of selected settings

FIGURE C-6: Font effects applied to text

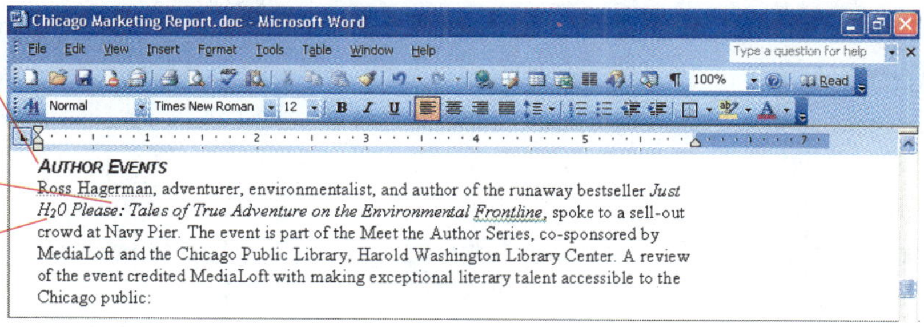

Subhead formatted in 12-point Arial, bold, italic, and small caps

Book title formatted in italic

Subscript text

FIGURE C-7: Character spacing effects applied to text

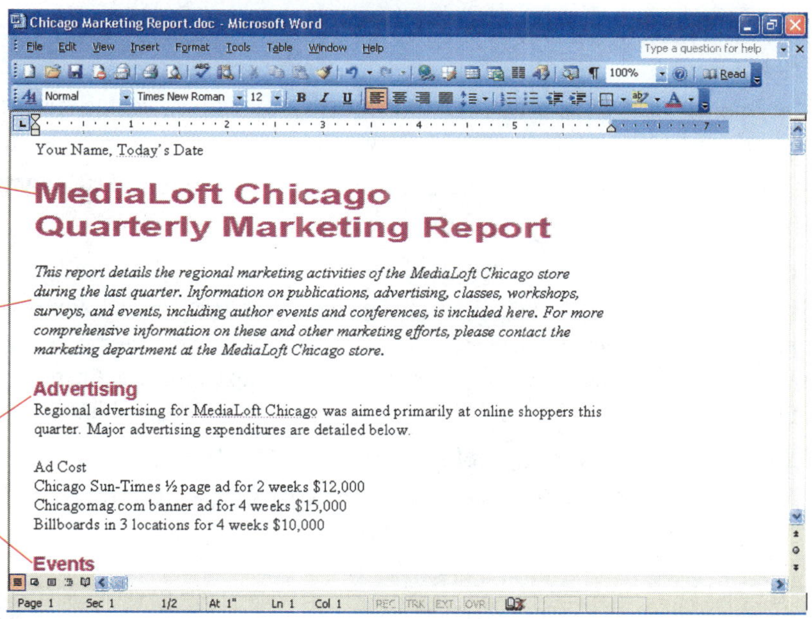

Report title formatted in bold with a character scale of 150%

Paragraph formatted in italic

Headings formatted in bold

Clues to Use

Changing the case of letters

The Change Case command on the Format menu allows you to quickly change letters from uppercase to lowercase—and vice versa—saving you the time it takes to retype text you want to change. To change the case of selected text, use the Change Case command to open the Change Case dialog box, then select the case style you want to use. Sentence case capitalizes the first letter of a sentence, title case capitalizes the first letter of each word, and toggle case switches all letters to the opposite case.

UNIT C

Word 2003

Changing Line and Paragraph Spacing

Increasing the amount of space between lines adds more white space to a document and can make it easier to read. Adding space between paragraphs can also open up a document and improve its appearance. You can change line and paragraph spacing using the Paragraph command on the Format menu. You can also use the Line Spacing list arrow to quickly change line spacing. You increase the line spacing of several paragraphs and add extra space under each heading to give the report a more open feel. You work with formatting marks turned on, so you can see the paragraph marks (¶).

STEPS

QUICK TIP

The check mark on the Line Spacing list indicates the current line spacing.

QUICK TIP

Word recognizes any string of text that ends with a paragraph mark as a paragraph, including titles, headings, and single lines in a list.

QUICK TIP

Adjusting the space between paragraphs is a more precise way to add white space to a document than inserting blank lines.

QUICK TIP

Using the Format Painter is not the same as using [F4]. Pressing [F4] repeats only the last action you took. You can use the Format Painter at any time to copy multiple format settings.

1. **Click the Show/Hide ¶ button on the Standard toolbar, place the insertion point in the italicized paragraph under the report title, then click the Line Spacing list arrow on the Formatting toolbar**

   The Line Spacing list opens. This list includes options for increasing the space between lines.

2. **Click 1.5**

   The space between the lines in the paragraph increases to 1.5 lines. Notice that you do not need to select an entire paragraph to change its paragraph formatting; simply place the insertion point in the paragraph you want to format.

3. **Scroll down until the heading Advertising is at the top of your screen, select the four-line list that begins with Ad Cost, click , then click 1.5**

   The line spacing between the selected paragraphs changes to 1.5. To change the paragraph-formatting features of more than one paragraph, you must select the paragraphs.

4. **Place the insertion point in the heading Advertising, click Format on the menu bar, then click Paragraph**

   The Paragraph dialog box opens, as shown in Figure C-8. You can use the Indents and Spacing tab to change line spacing and the spacing above and below paragraphs. Spacing between paragraphs is measured in points.

5. **Click the After up arrow in the Spacing section so that 6 pt appears, then click OK**

   Six points of space are added below the Advertising heading paragraph.

6. **Select Advertising, then click the Format Painter button on the Standard toolbar**

   The pointer changes to . The **Format Painter** is a powerful Word feature that allows you to copy all the format settings applied to the selected text to other text that you want to format the same way. The Format Painter is especially useful when you want to copy multiple format settings, but you can also use it to copy individual formats.

7. **Select Events with the pointer, then deselect the text**

   Six points of space are added below the Events heading paragraph and the pointer changes back to the I-beam pointer. Compare your document with Figure C-9.

8. **Select Events, then double-click**

   Double-clicking the Format Painter button allows the Format Painter to remain active until you turn it off. By keeping the Format Painter turned on you can apply formatting to multiple items.

9. **Scroll down, select the headings Classes & Workshops, Publications, and Surveys with the pointer, then click to turn off the Format Painter**

   The headings are formatted in 14-point Arial, bold, plum, with six points of space added below each heading paragraph.

10. **Press [Ctrl][Home], click , then click the Save button on the Standard toolbar**

FIGURE C-8: Indents and Spacing tab in Paragraph dialog box

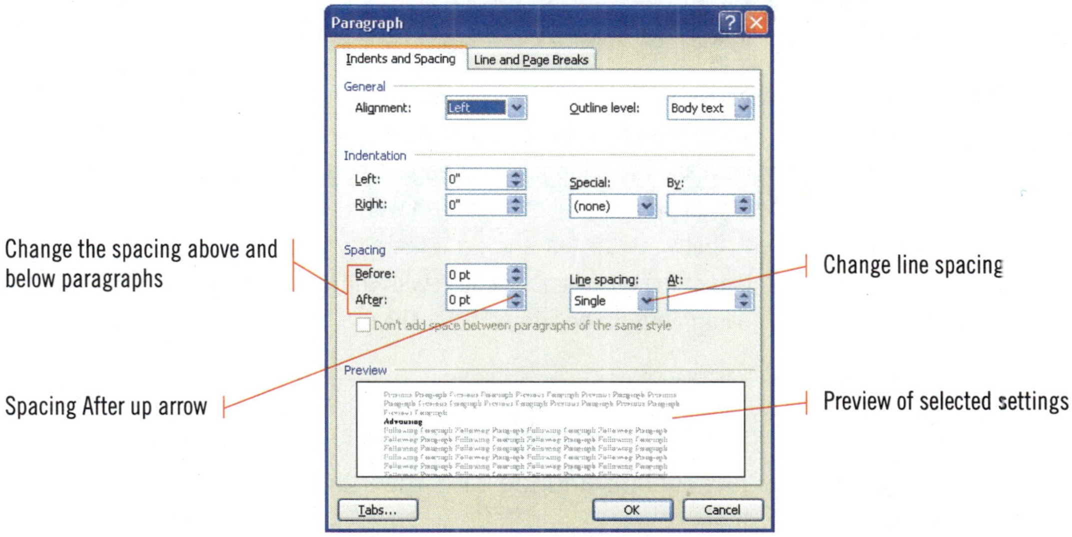

FIGURE C-9: Line and paragraph spacing applied to document

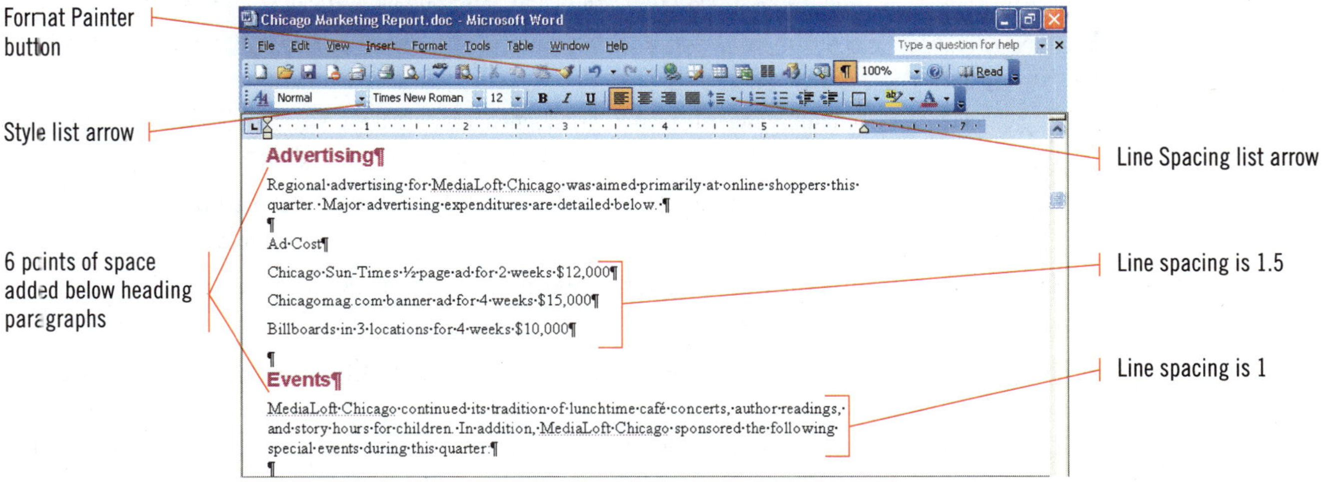

Clues to Use

Formatting with styles

You can also apply multiple format settings to text in one step by applying a style. A **style** is a set of formats, such as font, font size, and paragraph alignment, that are named and stored together. Styles can be applied to text, paragraphs, lists, and tables. To work with styles, click the Styles and Formatting button on the Formatting toolbar to open the Styles and Formatting task pane, shown in Figure C-10. The task pane displays the list of available styles and the formats you have created for the current document. To view all the styles available in Word, click the Show list arrow at the bottom of the task pane, then click All Styles.

A **character style**, indicated by **a** in the list of styles, includes character format settings, such as font and font size. A **paragraph style**, indicated by ¶ in the list, is a combination of character and paragraph formats, such as font, font size, paragraph alignment, paragraph spacing, indents, and bullets and numbering. A **table style** indicated by ⊞ in the list, includes format settings for text in tables, as well as for table borders, shading, and alignment. Finally, a **list style**, indicated by ☰ in the list, includes indent and numbering format settings for an outline numbered list.

To apply a style, select the text, paragraph, or table you want to format, then click the style name in the Pick formatting to apply list box. To remove styles from text, select the text, then click Clear Formatting in the Pick formatting to apply list box. You can also apply and remove styles using the Style list arrow on the Formatting toolbar.

FIGURE C-10: Styles and Formatting task pane

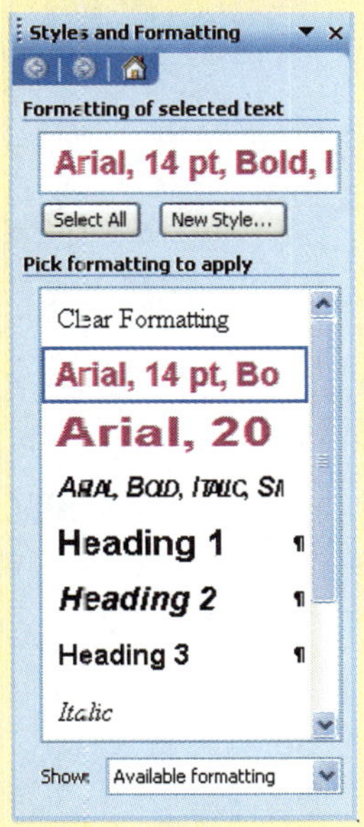

UNIT C

Word 2003

Aligning Paragraphs

Changing paragraph alignment is another way to enhance a document's appearance. Paragraphs are aligned relative to the left and right margins in a document. By default, text is **left-aligned**, which means it is flush with the left margin and has a ragged right edge. Using the alignment buttons on the Formatting toolbar, you can **right-align** a paragraph—make it flush with the right margin—or **center** a paragraph so that it is positioned evenly between the left and right margins. You can also **justify** a paragraph so that both the left and right edges of the paragraph are flush with the left and right margins. You change the alignment of several paragraphs at the beginning of the report to make it more visually interesting.

STEPS

1. **Replace Your Name, Today's Date with your name, a comma, and the date**
2. **Select your name, the comma, and the date, then click the Align Right button on the Formatting toolbar**
   The text is aligned with the right margin. In Normal view, the junction of the white and shaded sections of the horizontal ruler indicates the location of the right margin. The left end of the ruler indicates the left margin.
3. **Place the insertion point between your name and the comma, press [Delete] to delete the comma, then press [Enter]**
   The new paragraph containing the date is also right-aligned. Pressing [Enter] in the middle of a paragraph creates a new paragraph with the same text and paragraph formatting as the original paragraph.
4. **Select the report title, then click the Center button on the Formatting toolbar**
   The two paragraphs that make up the title are centered between the left and right margins.
5. **Place the insertion point in the Advertising heading, then click**
   The Advertising heading is centered.
6. **Place the insertion point in the italicized paragraph under the report title, then click the Justify button**
   The paragraph is aligned with both the left and right margins, as shown in Figure C-11. When you justify a paragraph, Word adjusts the spacing between words so that each line in the paragraph is flush with the left and the right margins.
7. **Place the insertion point in MediaLoft in the report title, click Format on the menu bar, then click Reveal Formatting**
   The Reveal Formatting task pane opens in the Word program window, as shown in Figure C-12. The Reveal Formatting task pane shows the formatting applied to the text and paragraph where the insertion point is located. You can use the Reveal Formatting task pane to check or change the formatting of any character, word, paragraph, or other aspect of a document.
8. **Select Advertising, then click the Alignment hyperlink in the Reveal Formatting task pane**
   The Paragraph dialog box opens with the Indents and Spacing tab displayed. It shows the settings for the selected text.
9. **Click the Alignment list arrow, click Left, click OK, then deselect the text**
   The Advertising heading is left-aligned.
10. **Close the Reveal Formatting task pane, then click the Save button on the Standard toolbar**

QUICK TIP

Click the Align Left button on the Formatting toolbar to left-align a paragraph.

FIGURE C-11: Modified paragraph alignment

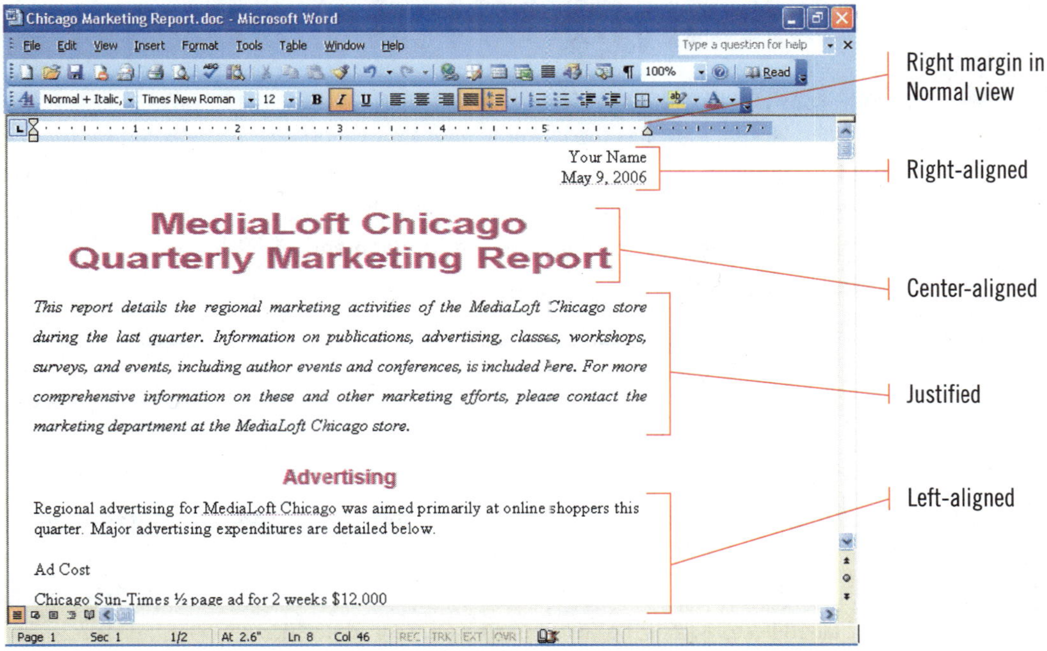

FIGURE C-12: Reveal Formatting task pane

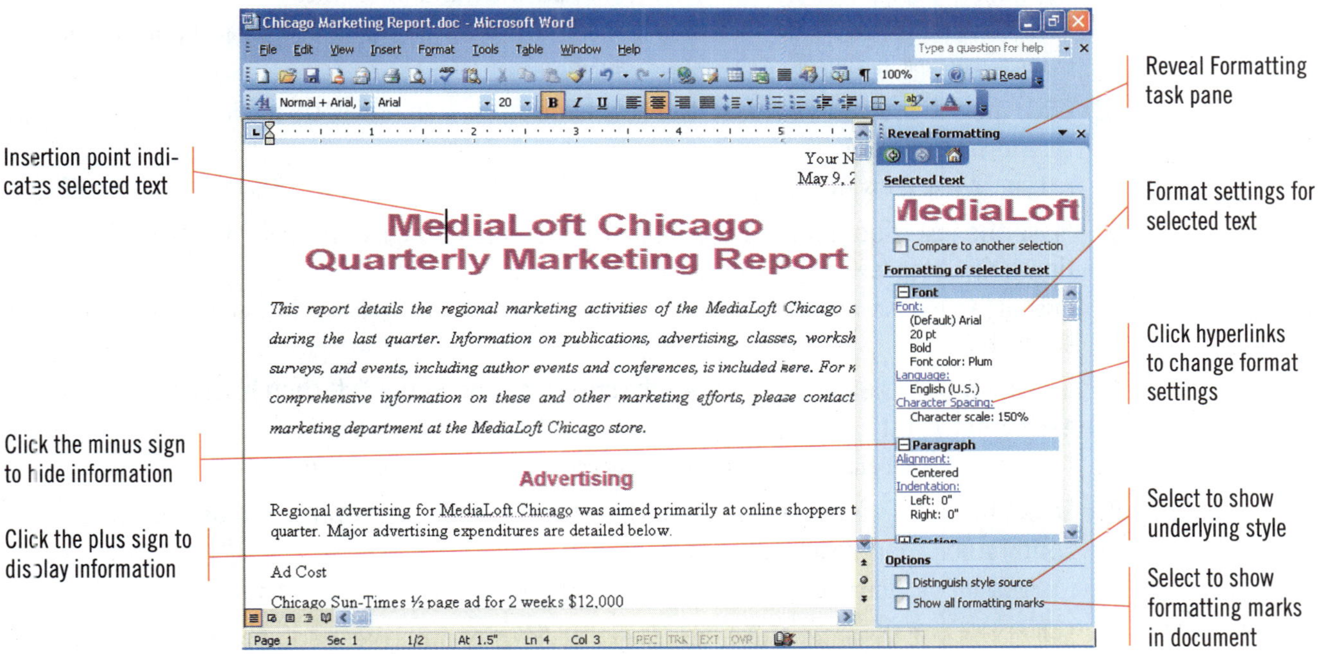

Clues to Use

Comparing formatting

When two words or paragraphs in a document do not look exactly the same but you are not sure how they are formatted differently, you can use the Reveal Formatting task pane to compare the two selections to determine the differences. To compare the formatting of two text selections, select the first instance, select the Compare to another selection check box in the Reveal Formatting task pane, and then select the second instance. Differences in formatting between the two selections are listed in the Formatting differences section in the Reveal Formatting task pane. You can then use the hyperlinks in the Formatting differences section to make changes to the formatting of the second selection. If you want to format the second selection so that it matches the first, you can click the list arrow next to the second selection in the Selected text section, and then click Apply Formatting of Original Selection on the menu that appears. On the same menu, you can also click Select All Text with Similar Formatting to select all the text in the document that is formatted the same, or Clear Formatting to return the formatting of the selected text to the default.

UNIT C

Word 2003

Working with Tabs

Tabs allow you to align text vertically at a specific location in a document. A **tab stop** is a point on the horizontal ruler that indicates the location at which to align text. By default, tab stops are located every ½" from the left margin, but you can also set custom tab stops. Using tabs, you can align text to the left, right, or center of a tab stop, or you can align text at a decimal point or bar character. You set tabs using the horizontal ruler or the Tabs command on the Format menu. You use tabs to format the information on advertising expenditures so it is easy to read.

STEPS

1. **Scroll down until the heading Advertising is at the top of your screen, then select the four-line list beginning with Ad Cost**
   Before you set tab stops for existing text, you must select the paragraphs for which you want to set tabs.
2. **Point to the tab indicator at the left end of the horizontal ruler**
   The icon that appears in the tab indicator indicates the active type of tab; pointing to the tab indicator displays a ScreenTip with the name of the active tab type. By default, left tab is the active tab type. Clicking the tab indicator scrolls through the types of tabs and indents.
3. **Click the tab indicator to see each of the available tab and indent types, make left tab the active tab type, then click the 1" mark on the horizontal ruler**
   A left tab stop is inserted at the 1" mark on the horizontal ruler. Clicking the horizontal ruler inserts a tab stop of the active type for the selected paragraph or paragraphs.
4. **Click the tab indicator twice so the Right Tab icon is active, then click the 4½" mark on the horizontal ruler**
   A right tab stop is inserted at the 4½" mark on the horizontal ruler, as shown in Figure C-13.
5. **Place the insertion point before Ad in the first line in the list, press [Tab], place the insertion point before Cost, then press [Tab]**
   Inserting a tab before Ad left-aligns the text at the 1" mark. Inserting a tab before Cost right-aligns Cost at the 4½" mark.
6. **Insert a tab at the beginning of each remaining line in the list, then insert a tab before each $ in the list**
   The paragraphs left-align at the 1" mark. The prices right-align at the 4½" mark.
7. **Select the four lines of tabbed text, drag the right tab stop to the 5" mark on the horizontal ruler, then deselect the text**
   Dragging the tab stop moves it to a new location. The prices right-align at the 5" mark.
8. **Select the last three lines of tabbed text, click Format on the menu bar, then click Tabs**
   The Tabs dialog box opens, as shown in Figure C-14. You can use the Tabs dialog box to set tab stops, change the position or alignment of existing tab stops, clear tab stops, and apply tab leaders to tabs. **Tab leaders** are lines that appear in front of tabbed text.
9. **Click 5" in the Tab stop position list box, click the 2 option button in the Leader section, click OK, deselect the text, then click the Save button on the Standard toolbar**
   A dotted tab leader is added before each 5" tab stop, as shown in Figure C-15.

TROUBLE

If the horizontal ruler is not visible, click Ruler on the View menu.

QUICK TIP

Never use the Spacebar to vertically align text; always use tabs or a table.

QUICK TIP

Place the insertion point in a paragraph to see the tab stops for that paragraph on the horizontal ruler.

FIGURE C-13: Left and right tab stops on the horizontal ruler

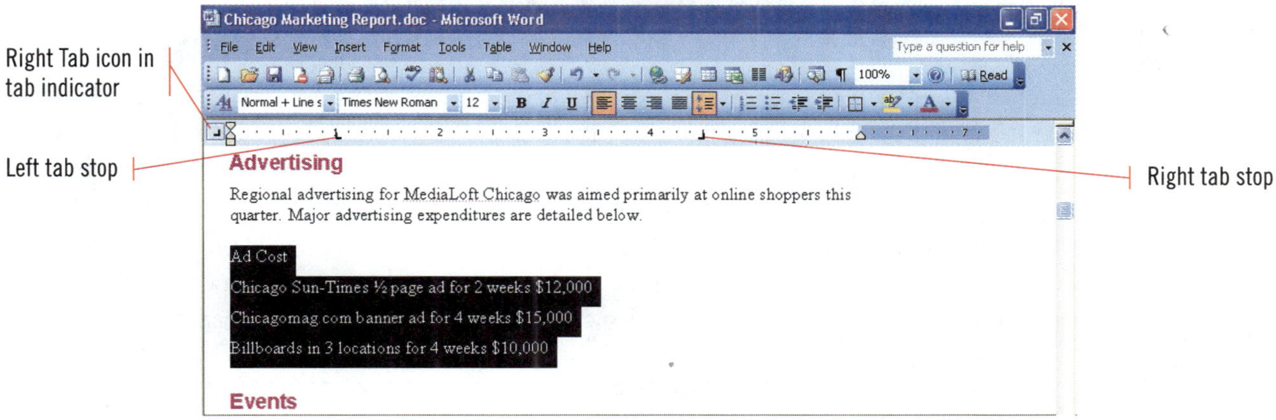

FIGURE C-14: Tabs dialog box

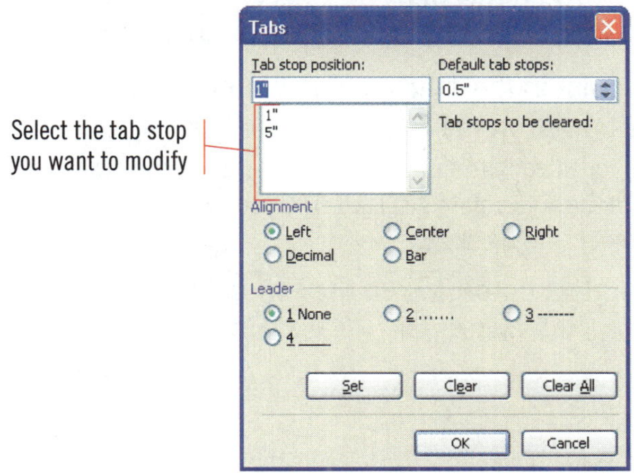

FIGURE C-15: Tab leaders

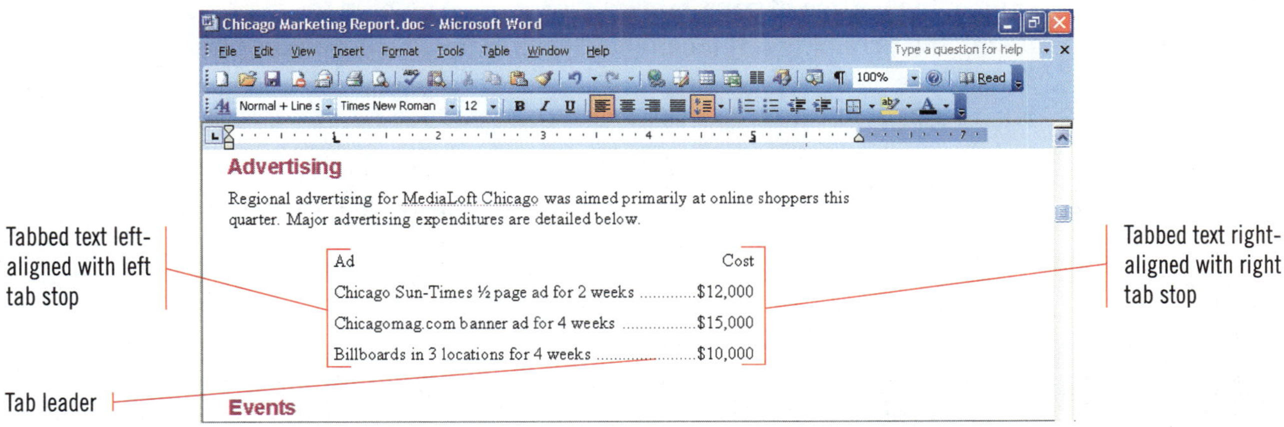

Clues to Use

Working with Click and Type

The **Click and Type** feature in Word allows you to automatically apply the paragraph formatting (alignment and indentation) necessary to insert text, graphics, or tables in a blank area of a document in Print Layout or Web Layout view. As you move the pointer around in a blank area of a document, the pointer changes depending on its location. Double-clicking with a click and type pointer in a blank area of a document automatically applies the appropriate alignment and indentation for that location, so that when you begin typing, the text is already formatted. The pointer shape indicates which formatting is applied at each location when you double-click. For example, if you click with the pointer, the text you type is center-aligned. Clicking with creates a left tab stop at the location of the insertion point so that the text you type is left-aligned at the tab stop. Clicking with right-aligns the text you type. The pointer creates left-aligned text with a first line indent. The best way to learn how to use Click and Type is to experiment in a blank document.

UNIT C

Word 2003

Working with Indents

When you **indent** a paragraph, you move its edge in from the left or right margin. You can indent the entire left or right edge of a paragraph, just the first line, or all lines except the first line. The **indent markers** on the horizontal ruler indicate the indent settings for the paragraph in which the insertion point is located. Dragging the indent markers to a new location on the ruler is one way to change the indentation of a paragraph; using the indent buttons on the Formatting toolbar is another. You can also use the Paragraph command on the Format menu to indent paragraphs. Table C-1 describes different types of indents and the methods for creating each. You indent several paragraphs in the report.

STEPS

1. **Press [Ctrl][Home], click the Print Layout View button on the horizontal scroll bar, click the Zoom list arrow on the Standard toolbar, then click Page Width**
   The document is displayed in Print Layout view, making it easier to see the document margins.
2. **Place the insertion point in the italicized paragraph under the title, then click the Increase Indent button on the Formatting toolbar**
   The entire paragraph is indented ½" from the left margin, as shown in Figure C-16. The indent marker also moves to the ½" mark on the horizontal ruler. Each time you click the Increase Indent button, the left edge of a paragraph moves another ½" to the right.
3. **Click the Decrease Indent button on the Formatting toolbar**
   The left edge of the paragraph moves ½" to the left, and the indent marker moves back to the left margin.
4. **Drag the First Line Indent marker to the ¼" mark on the horizontal ruler as shown in Figure C-17**
   The first line of the paragraph is indented ¼". Dragging the first line indent marker indents only the first line of a paragraph.
5. **Scroll to the bottom of page 1, place the insertion point in the quotation (the last paragraph), then drag the Left Indent marker to the ½" mark on the horizontal ruler**
   When you drag the Left Indent marker, the First Line and Hanging Indent markers move as well. The left edge of the paragraph is indented ½" from the left margin.
6. **Drag the Right Indent marker to the 5½" mark on the horizontal ruler**
   The right edge of the paragraph is indented ½" from the right margin, as shown in Figure C-18.
7. **Click the Save button on the Standard toolbar**

QUICK TIP

Press [Tab] at the beginning of a paragraph to indent the first line ½". You can also set a custom indent using the Indents and Spacing tab in the Paragraph dialog box.

TROUBLE

Take care to drag only the First Line Indent marker. If you make a mistake, click the Undo button, then try again.

TABLE C-1: Types of indents

indent type	description	to create
Left indent	The left edge of a paragraph is moved in from the left margin	Drag the Left Indent marker right to the position where you want the left edge of the paragraph to align, or click the Increase Indent button to indent the paragraph in ½" increments
Right indent	The right edge of a paragraph is moved in from the right margin	Drag the Right Indent marker left to the position where you want the right edge of the paragraph to end
First-line indent	The first line of a paragraph is indented more than the subsequent lines	Drag the First Line Indent marker right to the position where you want the first line of the paragraph to start
Hanging indent	The subsequent lines of a paragraph are indented more than the first line	Drag the Hanging Indent marker right to the position where you want the hanging indent to start
Negative indent (or Outdent)	The left edge of a paragraph is moved to the left of the left margin	Drag the Left Indent marker left to the position where you want the negative indent to start

FIGURE C-16: Indented paragraph

FIGURE C-17: Dragging the First Line Indent marker

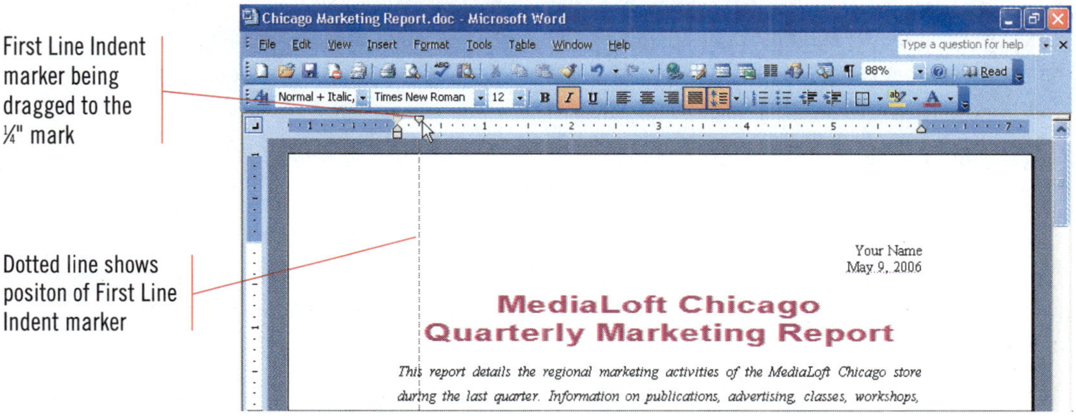

FIGURE C-18: Paragraph indented from the left and right

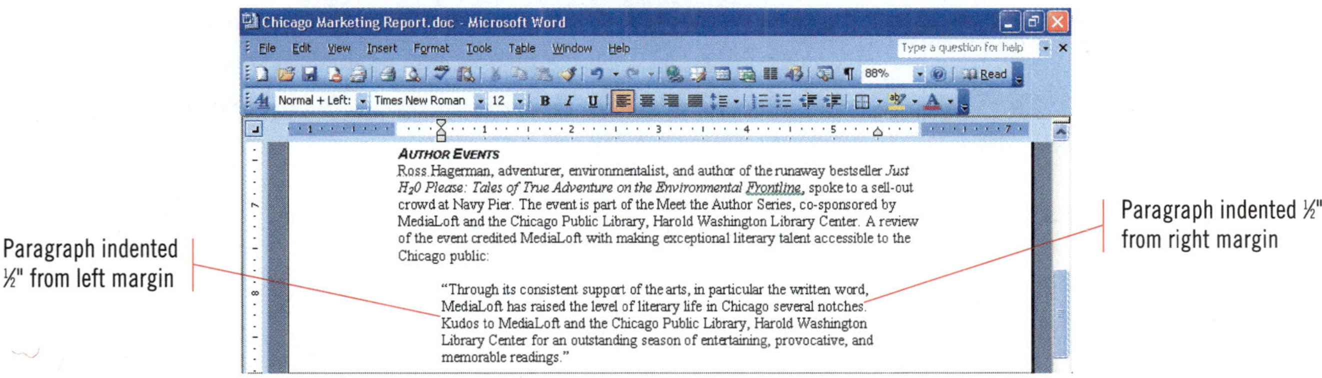

Clues to Use

Clearing formatting

If you are unhappy with the way text is formatted, you can use the Clear Formats command to return the text to the default format settings. By default, text is formatted in 12-point Times New Roman and paragraphs are left-aligned and single-spaced with no indents.

To clear formatting from text, select the text you want to clear, point to Clear on the Edit menu, then click Formats. Alternately, click the Styles list arrow on the Formatting toolbar, then click Clear Formatting.

Adding Bullets and Numbering

Formatting a list with bullets or numbering can help to organize the ideas in a document. A **bullet** is a character, often a small circle, that appears before the items in a list to add emphasis. Formatting a list as a numbered list helps illustrate sequences and priorities. You can quickly format a list with bullets or numbering by using the Bullets and Numbering buttons on the Formatting toolbar. You can also use the Bullets and Numbering command on the Format menu to change or customize bullet and numbering styles. You format the lists in your report with numbers and bullets.

STEPS

1. **Scroll down until the first paragraph on the second page (Authors on our...) is at the top of your screen**
2. **Select the three-line list of names under the paragraph, then click the Numbering button on the Formatting toolbar**
   The paragraphs are formatted as a numbered list.
3. **Place the insertion point after Jack Seneschal, press [Enter], then type Polly Flanagan**
   Pressing [Enter] in the middle of the numbered list creates a new numbered paragraph and automatically renumbers the remainder of the list. Similarly, if you delete a paragraph from a numbered list, Word automatically renumbers the remaining paragraphs.
4. **Click 1 in the list**
   Clicking a number in a list selects all the numbers, as shown in Figure C-19.
5. **Click the Bold button on the Formatting toolbar**
   The numbers are all formatted in bold. Notice that the formatting of the items in the list does not change when you change the formatting of the numbers. You can also use this technique to change the formatting of bullets in a bulleted list.
6. **Select the list of classes and workshops under the Classes & Workshops heading, scrolling down if necessary, then click the Bullets button on the Formatting toolbar**
   The five paragraphs are formatted as a bulleted list.
7. **With the list still selected, click Format on the menu bar, then click Bullets and Numbering**
   The Bullets and Numbering dialog box opens with the Bulleted tab displayed, as shown in Figure C-20. You use this dialog box to apply bullets and numbering to paragraphs, or to change the style of bullets or numbers.
8. **Click the Square bullets box or select another style if square bullets are not available to you, click OK, then deselect the text**
   The bullet character changes to a small square, as shown in Figure C-21.
9. **Click the Save button on the Standard toolbar**

QUICK TIP
To change the numbers to letters, Roman numerals, or another numbering style, right-click the list, click Bullets and Numbering, then select a new numbering style on the Numbered tab.

QUICK TIP
To remove a bullet or number, select the paragraph(s), then click or .

Clues to Use

Creating outlines

You can create lists with hierarchical structures by applying an outline numbering style to a list. To create an outline, begin by applying an outline numbering style from the Outline Numbered tab in the Bullets and Numbering dialog box, then type your outline, pressing [Enter] after each item. To demote items to a lower level of importance in the outline, place the insertion point in the item, then click the Increase Indent button on the Formatting toolbar. Each time you indent a paragraph, the item is demoted to a lower lever in the outline. Similarly, you can use the Decrease Indent button to promote an item to a higher level in the outline. You can also create a hierarchical structure in any bulleted or numbered list by using and to demote and promote items in the list. To change the outline numbering style applied to a list, select a new style from the Outline Numbered tab in the Bullets and Numbering dialog box.

FIGURE C-19: Numbered list

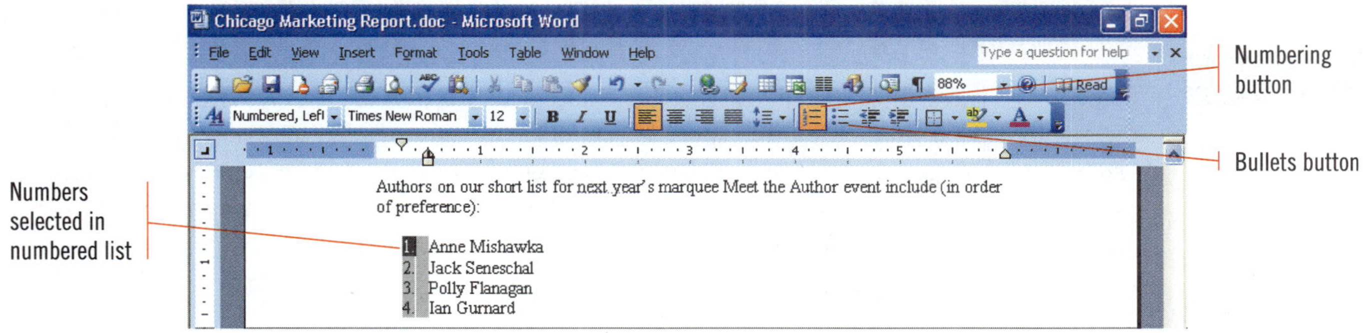

FIGURE C-20: Bulleted tab in the Bullets and Numbering dialog box

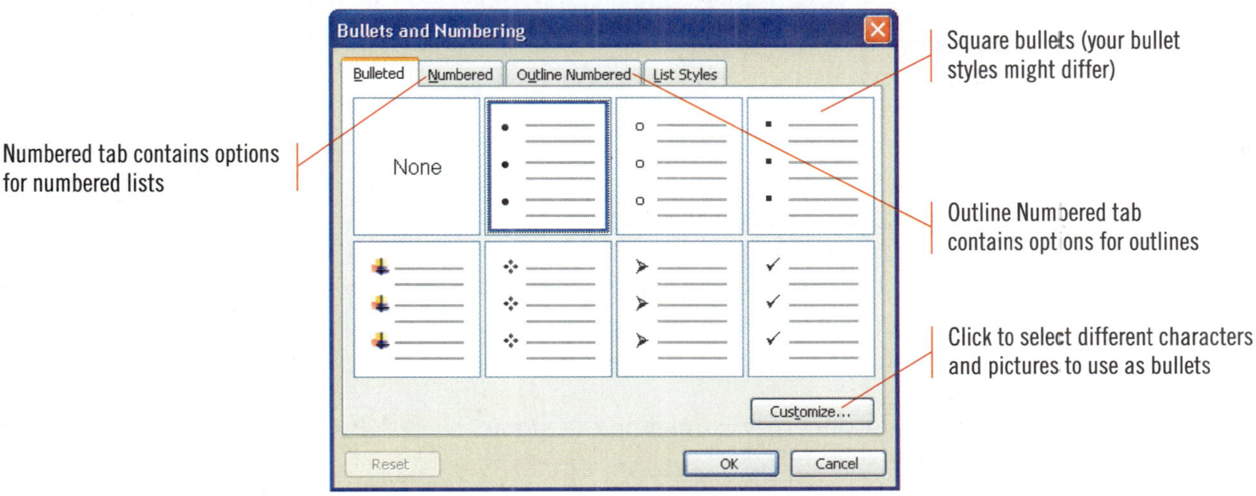

FIGURE C-21: Square bullets applied to list

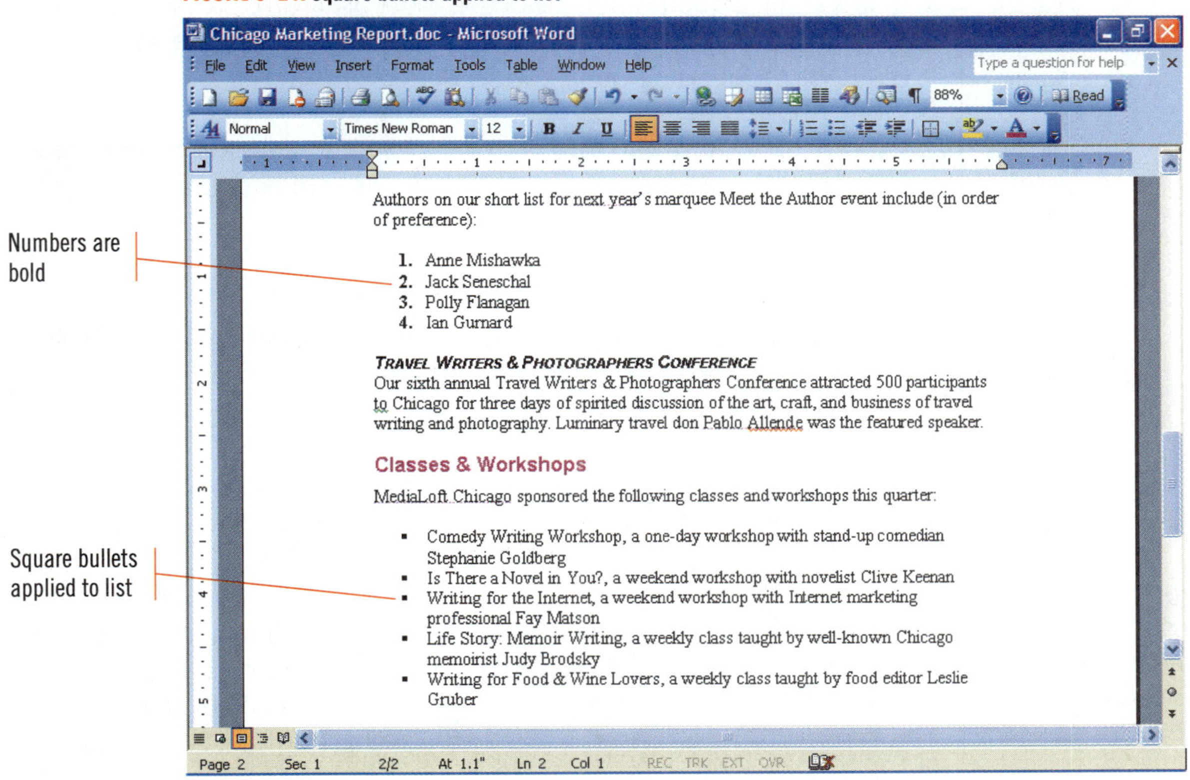

Word 2003

UNIT
C
Word 2003

Adding Borders and Shading

Borders and shading can add color and splash to a document. **Borders** are lines you add above, below, to the side, or around words or a paragraph. You can format borders using different line styles, colors, and widths. **Shading** is a color or pattern you apply behind words or paragraphs to make them stand out on a page. You apply borders and shading using the Borders and Shading command on the Format menu. You enhance the advertising expenses table by adding shading to it. You also apply a border under every heading to visually punctuate the sections of the report.

STEPS

1. **Scroll up until the heading Advertising is at the top of your screen**

2. **Select the four paragraphs of tabbed text under the Advertising heading, click Format on the menu bar, click Borders and Shading, then click the Shading tab**

   The Shading tab in the Borders and Shading dialog box is shown in Figure C-22. You use this tab to apply shading to words and paragraphs.

3. **Click the Lavender box in the bottom row of the Fill section, click OK, then deselect the text**

   Lavender shading is applied to the four paragraphs. Notice that the shading is applied to the entire width of the paragraphs, despite the tab settings.

4. **Select the four paragraphs, drag the Left Indent marker to the ¾" mark on the horizontal ruler, drag the Right Indent marker to the 5¼" mark, then deselect the text**

   The shading for the paragraphs is indented from the left and right, making it look more attractive.

5. **Select Advertising, click Format on the menu bar, click Borders and Shading, then click the Borders tab**

   The Borders tab is shown in Figure C-23. You use this tab to add boxes and lines to words or paragraphs.

6. **Click the Custom box in the Setting section, click the Width list arrow, click ¾ pt, click the Bottom Border button in the Preview section, click OK, then deselect the text**

   A ¾-point black border is added below the Advertising paragraph.

7. **Click Events, press [F4], scroll down and use [F4] to add a border under each plum heading, press [Ctrl] [Home], then click the Save button on the Standard toolbar**

   The completed document is shown in Figure C-24.

8. **Click the Print button, close the document, then exit Word**

   A copy of the report prints. Depending on your printer, colors might appear differently when you print. If you are using a black-and-white printer, colors will print in shades of gray.

QUICK TIP

When creating custom borders, it's important to select the style, color, and width settings before applying the borders in the Preview section.

Clues to Use

Highlighting text in a document

The Highlight tool allows you to mark and find important text in a document. **Highlighting** is transparent color that is applied to text using the Highlight pointer. To highlight text, click the Highlight list arrow on the Formatting toolbar, select a color, then use the I-beam part of the pointer to select the text. Click to turn off the Highlight pointer. To remove highlighting, select the highlighted text, click, then click None. Highlighting prints, but it is used most effectively when a document is viewed on screen.

FIGURE C-22: **Shading tab in Borders and Shading dialog box**

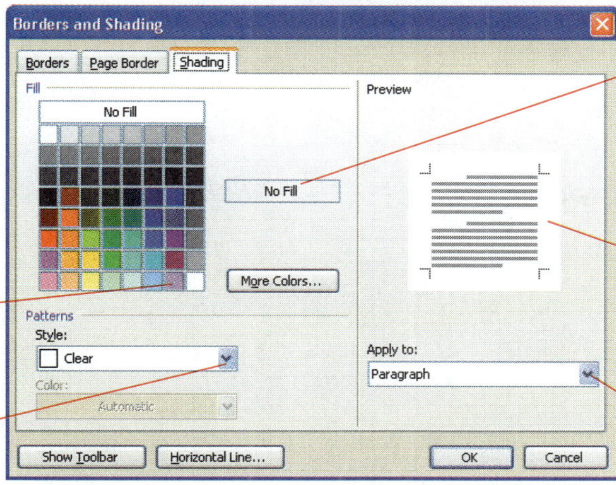

FIGURE C-23: **Borders tab in Borders and Shading dialog box**

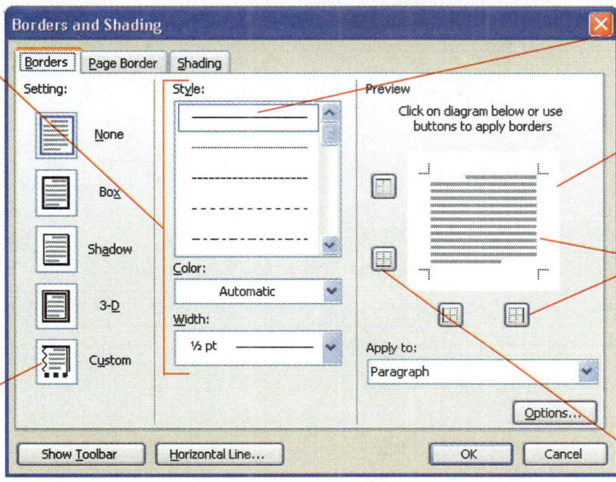

FIGURE C-24: **Borders and shading applied to the document**

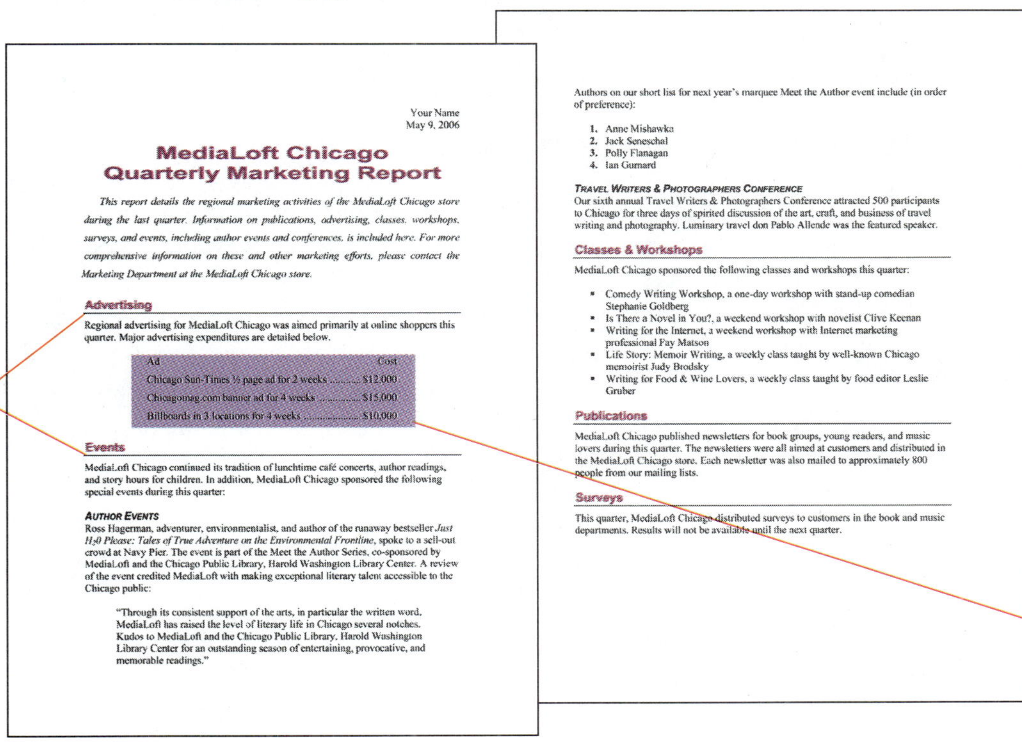

Your Name
May 9, 2006

MediaLoft Chicago
Quarterly Marketing Report

This report details the regional marketing activities of the MediaLoft Chicago store during the last quarter. Information on publications, advertising, classes, workshops, surveys, and events, including author events and conferences, is included here. For more comprehensive information on these and other marketing efforts, please contact the Marketing Department at the MediaLoft Chicago store.

Advertising

Regional advertising for MediaLoft Chicago was aimed primarily at online shoppers this quarter. Major advertising expenditures are detailed below.

Ad	Cost
Chicago Sun-Times ½ page ad for 2 weeks	$12,000
Chicagomag.com banner ad for 4 weeks	$15,000
Billboards in 3 locations for 4 weeks	$10,000

Events

MediaLoft Chicago continued its tradition of lunchtime café concerts, author readings, and story hours for children. In addition, MediaLoft Chicago sponsored the following special events during this quarter:

AUTHOR EVENTS

Ross Hagerman, adventurer, environmentalist, and author of the runaway bestseller *Just H₂0 Please: Tales of True Adventure on the Environmental Frontline*, spoke to a sell-out crowd at Navy Pier. The event is part of the Meet the Author Series, co-sponsored by MediaLoft and the Chicago Public Library, Harold Washington Library Center. A review of the event credited MediaLoft with making exceptional literary talent accessible to the Chicago public:

> "Through its consistent support of the arts, in particular the written word, MediaLoft has raised the level of literary life in Chicago several notches. Kudos to MediaLoft and the Chicago Public Library, Harold Washington Library Center for an outstanding season of entertaining, provocative, and memorable readings."

Authors on our short list for next year's marquee Meet the Author event include (in order of preference):

1. Anne Mishawka
2. Jack Seneschal
3. Polly Flanagan
4. Ian Gurnard

TRAVEL WRITERS & PHOTOGRAPHERS CONFERENCE

Our sixth annual Travel Writers & Photographers Conference attracted 500 participants to Chicago for three days of spirited discussion of the art, craft, and business of travel writing and photography. Luminary travel don Pablo Allende was the featured speaker.

Classes & Workshops

MediaLoft Chicago sponsored the following classes and workshops this quarter:

- Comedy Writing Workshop, a one-day workshop with stand-up comedian Stephanie Goldberg
- Is There a Novel in You?, a weekend workshop with novelist Clive Keenan
- Writing for the Internet, a weekend workshop with Internet marketing professional Fay Matson
- Life Story: Memoir Writing, a weekly class taught by well-known Chicago memoirist Judy Brodsky
- Writing for Food & Wine Lovers, a weekly class taught by food editor Leslie Gruber

Publications

MediaLoft Chicago published newsletters for book groups, young readers, and music lovers during this quarter. The newsletters were all aimed at customers and distributed in the MediaLoft Chicago store. Each newsletter was also mailed to approximately 800 people from our mailing lists.

Surveys

This quarter, MediaLoft Chicago distributed surveys to customers in the book and music departments. Results will not be available until the next quarter.

Practice

▼ CONCEPTS REVIEW

Label each element of the Word program window shown in Figure C-25.

FIGURE C-25

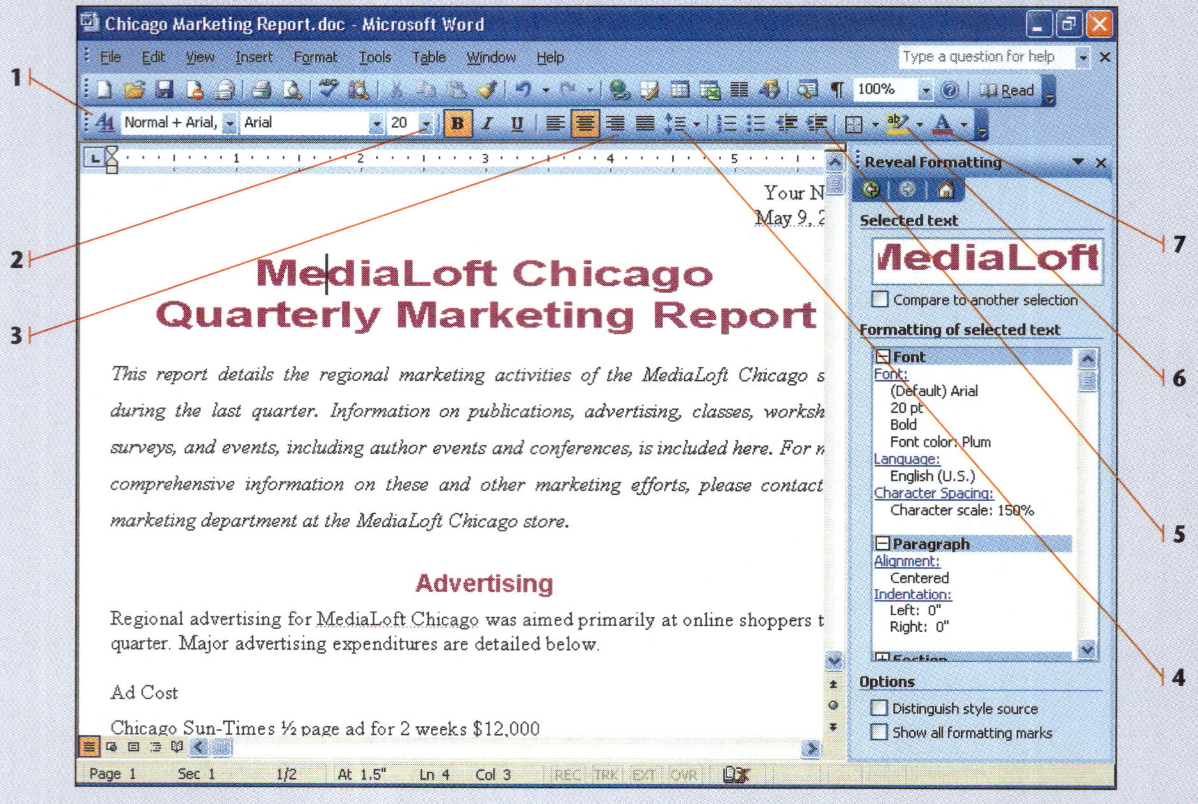

Match each term with the statement that best describes it.

8. Bold
9. Shading
10. Point
11. Style
12. Italic
13. Highlight
14. Bullet
15. Border

a. A character that appears at the beginning of a paragraph to add emphasis
b. Transparent color that is applied to text to mark it in a document
c. A text style in which characters are slanted
d. Color or a pattern that is applied behind text to make it look attractive
e. A set of format settings
f. A unit of measurement equal to 1/72 of an inch
g. A line that can be applied above, below, or to the sides of a paragraph
h. A text style in which characters are darker and thicker

Select the best answer from the list of choices.

16. Which button is used to align a paragraph with both the left and right margins?

a. 

b. 

c. 

d. 

17. What is Arial?

a. A style

b. A character format

c. A text effect

d. A font

18. What is the most precise way to increase the amount of white space between two paragraphs?

a. Insert an extra blank line between the paragraphs.

b. Change the line spacing of the paragraphs.

c. Indent the paragraphs.

d. Use the Paragraph command to change the spacing below the first paragraph.

19. What element of the Word program window can be used to check the tab settings applied to text?

a. Formatting toolbar

b. Standard toolbar

c. Reveal Formatting task pane

d. Styles and Formatting task pane

20. Which command would you use to apply color behind a paragraph?

a. Background

b. Styles and Formatting

c. Borders and Shading

d. Paragraph

▼ SKILLS REVIEW

1. Format with fonts.

a. Start Word, open the file WD C-2.doc from the drive and folder where your Data Files are located, save it as **EDA Report**, then scroll through the document to get a feel for its contents.

b. Press [Ctrl][Home], format the report title **Richmond Springs Economic Development Report Executive Summary** in 26-point Tahoma. Choose a different font if Tahoma is not available to you.

c. Change the font color of the report title to Teal, then press [Enter] after Springs in the title.

d. Place the insertion point in the first body paragraph under the title, then add a two-line drop cap to the paragraph using the Dropped position.

e. Format each of the following headings in 14-point Tahoma with the Teal font color: **Mission Statement**, **Guiding Principles**, **Issues**, **Proposed Actions**.

f. Press [Ctrl][Home], then save your changes to the report.

2. Change font styles and effects.

a. Apply bold to the report title and to each heading in the report.

b. Show formatting marks, then format the paragraph under the Mission Statement heading in italic.

c. Format **Years Population Growth**, the first line in the four-line list under the Issues heading, in bold, small caps, with a Teal font color.

d. Change the font color of the next two lines under Years Population Growth to Teal.

e. Format the line **Source: Office of State Planning** in italic.

f. Scroll to the top of the report, change the character scale of **Richmond Springs Economic Development Report** to 80%, then save your changes.

3. **Change line and paragraph spacing.**
   a. Change the line spacing of the three-line list under the first body paragraph to 1.5 lines.
   b. Add 12 points of space before the Executive Summary line in the title.
   c. Add 12 points of space after each heading in the report (but not the title).
   d. Add 6 points of space after each paragraph in the list under the Guiding Principles heading.
   e. Add 6 points of space after each paragraph under the Proposed Actions heading.
   f. Press [Ctrl][Home], then save your changes to the report.

4. **Align paragraphs.**
   a. Press [Ctrl][A] to select the entire document, then justify all the paragraphs.
   b. Center the three-line report title.
   c. Press [Ctrl][End], type your name, press [Enter], type the current date, then right-align your name and the date.
   d. Save your changes to the report.

5. **Work with tabs.**
   a. Scroll up and select the four-line list of population information under the Issues heading.
   b. Set left tab stops at the 1¾" mark and the 3" mark.
   c. Insert a tab at the beginning of each line in the list.
   d. In the first line, insert a tab before Population. In the second line, insert a tab before 4.5%. In the third line, insert a tab before 53%.
   e. Select the first three lines, then drag the second tab stop to the 2¾" mark on the horizontal ruler.
   f. Press [Ctrl][Home], then save your changes to the report.

6. **Work with indents.**
   a. Indent the paragraph under the Mission Statement heading ½" from the left and ½" from the right.
   b. Indent the first line of the paragraph under the Guiding Principles heading ½".
   c. Indent the first line of the three body paragraphs under the Issues heading ½".
   d. Press [Ctrl][Home], then save your changes to the report.

7. **Add bullets and numbering.**
   a. Apply bullets to the three-line list under the first body paragraph.
   b. Change the bullet style to small black circles (or choose another bullet style if small black circles are not available to you).
   c. Change the font color of the bullets to Teal.
   d. Scroll down until the Guiding Principles heading is at the top of your screen.
   e. Format the six-paragraph list under Guiding Principles as a numbered list.
   f. Format the numbers in 12-point Tahoma bold, then change the font color to Teal.
   g. Scroll down until the Proposed Actions heading is at the top of your screen, then format the paragraphs under the heading as a bulleted list using check marks as the bullet style. If checkmarks are not available, click Reset or choose another bullet style.
   h. Change the font color of the bullets to Teal, press [Ctrl][Home], then save your changes to the report.

8. **Add borders and shading.**
   a. Change the font color of the report title to Light Yellow, then apply Teal shading.
   b. Add a 1-point Teal border below the Mission Statement heading.
   c. Use the Format Painter to copy the formatting of the Mission Statement heading to the other headings in the report.
   d. Under the Issues heading, select the first three lines of tabbed text, which are formatted in Teal.

▼ SKILLS REVIEW (CONTINUED)

e. Apply Light Yellow shading to the paragraphs, then add a 1-point Teal box border around the paragraphs.

f. Indent the shading and border around the paragraphs 1½" from the left and 1½" from the right.

g. Press [Ctrl][Home], save your changes to the report, view the report in Print Preview, then print a copy. The formatted report is shown in Figure C-26.

h. Close the file and exit Word.

FIGURE C-26

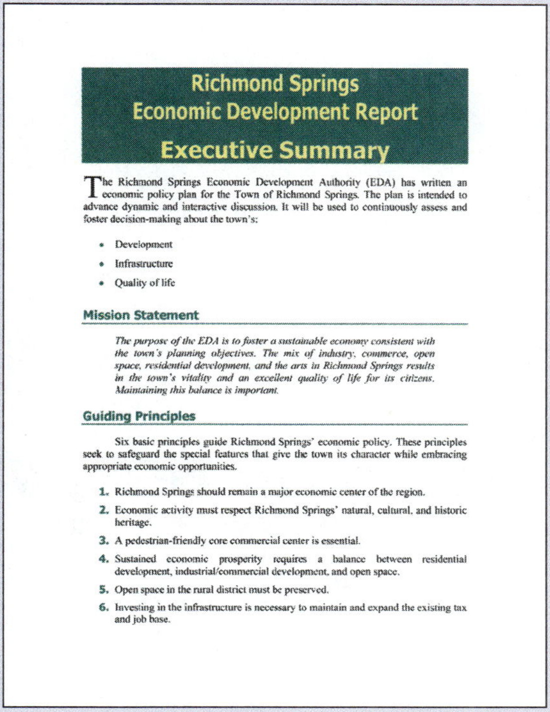

Richmond Springs
Economic Development Report
Executive Summary

The Richmond Springs Economic Development Authority (EDA) has written an economic policy plan for the Town of Richmond Springs. The plan is intended to advance dynamic and interactive discussion. It will be used to continuously assess and foster decision-making about the town's:

- Development
- Infrastructure
- Quality of life

Mission Statement

The purpose of the EDA is to foster a sustainable economy consistent with the town's planning objectives. The mix of industry, commerce, open space, residential development, and the arts in Richmond Springs results in the town's vitality and an excellent quality of life for its citizens. Maintaining this balance is important.

Guiding Principles

Six basic principles guide Richmond Springs' economic policy. These principles seek to safeguard the special features that give the town its character while embracing appropriate economic opportunities.

1. Richmond Springs should remain a major economic center of the region.
2. Economic activity must respect Richmond Springs' natural, cultural, and historic heritage.
3. A pedestrian-friendly core commercial center is essential.
4. Sustained economic prosperity requires a balance between residential development, industrial/commercial development, and open space.
5. Open space in the rural district must be preserved.
6. Investing in the infrastructure is necessary to maintain and expand the existing tax and job base.

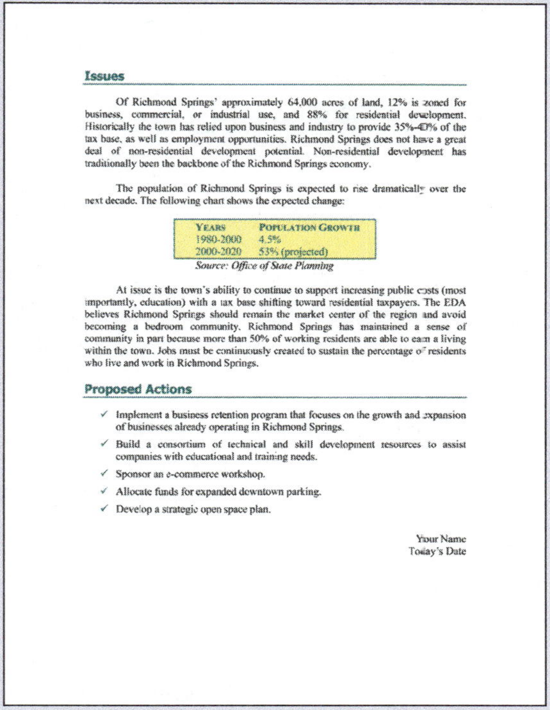

Issues

Of Richmond Springs' approximately 64,000 acres of land, 12% is zoned for business, commercial, or industrial use, and 88% for residential development. Historically the town has relied upon business and industry to provide 35%-40% of the tax base, as well as employment opportunities. Richmond Springs does not have a great deal of non-residential development potential. Non-residential development has traditionally been the backbone of the Richmond Springs economy.

The population of Richmond Springs is expected to rise dramatically over the next decade. The following chart shows the expected change:

YEARS	POPULATION GROWTH
1980-2000	4.5%
2000-2020	53% (projected)

Source: Office of State Planning

At issue is the town's ability to continue to support increasing public costs (most importantly, education) with a tax base shifting toward residential taxpayers. The EDA believes Richmond Springs should remain the market center of the region and avoid becoming a bedroom community. Richmond Springs has maintained a sense of community in part because more than 50% of working residents are able to earn a living within the town. Jobs must be continuously created to sustain the percentage of residents who live and work in Richmond Springs.

Proposed Actions

- ✓ Implement a business retention program that focuses on the growth and expansion of businesses already operating in Richmond Springs.
- ✓ Build a consortium of technical and skill development resources to assist companies with educational and training needs.
- ✓ Sponsor an e-commerce workshop.
- ✓ Allocate funds for expanded downtown parking.
- ✓ Develop a strategic open space plan.

Your Name
Today's Date

▼ INDEPENDENT CHALLENGE 1

You are an estimator for Zephir Construction in the Australian city of Wollongong. You have drafted an estimate for a home renovation job, and need to format it. It's important that your estimate have a clean, striking design, and reflect your company's professionalism.

a. Start Word, open the file WD C-3.doc from the drive and folder where your Data Files are located, save it as **Zephir Construction**, then read the document to get a feel for its contents. Figure C-27 shows how you will format the letterhead.

FIGURE C-27

ZEPHIRConstruction
73 Corrimal Street, Wollongong, NSW 2500
Tel: 02-4225-3202; www.zephir.com.au

b. In the first paragraph, format **ZEPHIR** in 24-point Arial Black, then apply bold. (*Hint*: Select a similar font if Arial Black is not available to you.)

c. Format **Construction** in 24-point Arial, then change the character scale to 90%.

d. Format the next two lines in 9-point Arial bold, center the three-line letterhead, then add a 1-point black border below the last line.

e. Format the title **Proposal of Renovation** in 16-point Arial Black, then center the title.

f. Format the following headings (including the colons) in 12-point Arial Black: **Date**, **Work to be performed for and at**, **Scope of work**, **Payment schedule**, and **Agreement**.

g. Format the 14-line list under **Scope of work** that begins with **Demo of all ...** as a numbered list, then apply bold to the numbers.

▼ INDEPENDENT CHALLENGE 1 (CONTINUED)

h. Change the paragraph spacing to add 4 points of space after each paragraph in the list. (*Hint*: Select 0 pt in the After text box, then type 4.)
i. With the list selected, set a right tab stop at the 5¾" mark, then insert tabs before every price in the list.
j. Apply bold to the two lines, **Total estimated job cost...** and **Approximate job time**... below the list.
k. Replace Your Name with your name in the signature block, select the signature block (Respectfully submitted through your name), set a left tab stop at the 3½" mark, then indent the signature block.
l. Examine the document carefully for formatting errors and make any necessary adjustments.
m. Save and print the document, then close the file and exit Word.

▼ INDEPENDENT CHALLENGE 2

Your employer, The Lange Center for Contemporary Arts in Halifax, Nova Scotia, is launching a membership drive. Your boss has written the text for a flyer advertising Lange membership, and asks you to format it so that it is eye catching and attractive.

a. Open the file WD C-4.doc from the drive and folder where your Data Files are located, save it as **Membership Flyer**, then read the document. Figure C-28 shows how you will format the first several paragraphs of the flyer.
b. Select the entire document and format it in 10-point Arial Narrow.
c. Center the first line, **Membership Drive**, and apply indigo shading to the paragraph. Format the text in 26-point Arial Narrow, bold, with a white font color. Expand the character spacing by 7 points.
d. Format the second line, **2006**, in 36-point Arial Black. Expand the character spacing by 25 points and change the character scale to 200%. Center the line.

FIGURE C-28

e. Format each **What we do for...** heading in 12-point Arial, bold, with an indigo font color. Add a single line ½-point border under each heading.
f. Format each subheading (**Gallery**, **Lectures**, **Library**, **All members...**, and **Membership Levels**) in 10-point Arial, bold. Add 3 points of spacing before each paragraph.
g. Indent each body paragraph ¼", except for the lines under the **What we do for YOU** heading.
h. Format the four lines under the All members... subheading as a bulleted list. Use a bullet symbol of your choice and format the bullets in the indigo color.
i. Indent the five lines under the Membership Levels heading ¼". For these five lines, set left tab stops at the 1¼" mark and the 2" mark on the horizontal ruler. Insert tabs before the price and before the word **All** in each of the five lines.
j. Format the name of each membership level (**Artistic**, **Conceptual**, etc.) in 10-point Arial, bold, italic, with an indigo font color.
k. Format the **For more information** heading in 14-point Arial, bold, with an indigo font color, then center the heading.
l. Format the last two lines in 11-point Arial Narrow, and center the lines. In the contact information, replace Your Name with your name, then apply bold to your name.

Advanced Challenge Exercise

ACE

- Change the font color of **2006** to 80% gray and add a shadow effect.
- Add an emboss effect to each subheading.
- Add a 3-point dotted black border above the **For more information** heading.

m. Examine the document carefully for formatting errors and make any necessary adjustments.
n. Save and print the flyer, then close the file and exit Word.

▼ INDEPENDENT CHALLENGE 3

One of your responsibilities as program coordinator at Solstice Mountain Sports is to develop a program of winter outdoor learning and adventure workshops. You have drafted a memo to your boss to update her on your progress. You need to format the memo so it is professional looking and easy to read.

FIGURE C-29

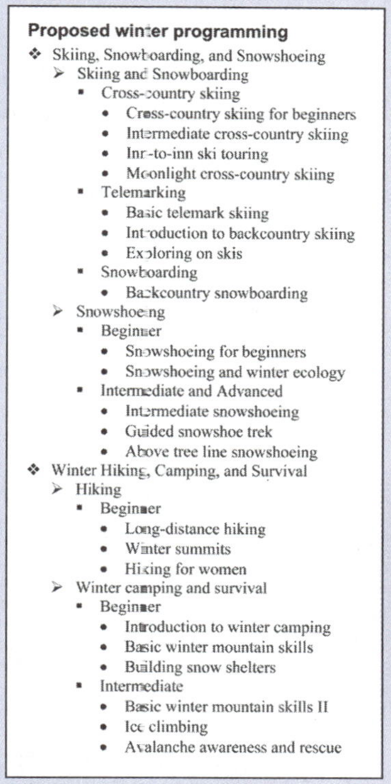

Proposed winter programming

- Skiing, Snowboarding, and Snowshoeing
  - Skiing and Snowboarding
    - Cross-country skiing
      - Cross-country skiing for beginners
      - Intermediate cross-country skiing
      - Inn-to-inn ski touring
      - Moonlight cross-country skiing
    - Telemarking
      - Basic telemark skiing
      - Introduction to backcountry skiing
      - Exploring on skis
    - Snowboarding
      - Backcountry snowboarding
  - Snowshoeing
    - Beginner
      - Snowshoeing for beginners
      - Snowshoeing and winter ecology
    - Intermediate and Advanced
      - Intermediate snowshoeing
      - Guided snowshoe trek
      - Above tree line snowshoeing
- Winter Hiking, Camping, and Survival
  - Hiking
    - Beginner
      - Long-distance hiking
      - Winter summits
      - Hiking for women
  - Winter camping and survival
    - Beginner
      - Introduction to winter camping
      - Basic winter mountain skills
      - Building snow shelters
    - Intermediate
      - Basic winter mountain skills II
      - Ice climbing
      - Avalanche awareness and rescue

a. Start Word, open the file WD C-5.doc from the drive and folder where your Data Files are located, then save it as **Solstice Memo**.

b. Select the heading **Solstice Mountain Sports Memorandum**, then apply the paragraph style Heading 1 to it. (*Hint:* Open the Styles and Formatting task pane, click the Show list arrow, click Available Styles if necessary, then click Heading 1.)

c. In the memo header, replace Today's Date and Your Name with the current date and your name.

d. Select the four-line memo header, set a left tab stop at the ¾" mark, then insert tabs before the date, the recipient's name, your name, and the subject of the memo.

e. Double-space the four lines in the memo header, then apply the character style Strong to **Date:**, **To:**, **From:**, and **Re:**.

f. Apply a 1½-point double line border below the blank line under the memo header. (*Hint*: Turn on formatting marks, select the paragraph symbol below the memo header, then apply a border below it.)

g. Apply the paragraph style Heading 3 to the headings **Overview**, **Workshops**, **Accommodation**, **Fees**, and **Proposed winter programming**.

h. Under the Fees heading, format the words **Workshop fees** and **Accommodation fees** in bold italic.

i. Add 6 points of space after the Workshop fees paragraph.

Advanced Challenge Exercise

- Format **Fees** as animated text using the Las Vegas Lights animation style.
- After Fees, type **Verify prices with the Moose Lodge**, then format the text as hidden text.
- In the Fees section, apply yellow highlighting to the prices.

j. On the second page of the document, format the list under the **Proposed winter programming** heading as an outline. Figure C-29 shows the hierarchical structure of the outline. (*Hint*: Format the list as an outline numbered list, then use the Increase Indent and Decrease Indent buttons to change the level of importance of each item.)

k. Change the outline numbering style to the bullet numbering style shown in Figure C-29, if necessary.

l. Save and print the document, then close the file and exit Word.

E-QUEST

▼ INDEPENDENT CHALLENGE 4

The fonts you choose for a document can have a major effect on the document's tone. Not all fonts are appropriate for use in a business document, and some fonts, especially those with a definite theme, are appropriate only for specific purposes. The World Wide Web includes hundreds of Web sites devoted to fonts and text design. Some Web sites sell fonts, others allow you to download fonts for free and install them on your computer. In this Independent Challenge, you will research Web sites related to fonts and find examples of fonts you can use in your work.

a. Start Word, open the file WD C-6.doc from the drive and folder where your Data Files are located, and save it as **Fonts**. This document contains the questions you will answer about the fonts you find.

b. Use your favorite search engine to search the Web for Web sites related to fonts. Use the keyword **font** to conduct your search.

c. Explore the fonts available for downloading. As you examine the fonts, notice that fonts fall into two general categories: serif fonts, which have a small stroke, called a serif, at the ends of each character, and sans serif fonts, which do not have a serif. Times New Roman is an example of a serif font and Arial is an example of a sans serif font.

d. Replace Your Name and Today's Date with the current date and your name, type your answers in the Fonts document, save it, print a copy, then close the file and exit Word.

▼ VISUAL WORKSHOP

Using the file WD C-7.doc found in the drive and folder where your Data Files are located, create the menu shown in Figure C-30. (*Hints*: Use Centaur or a similar font. Change the font size of the heading to 56 points, scale the font to 90%, and expand the spacing by 1 point. For the rest of the text, change the font size of the daily specials to 18 points and the descriptions to 14 points. Format the prices using tabs. Use paragraph spacing to adjust the spacing between paragraphs so that all the text fits on one page.) Save the menu as **Melting Pot Specials**, then print a copy.

FIGURE C-30

The Melting Pot Café

Daily Specials

Monday: Veggie Chili
Hearty veggie chili with melted cheddar in our peasant French bread bowl. Topped with sour cream & scallions....$5.95

Tuesday: Greek Salad
Our large garden salad with kalamata olives, feta cheese, and garlic vinaigrette. Served with an assortment of rolls....$5.95

Wednesday: French Dip
Lean roast beef topped with melted cheddar on our roasted garlic roll. Served with a side of au jus and red bliss mashed potatoes....$6.95

Thursday: Chicken Cajun Bleu
Cajun chicken, chunky blue cheese, cucumbers, leaf lettuce, and tomato on our roasted garlic roll....$6.50

Friday: Clam Chowder
Classic New England thick, rich, clam chowder in our peasant French bread bowl. Served with a garden salad....$5.95

Saturday: Hot Chicken and Gravy
Delicious chicken and savory gravy served on a thick slice of toasted honest white. Served with red bliss mashed potatoes....$6.95

Sunday: Turkey-Bacon Club
Double-decker roasted turkey, crisp bacon, leaf lettuce, tomato, and sun-dried tomato mayo on toasted triple seed....$6.50

Chef: Your Name

UNIT
D
Word 2003

Formatting Documents

OBJECTIVES

- Set document margins
- Divide a document into sections
- Insert page breaks
- Insert page numbers
- Add headers and footers
- Edit headers and footers
- Format columns
- Insert a table
- Insert WordArt
- Insert clip art

SAM

If you have a SAM user profile, you may have access to hands-on instruction, practice, and assessment of the skills covered in this unit. Log in to your SAM account and go to your assignments page to see what your instructor has assigned.

The page-formatting features of Word allow you to creatively lay out and design the pages of your documents. In this unit, you learn how to change the document margins, determine page orientation, add page numbers, and insert headers and footers. You also learn how to format text in columns and how to illustrate your documents with tables, clip art, and WordArt. You have written and formatted the text for the quarterly newsletter for the marketing staff. You are now ready to lay out and design the newsletter pages. You plan to organize the articles in columns and to illustrate the newsletter with a table, clip art, and WordArt.

UNIT
D
Word 2003

Setting Document Margins

Changing a document's margins is one way to change the appearance of a document and control the amount of text that fits on a page. The **margins** of a document are the blank areas between the edge of the text and the edge of the page. When you create a document in Word, the default margins are 1" at the top and bottom of the page, and 1.25" on the left and right sides of the page. You can adjust the size of a document's margins using the Page Setup command on the File menu, or using the rulers. The newsletter should be a four-page document when finished. You begin formatting the pages by reducing the size of the document margins so that more text fits on each page.

STEPS

1. **Start Word, open the file WD D-1.doc from the drive and folder where your Data Files are located, then save it as MediaLoft Buzz**
   The newsletter opens in Print Layout view.
2. **Scroll through the newsletter to get a feel for its contents, then press [Ctrl][Home]**
   The newsletter is currently five pages long. Notice the status bar indicates the page where the insertion point is located and the total number of pages in the document.
3. **Click File on the menu bar, click Page Setup, then click the Margins tab in the Page Setup dialog box if it is not already selected**
   The Margins tab in the Page Setup dialog box is shown in Figure D-1. You can use the Margins tab to change the top, bottom, left, or right document margins, to change the orientation of the pages from portrait to landscape, and to alter other page layout settings. **Portrait orientation** means a page is taller than it is wide; **landscape orientation** means a page is wider than it is tall. This newsletter uses portrait orientation.
4. **Click the Top down arrow three times until 0.7" appears, then click the Bottom down arrow until 0.7" appears**
   The top and bottom margins of the newsletter will be .7". Notice that the margins in the Preview section of the dialog box change as you adjust the margin settings.

> **QUICK TIP**
> The minimum allowable margin settings depend on your printer and the size of the paper you are using. Word displays a warning message if you set margins that are too narrow for your printer.

5. **Press [Tab], type .7 in the Left text box, press [Tab], then type .7 in the Right text box**
   The left and right margins of the newsletter will also be .7". You can change the margin settings by using the arrows or by typing a value in the appropriate text box.
6. **Click OK**
   The document margins change to .7", as shown in Figure D-2. The bar at the intersection of the white and shaded areas on the horizontal and vertical rulers indicates the location of the margin. You can also change a document's margins by dragging the bar to a new location.
7. **Click the Zoom list arrow on the Standard toolbar, then click Two Pages**
   The first two pages of the document appear in the document window.

> **QUICK TIP**
> Use the Reveal Formatting task pane to quickly check the margin, orientation, paper size, and other page layout settings for a document.

8. **Scroll down to view all five pages of the newsletter, press [Ctrl][Home], click the Zoom list arrow, click Page Width, then click the Save button on the Standard toolbar to save the document**

FIGURE D-1: Margins tab in Page Setup dialog box

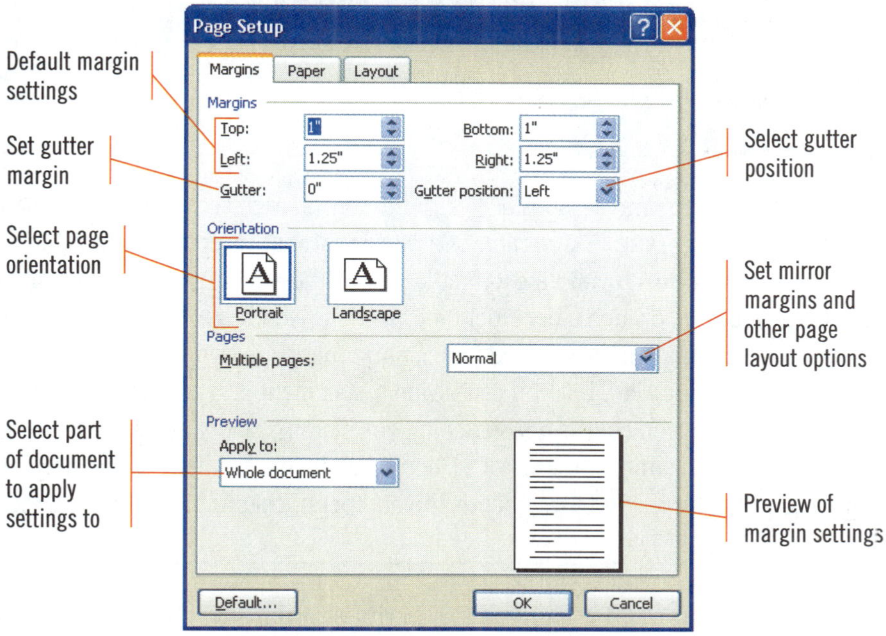

FIGURE D-2: Newsletter with smaller margins

Clues to Use

Changing orientation, margin settings, and paper size

By default, the documents you create in Word use an 8½" × 11" paper size in portrait orientation with the default margin settings. You can adjust these settings in the Page Setup dialog box to create documents that are a different size, shape, or layout. On the Margins tab, change the orientation of the pages by selecting Portrait or Landscape. To change the layout of multiple pages, use the Multiple pages list arrow to create pages that use mirror margins, that include two pages per sheet of paper, or that are formatted like a folded booklet. **Mirror margins** are used in documents with facing pages, such as a magazine, where the margins on the left page of the document are a mirror image of the margins on the right page. Documents with mirror margins have inside and outside margins, rather than right and left margins. Another type of margin is a gutter margin, which is used in documents that are bound, such as books. A **gutter** adds extra space to the left, top, or inside margin to allow for the binding. Add a gutter to a document by adjusting the setting in the Gutter text box on the Margins tab. If you want to change the size of the paper used in a document, use the Paper tab in the Page Setup dialog box. Use the Paper size list arrow to select a standard paper size, or enter custom measurements in the Width and Height text boxes.

UNIT D

Word 2003

Dividing a Document into Sections

Dividing a document into sections allows you to format each section of the document with different page layout settings. A **section** is a portion of a document that is separated from the rest of the document by section breaks. **Section breaks** are formatting marks that you insert in a document to show the end of a section. Once you have divided a document into sections, you can format each section with different column, margin, page orientation, header and footer, and other page layout settings. By default, a document is formatted as a single section, but you can divide a document into as many sections as you like. You want to format the body of the newsletter in two columns, but leave the masthead and the headline "News Bites" as a single column. You insert a section break before the body of the newsletter to divide the document into two sections, and then change the number of columns in the second section to two.

STEPS

1. **Click the Show/Hide ¶ button on the Standard toolbar to display formatting marks if they are not visible**

   Turning on formatting marks allows you to see the section breaks you insert in a document.

2. **Place the insertion point before the headline Web Marketing Solutions to be..., click Insert on the menu bar, then click Break**

   The Break dialog box opens, as shown in Figure D-3. You use this dialog box to insert different types of section breaks. Table D-1 describes the different types of section breaks.

3. **Click the Continuous option button, then click OK**

   Word inserts a continuous section break, shown as a dotted double line, above the headline. A continuous section break begins a new section of the document on the same page. The document now has two sections. Notice that the status bar indicates that the insertion point is in section 2.

4. **With the insertion point in section 2, click the Columns button on the Standard toolbar**

   A grid showing four columns opens. You use the grid to select the number of columns you want to create.

5. **Point to the second column on the grid, then click**

   Section 2 is formatted in two columns, as shown in Figure D-4. The text in section 1 remains formatted in a single column. Notice the status bar now indicates the document is four pages long. Formatting text in columns is another way to increase the amount of text that fits on a page.

6. **Click the Zoom list arrow on the Standard toolbar, click Two Pages, then scroll down to examine all four pages of the document**

   The text in section 2—all the text below the continuous section break—is formatted in two columns. Text in columns flows automatically from the bottom of one column to the top of the next column.

7. **Press [Ctrl][Home], click the Zoom list arrow, click Page Width, then save the document**

QUICK TIP

When you insert a section break at the beginning of a paragraph, Word inserts the break at the end of the previous paragraph. A section break stores the formatting information for the preceding section.

TABLE D-1: Types of section breaks

section	function
Next page	Begins a new section and moves the text following the break to the top of the next page
Continuous	Begins a new section on the same page
Even page	Begins a new section and moves the text following the break to the top of the next even-numbered page
Odd page	Begins a new section and moves the text following the break to the top of the next odd-numbered page

FIGURE D-3: Break dialog box

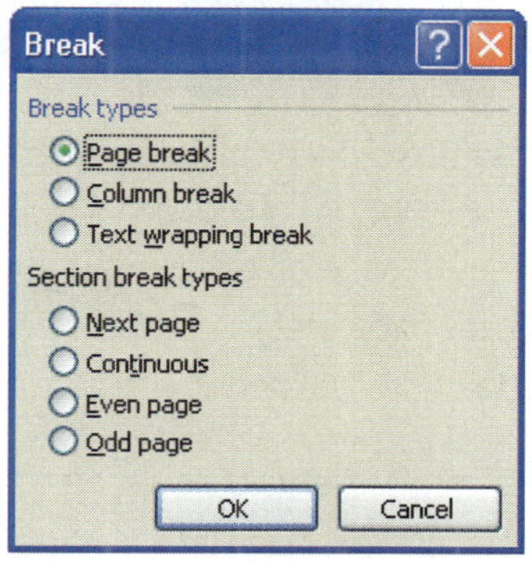

FIGURE D-4: Continuous section break and columns

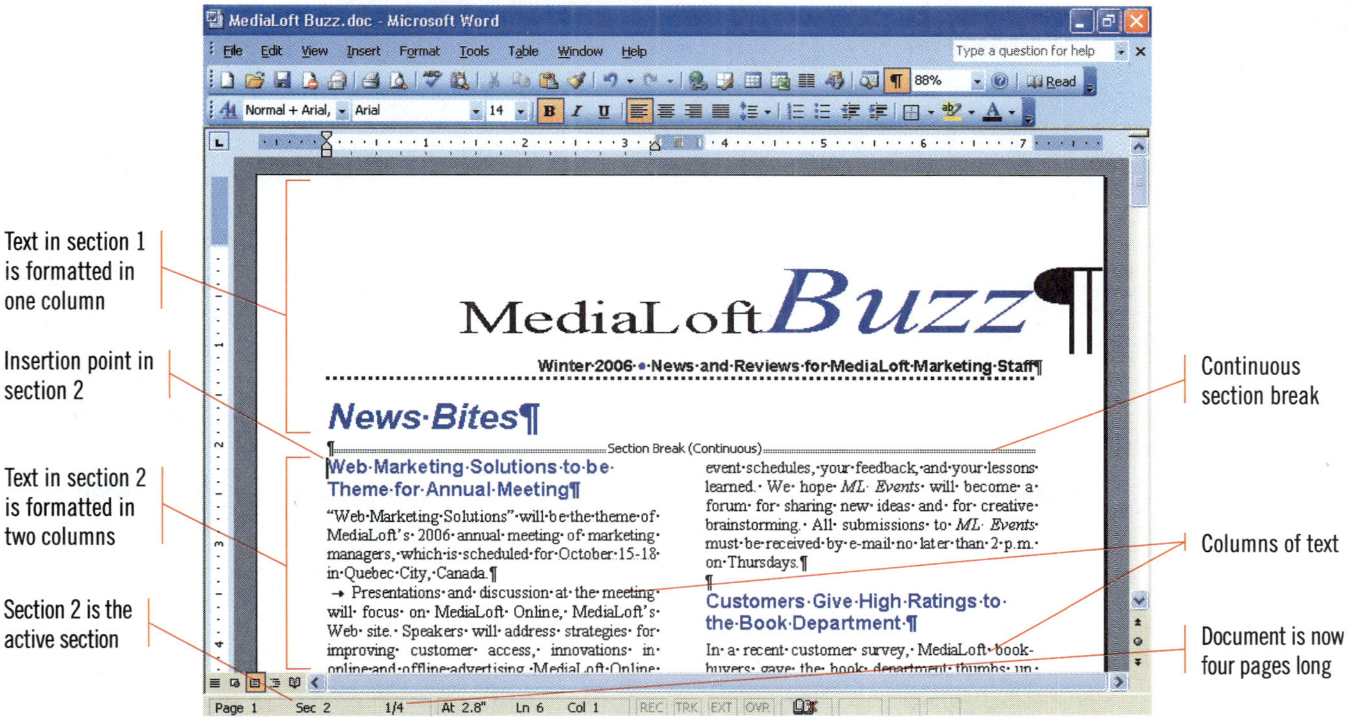

Clues to Use

Changing page layout settings for a section

Dividing a document into sections allows you to vary the layout of a document. In addition to applying different column settings to sections, you can apply different margins, page orientation, paper size, vertical alignment, header and footer, page numbering, and other page layout settings. For example, if you are formatting a report that includes a table with many columns, you might want to change the table's page orientation to landscape so that it is easier to read. To do this, you would insert a section break before and after the table to create a section that contains only the table. Then you would use the Margins tab in the Page Setup dialog box to change the page orientation of the section that contains the table to landscape.

To change the page layout settings for an individual section, place the insertion point in the section, open the Page Setup (or Columns) dialog box, select the options you want to change, click the Apply to list arrow, click This section, then click OK. When you select This section in the Apply to list box, the settings are applied to the current section only. If you select Whole document in the Apply to list box, the settings are applied to all the sections in the document.

Inserting Page Breaks

As you type text in a document, Word automatically inserts an **automatic page break** (also called a soft page break) when you reach the bottom of a page, allowing you to continue typing on the next page. You can also force text onto the next page of a document by using the Break command to insert a **manual page break** (also called a hard page break). You insert manual page breaks where you know you want to begin each new page of the newsletter.

STEPS

1. **Scroll down to the bottom of page 1, place the insertion point before the headline Career Corner, click Insert on the menu bar, then click Break**
   The Break dialog box opens. You also use this dialog box to insert page, column, and text-wrapping breaks. Table D-2 describes these types of breaks.
2. **Make sure the Page break option button is selected, then click OK**
   Word inserts a manual page break before "Career Corner" and moves all the text following the page break to the beginning of the next page, as shown in Figure D-5. The page break appears as a dotted line in Print Layout view when formatting marks are displayed. Page break marks are visible on the screen but do not print. Manual and automatic page breaks are always visible in Normal view.
3. **Scroll down to the bottom of page 2, place the insertion point before the headline Webcasts Slated for Spring, press and hold [Ctrl], then press [Enter]**
   Pressing [Ctrl][Enter] is a fast way to insert a manual page break. The headline is forced to the top of the third page.
4. **Scroll down page 3, place the insertion point before the headline Staff News, then press [Ctrl][Enter]**
   The headline is forced to the top of the fourth page.
5. **Press [Ctrl][Home], click the Zoom list arrow on the Standard toolbar, then click Two Pages**
   The first two pages of the document are displayed, as shown in Figure D-6.
6. **Scroll down to view pages 3 and 4, click the Zoom list arrow, click Page Width, then save the document**

QUICK TIP

To delete a break, double-click the break to select it, then press [Delete].

QUICK TIP

To fit more text on the screen in Print Layout view, you can hide the white space on the top and bottom of each page and the gray space between pages. To toggle between hiding and showing white space, move the pointer to the top of a page until the pointer changes to , then click.

Clues to Use

Vertically aligning text on a page

By default, text is vertically aligned with the top margin of a page, but you can change the vertical alignment of text so that it is centered between the top and bottom margins, justified between the top and bottom margins, or aligned with the bottom margin of the page. You vertically align text on a page only when the text does not fill the page; for example, if you are creating a flyer or a title page for a report. To change the vertical alignment of text in a section (or a document), place the insertion point in the section you want to align, open the Page Setup dialog box, use the Vertical alignment list arrow on the Layout tab to select the alignment you want—top, center, justified, or bottom—use the Apply to list arrow to select the part of the document you want to align, and then click OK.

FIGURE D-5: Manual page break in document

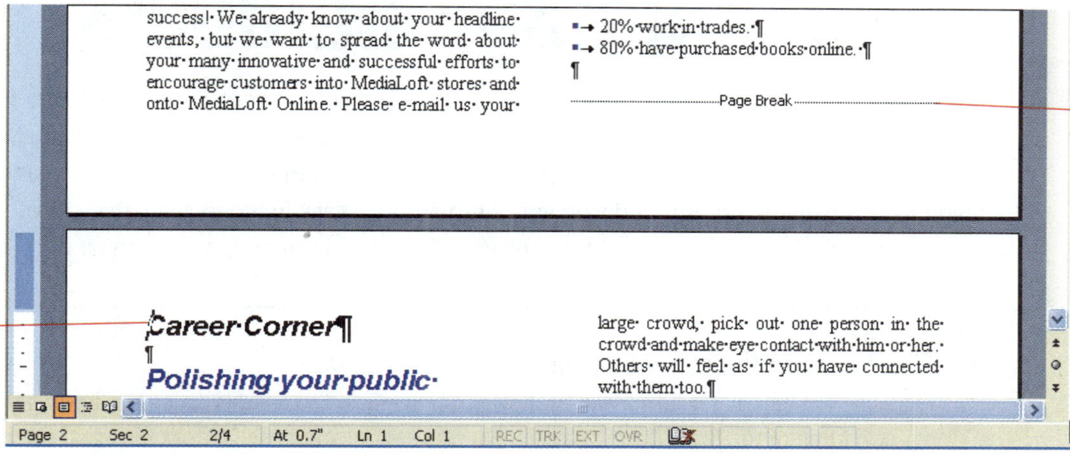

FIGURE D-6: Pages 1 and 2

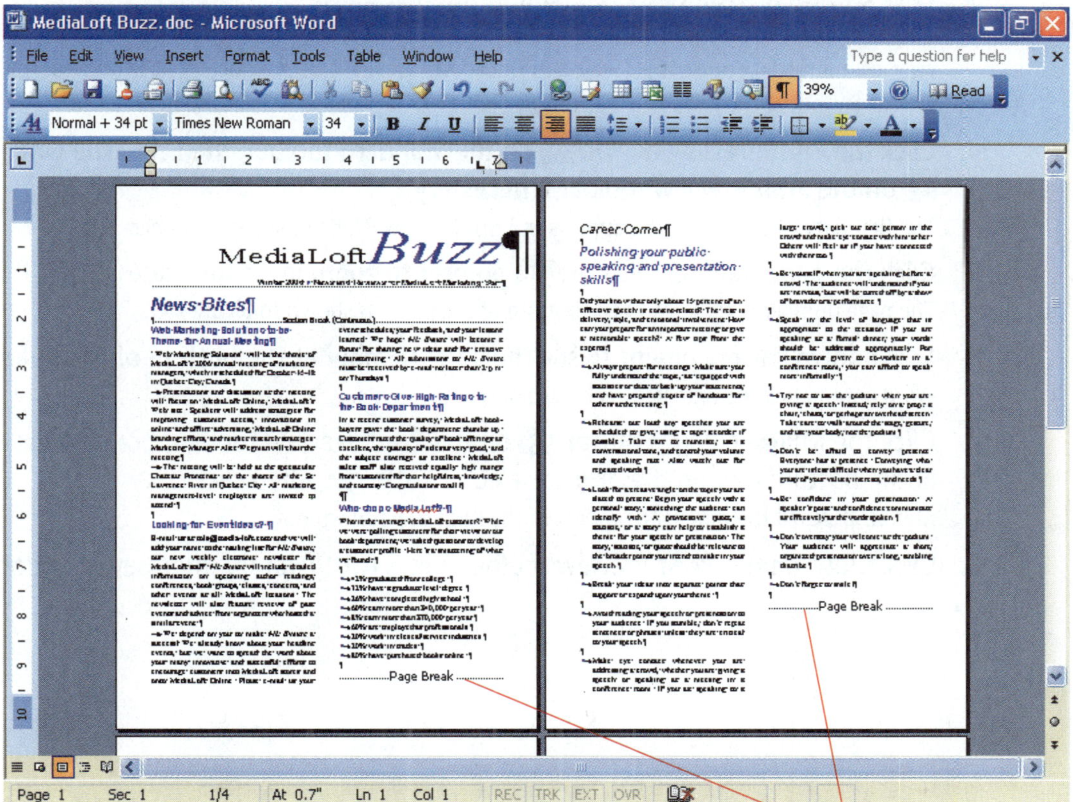

Word 2003

TABLE D-2: Types of breaks

break	function
Page break	Forces the text following the break to begin at the top of the next page
Column break	Forces the text following the break to begin at the top of the next column
Text wrapping break	Forces the text following the break to begin at the beginning of the next line

UNIT D
Word 2003

Inserting Page Numbers

If you want to number the pages of a multiple-page document, you can insert a page number field at the top or bottom of each page. A **field** is a code that serves as a placeholder for data that changes in a document, such as a page number or the current date. When you use the Page Numbers command on the Insert menu to add page numbers to a document, Word automatically numbers the pages for you. You insert a page number field so that page numbers will appear at the bottom of each page in the document.

STEPS

1. **Click Insert on the menu bar, then click Page Numbers**
   The Page Numbers dialog box opens, as shown in Figure D-7. You use this dialog box to specify the position—top or bottom of the page—and the alignment for the page numbers. Bottom of page (Footer) is the default position.

> **QUICK TIP**
> You can also align page numbers with the left, right, inside, or outside margins of a document.

2. **Click the Alignment list arrow, then click Center**
   The page numbers will be centered between the left and right margins at the bottom of each page.
3. **Click OK, then scroll to the bottom of the first page**
   The page number 1 appears in gray at the bottom of the first page, as shown in Figure D-8. The number is gray, or dimmed, because it is located in the Footer area. When the document is printed, the page numbers appear as normal text. You will learn more about headers and footers in the next lesson.
4. **Click the Print Preview button on the Standard toolbar, then click the One Page button on the Print Preview toolbar if necessary**
   The first page of the newsletter appears in Print Preview. Notice the page number.
5. **Click the page number with the pointer to zoom in on the page**
   The page number is centered at the bottom of the page, as shown in Figure D-9.
6. **Scroll down the document to see the page number at the bottom of each page**
   Word automatically numbered each page of the newsletter.

> **QUICK TIP**
> To display more than six pages of a document in Print Preview, drag to expand the Multiple Pages grid.

7. **Click the Multiple Pages button on the Print Preview toolbar, point to the second box in the bottom row on the grid to select 2 × 2 pages, then click**
   All four pages of the newsletter appear in the Print Preview window.
8. **Click Close on the Print Preview toolbar, press [Ctrl][Home], then save the document**

Clues to Use

Inserting the date and time

Using the Date and Time command on the Insert menu, you can insert the current date or the current time into a document, either as a field or as static text. Word uses the clock on your computer to compute the current date and time. To insert the current date or time at the location of the insertion point, click Date and Time on the Insert menu, then select the date or time format you want to use from the list of available formats in the Date and Time dialog box. If you want to insert the date or time as a field that is updated automatically each time you open or print the document, select the Update automatically check box, and then click OK. If you want the current date or time to remain in the document as static text, deselect the Update automatically check box, and then click OK.

FIGURE D-7: Page Numbers dialog box

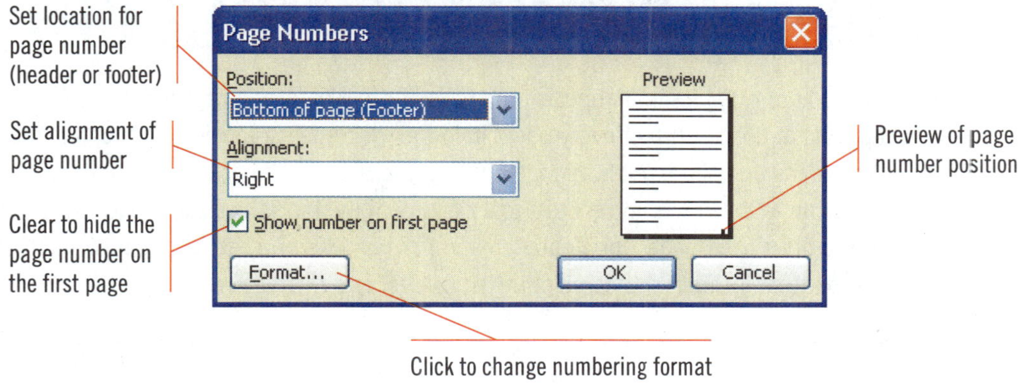

FIGURE D-8: Page number in document

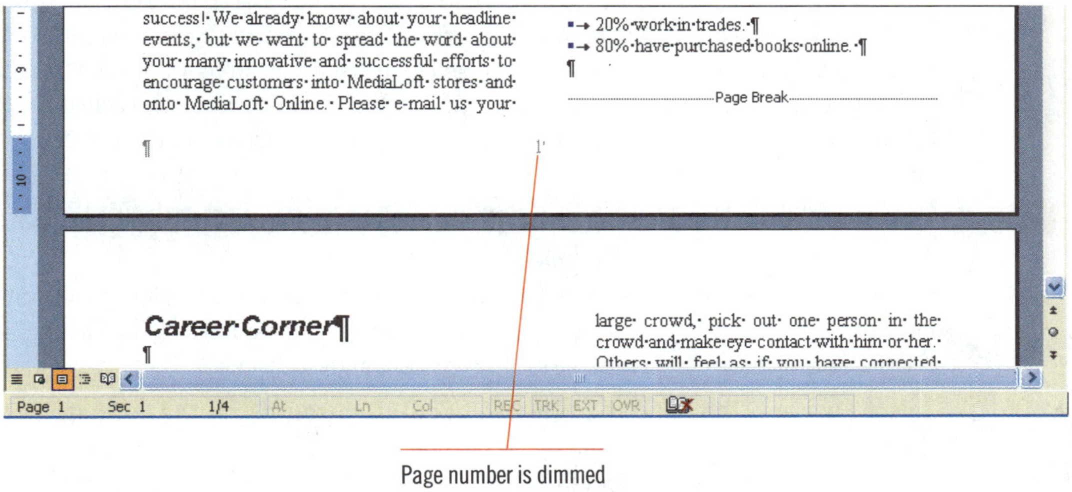

FIGURE D-9: Page number in Print Preview

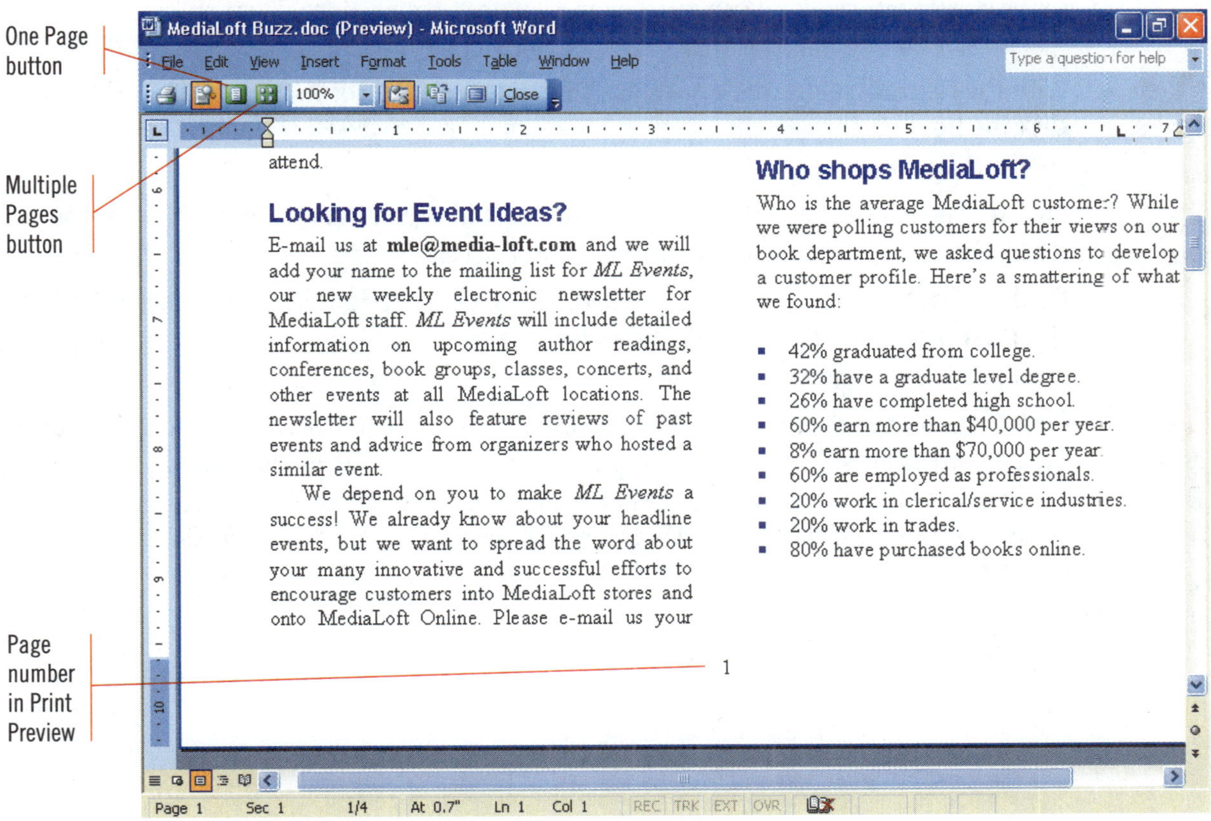

Word 2003

UNIT D

Word 2003

Adding Headers and Footers

A **header** is text or graphics that appears at the top of every page of a document. A **footer** is text or graphics that appears at the bottom of every page. In longer documents, headers and footers often contain information such as the title of the publication, the title of the chapter, the name of the author, the date, or a page number. You can add headers and footers to a document by using the Header and Footer command on the View menu to open the Header and Footer areas, and then inserting text and graphics in them. You create a header that includes the name of the newsletter and the current date.

STEPS

1. **Click View on the menu bar, then click Header and Footer**

   The Header and Footer areas open and the document text is dimmed, as shown in Figure D-10. When the document text is dimmed, it cannot be edited. The Header and Footer toolbar also opens. It includes buttons for inserting standard text into headers and footers and for navigating between headers and footers. See Table D-3. The Header and Footer areas of a document are independent of the document itself and must be formatted separately. For example, if you select all the text in a document and then change the font, the header and footer font does not change.

2. **Type Buzz in the Header area, press [Spacebar] twice, then click the Insert Date button on the Header and Footer toolbar**

   Clicking the Insert Date button inserts a date field into the header. The date is inserted using the default date format (usually month/date/year, although your default date format might be different). The word "Buzz" and the current date will appear at the top of every page in the document.

3. **Select Buzz and the date, then click the Center button on the Formatting toolbar**

   The text is centered in the Header area. In addition to the alignment buttons on the Formatting toolbar, you can use tabs to align text in the Header and Footer areas. Notice the tab stops shown on the ruler. The tab stops are the default tab stops for the Header and Footer areas and are based on the default margin settings. If you change the margins in a document, you can adjust the tab stops in the Header or Footer area to align with the new margin settings.

4. **With the text still selected, click the Font list arrow on the Formatting toolbar, click Arial, click the Bold button B, then click in the Header area to deselect the text**

   The header text is formatted in 12-point Arial bold.

5. **Click the Switch Between Header and Footer button on the Header and Footer toolbar**

   The insertion point moves to the Footer area, where a page number field is centered in the Footer area.

6. **Double-click the page number to select the field, click the Font list arrow, click Arial, click B, then click in the Footer area to deselect the field**

   The page number is formatted in 12-point Arial bold.

7. **Click Close on the Header and Footer toolbar, save the document, then scroll down until the bottom of page 1 and the top of page 2 appear in the document window**

   The Header and Footer areas close and the header and footer text is dimmed, as shown in Figure D-11. The header text—"Buzz" and the current date—appear at the top of every page in the document, and a page number appears at the bottom of every page.

QUICK TIP

You can change the date format by right-clicking the field, clicking Edit Field on the shortcut menu, and then selecting a new date format in the Field properties list in the Field dialog box.

QUICK TIP

Unless you set different headers and footers for different sections, the information you insert in any Header or Footer area appears on every page in the document.

QUICK TIP

To change the distance between the header and footer and the edge of the page, change the From edge settings on the Layout tab in the Page Setup dialog box.

FIGURE D-10: Header area

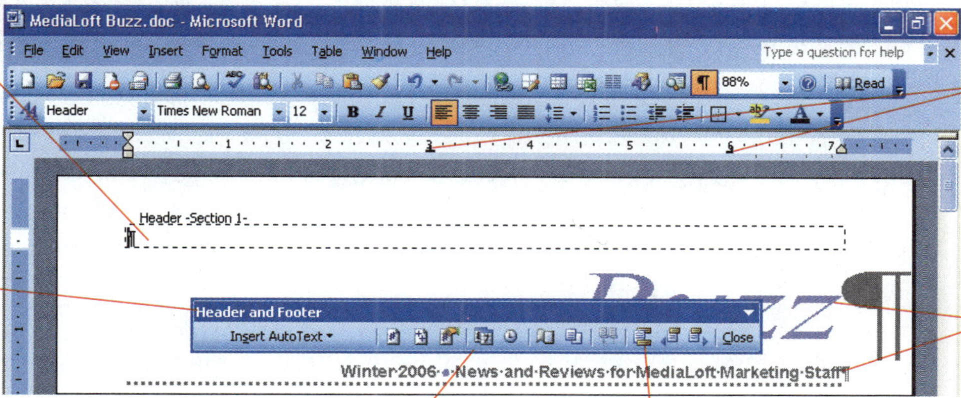

FIGURE D-11: Header and footer in document

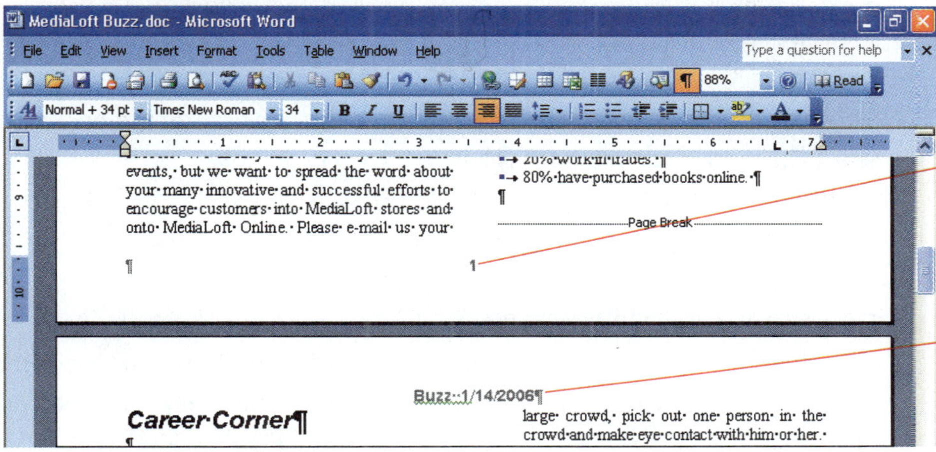

TABLE D-3: Buttons on the Header and Footer toolbar

button	function
Insert AutoText	Inserts an AutoText entry, such as a field for the filename, or the author's name
Insert Page Number	Inserts a field for the page number so that the pages are numbered automatically
Insert Number of Pages	Inserts a field for the total number of pages in the document
Format Page Number	Opens the Page Number Format dialog box; use to change the numbering format or to begin automatic page numbering with a specific number
Insert Date	Inserts a field for the current date
Insert Time	Inserts a field for the current time
Page Setup	Opens the Page Setup dialog box
Show/Hide Document Text	Hides and displays the document text
Link to Previous	Switches the link between headers and footers in adjoining sections on and off; use to make headers and footers in adjoining sections the same or different
Switch Between Header and Footer	Moves the insertion point between the Header and Footer areas
Show Previous	Moves the insertion point to the header or footer in the next section
Show Next	Moves the insertion point to the header or footer in the previous section

UNIT D
Word 2003

Editing Headers and Footers

To change header and footer text or to alter the formatting of headers and footers, you must first open the Header and Footer areas. You open headers and footers by using the Header and Footer command on the View menu or by double-clicking a header or footer in Print Layout view. You modify the header by adding a small circle symbol between "Buzz" and the date. You also add a border under the header text to set it off from the rest of the page. Finally, you remove the header and footer text from the first page of the document.

STEPS

1. **Place the insertion point at the top of page 2, position the pointer over the header text at the top of page 2, then double-click**
   The Header and Footer areas open.

> **QUICK TIP**
> To insert a character such as an em dash (—) or an ellipsis (...), select the character on the Special Characters tab in the Symbol dialog box, then click Insert.

2. **Place the insertion point between the two spaces after Buzz, click Insert on the menu bar, then click Symbol**
   The Symbol dialog box opens and is similar to Figure D-12. **Symbols** are special characters, such as graphics, shapes, and foreign language characters, that you can insert into a document. The symbols shown in Figure D-12 are the symbols included with the (normal text) font. You can use the Font list arrow on the Symbols tab to view the symbols included with each font on your computer.

> **TROUBLE**
> If you cannot locate the symbol, type 25CF in the Character code text box.

3. **Scroll the list of symbols if necessary to locate the black circle symbol shown in Figure D-12, select the black circle symbol, click Insert, then click Close**
   A circle symbol is added at the location of the insertion point.
4. **With the insertion point in the header text, click Format on the menu bar, then click Borders and Shading**
   The Borders and Shading dialog box opens.
5. **Click the Borders tab if it is not already selected, click Custom in the Setting section, click the dotted line in the Style scroll box (the second line style), click the Width list arrow, click 2¼ pt, click the Bottom border button in the Preview section, make sure Paragraph is selected in the Apply to list box, click OK, click Close on the Header and Footer toolbar, then scroll as needed to see the top of page 2**
   A dotted line border is added below the header text, as shown in Figure D-13.
6. **Press [Ctrl][Home] to move the insertion point to the beginning of the document**
   The newsletter already includes the name of the document at the top of the first page, making the header information redundant. You can modify headers and footers so that the header and footer text does not appear on the first page of a document or a section.
7. **Click File on the menu bar, click Page Setup, then click the Layout tab**
   The Layout tab of the Page Setup dialog box includes options for creating a different header and footer for the first page of a document or a section, and for creating different headers and footers for odd- and even-numbered pages. For example, in a document with facing pages, such as a magazine, you might want the publication title to appear in the left-page header and the publication date to appear in the right-page header.

> **QUICK TIP**
> You can enter different text in the First Page Header and First Page Footer areas when the Different first page check box is selected.

8. **Click the Different first page check box to select it, click the Apply to list arrow, click Whole document, then click OK**
   The header and footer text is removed from the Header and Footer areas on the first page.
9. **Scroll to see the header and footer on pages 2, 3, and 4, then save the document**

FIGURE D-12: Symbol dialog box

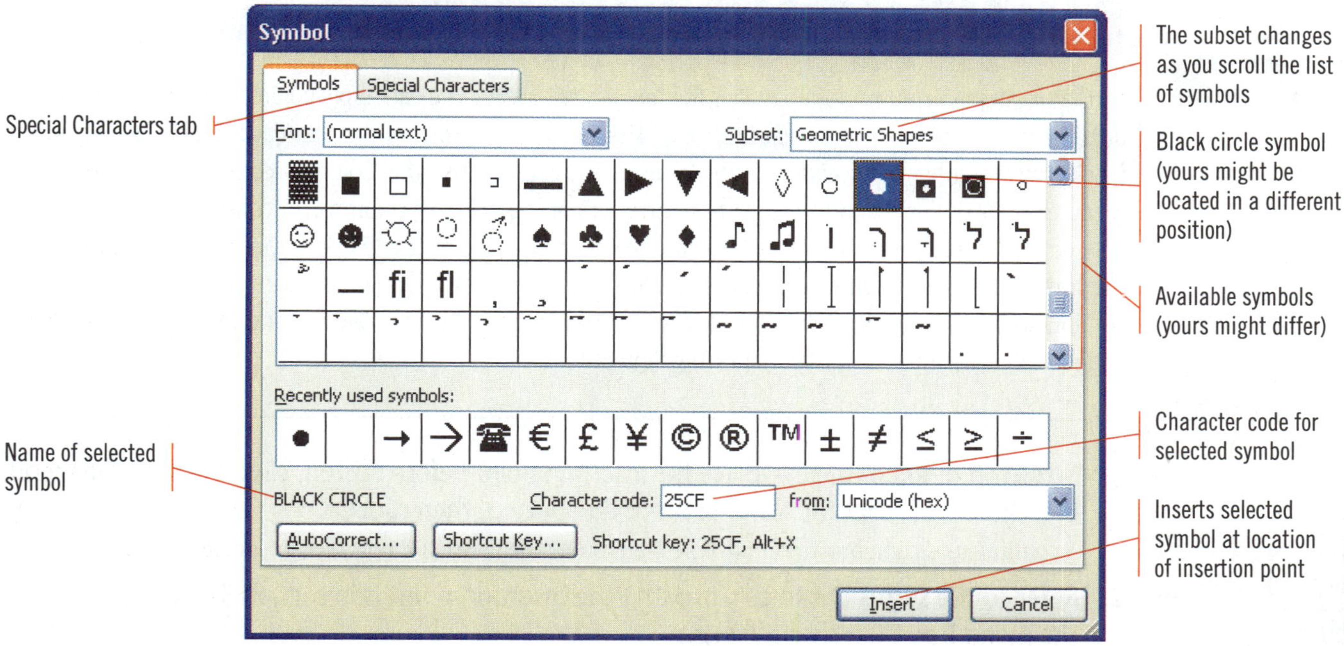

FIGURE D-13: Symbol and border added to header

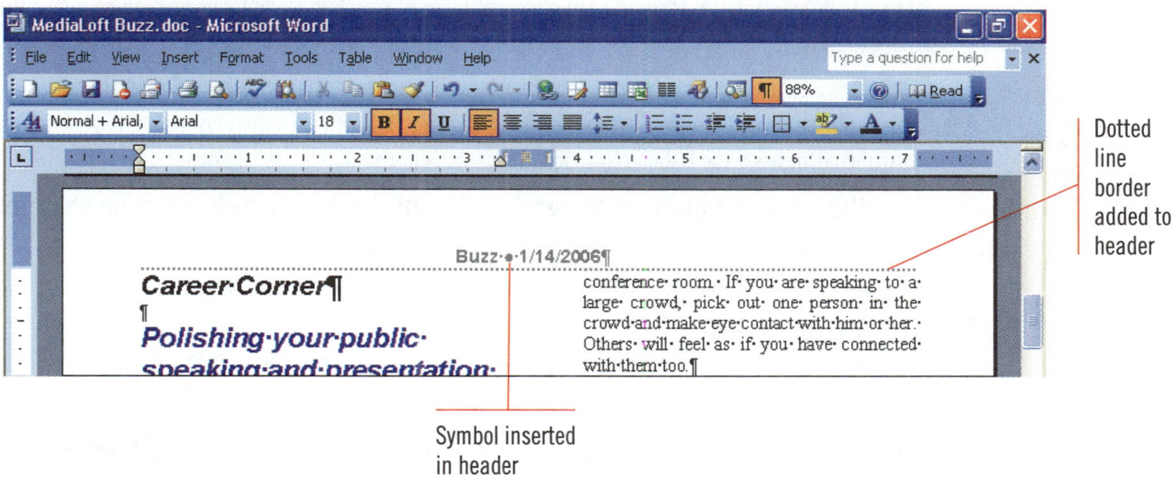

Clues to Use

Inserting and creating AutoText entries

Word includes a number of built-in AutoText entries, including salutations and closings for letters, as well as information for headers and footers. To insert a built-in AutoText entry at the location of the insertion point, point to AutoText on the Insert menu, point to a category on the AutoText menu, then click the AutoText entry you want to insert. You can also use the Insert AutoText button on the Header and Footer toolbar to insert an AutoText entry from the Header/Footer category into a header or footer.

The Word AutoText feature also allows you to store text and graphics that you use frequently so that you can easily insert them in a document. To create a custom AutoText entry, enter the text or graphic you want to store—such as a company name or logo—in a document, select it, point to AutoText on the Insert menu, and then click New. In the Create AutoText dialog box, type a name for your AutoText entry, then click OK. The text or graphic is saved as a custom AutoText entry. To insert a custom AutoText entry in a document, point to AutoText on the Insert menu, click AutoText, select the entry name on the AutoText tab in the AutoCorrect dialog box, click Insert, then click OK.

Formatting Columns

Formatting text in columns often makes the text easier to read. You can apply column formatting to a whole document, to a section, or to selected text. The Columns button on the Standard toolbar allows you to quickly create columns of equal width. In addition, you can use the Columns command on the Format menu to create columns and to customize the width and spacing of columns. To control the way text flows between columns, you can insert a **column break**, which forces the text following the break to move to the top of the next column. You can also balance columns of unequal length on a page by inserting a continuous section break at the end of the last column on the page. You format the Staff News page in three columns, and then adjust the flow of text.

STEPS

1. **Scroll to the top of page 4, place the insertion point before Boston, click Insert on the menu bar, click Break, click the Continuous option button, then click OK**
   A continuous section break is inserted before Boston. The newsletter now contains three sections.

QUICK TIP
To change the width and spacing of existing columns, you can use the Columns dialog box or drag the column markers on the horizontal ruler.

2. **Refer to the status bar to confirm that the insertion point is in section 3, click Format on the menu bar, then click Columns**
   The Columns dialog box opens, as shown in Figure D-14.
3. **Select Three in the Presets section, click the Spacing down arrow twice until 0.3" appears, select the Line between check box, then click OK**
   All the text in section 3 is formatted in three columns of equal width with a line between the columns, as shown in Figure D-15.

QUICK TIP
To create a banner headline that spans the width of a page, select the headline text, click the Columns button, then click 1 Column.

4. **Click the Zoom list arrow on the Standard toolbar, then click Whole Page**
   Notice that the third column of text is much shorter than the first two columns. Page 4 would look better if the three columns were balanced—each the same length.
5. **Place the insertion point at the end of the third column, click Insert on the menu bar, click Break, click the Continuous option button, then click OK**
   The columns in section 3 adjust to become roughly the same length.
6. **Scroll up to page 3**
   The two columns on page 3 are also uneven. You want the information about Jack Niven to appear at the top of the second column.

QUICK TIP
If a section contains a column break, you cannot balance the columns by inserting a continuous section break.

7. **Click the Zoom list arrow, click Page Width, scroll down page 3, place the insertion point before the heading Jack Niven, click Insert on the menu bar, click Break, click the Column break option button, then click OK**
   The text following the column break is forced to the top of the next column.
8. **Click the Zoom list arrow, click Two Pages, then save the document**
   The columns on pages 3 and 4 are formatted as shown in Figure D-16.

Clues to Use

Hyphenating text in a document

Hyphenating a document is another way to control the flow of text in columns. Hyphens are small dashes that break words that fall at the end of a line. Hyphenation diminishes the gaps between words in justified text and reduces ragged right edges in left-aligned text. If a document includes narrow columns, hyphenating the text can help give the pages a cleaner look. To hyphenate a document automatically, point to Language on the Tools menu, click Hyphenation, select the Automatically hyphenate document check box in the Hyphenation dialog box, and then click OK. You can also use the Hyphenation dialog box to change the hyphenation zone—the distance between the margin and the end of the last word in the line. A smaller hyphenation zone results in a greater number of hyphenated words and a cleaner look to columns of text.

FIGURE D-14: Columns dialog box

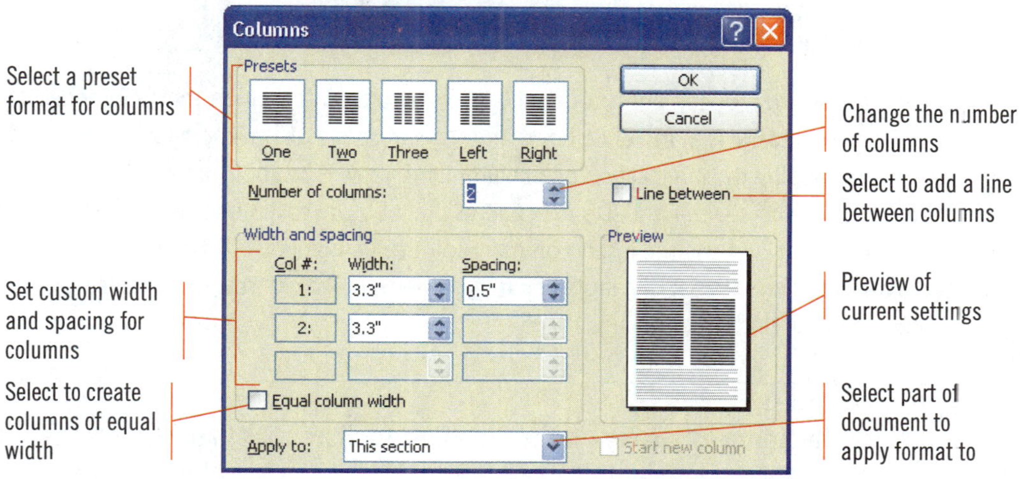

FIGURE D-15: Text formatted in three columns

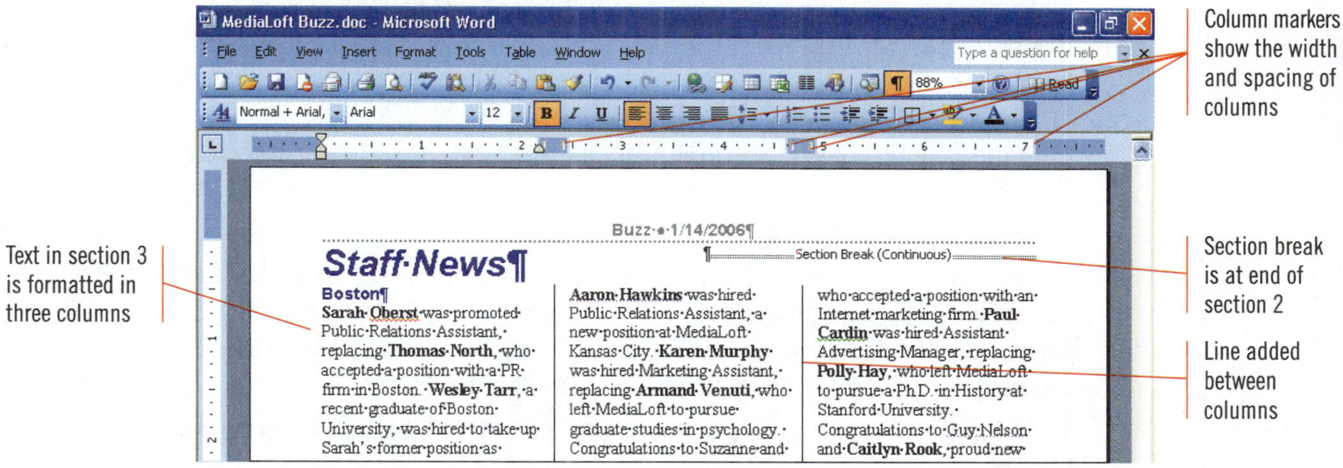

FIGURE D-16: Columns on pages 3 and 4 of the newsletter

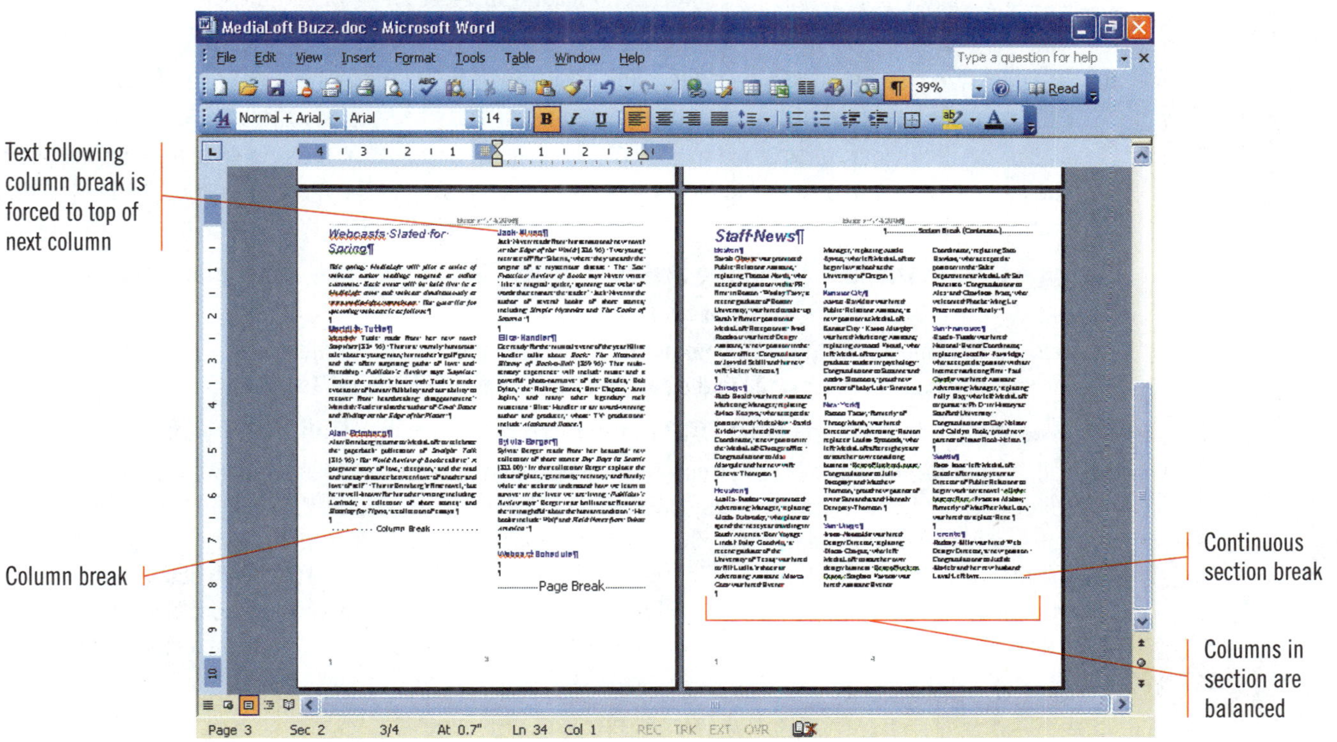

Word 2003

UNIT D

Word 2003

Inserting a Table

Adding a table to a document is a useful way to illustrate information that is intended for quick reference and analysis. A **table** is a grid of columns and rows of cells that you can fill with text and graphics. A **cell** is the box formed by the intersection of a column and a row. The lines that divide the columns and rows of a table and help you see the grid-like structure of the table are called **borders**. A simple way to insert a table into a document is to use the Insert command on the Table menu. This command allows you to determine the dimensions and format of a table before it is inserted. You add a table showing the schedule for Webcasts to the bottom of page 3.

STEPS

1. **Click the Zoom list arrow on the Standard toolbar, click Page Width, then scroll down page 3 until the heading Webcast Schedule is at the top of your screen**
   The bottom of page three is displayed.
2. **Place the insertion point before the heading Webcast Schedule, click Insert on the menu bar, click Break, click the Continuous option button, then click OK**
   A continuous section break is inserted before the heading Webcast Schedule. The document now includes four sections, with the heading Webcast Schedule in the third section.
3. **Click the Columns button on the Standard toolbar, point to the first column on the grid, then click**
   Section 3 is formatted as a single column.
4. **Place the insertion point before the second paragraph mark below the heading Webcast Schedule, click Table on the menu bar, point to Insert, then click Table**
   The Insert Table dialog box opens, as shown in Figure D-17. You use this dialog box to create a blank table with a set number of columns and rows, and to choose an option for sizing the width of the columns in the table.
5. **Type 4 in the Number of columns text box, press [Tab], type 6 in the Number of rows text box, make sure the Fixed column width option button is selected, then click AutoFormat**
   The Table AutoFormat dialog box opens. You use this dialog box to apply a table style to the table. Table styles include format settings for the text, borders, and shading in a table. A preview of the selected style appears in the Preview section of the dialog box.
6. **Scroll down the list of table styles, click Table Grid 8, clear the First column, Last row, and Last column check boxes in the Apply special formats to section, then click OK twice**
   A blank table with four columns and six rows is inserted in the document at the location of the insertion point. The table is formatted in the Table Grid 8 style, with blue shading in the header row and blue borders that define the table cells. The insertion point is in the upper-left cell of the table, the first cell in the header row.
7. **Type Date in the first cell in the first row, press [Tab], type Time, press [Tab], type Guest, press [Tab], type Store, then press [Tab]**
   Pressing [Tab] moves the insertion point to the next cell in the row. At the end of a row, pressing [Tab] moves the insertion point to the first cell in the next row. You can also click in a cell to move the insertion point to it.
8. **Type the text shown in Figure D-18 in the table cells, pressing [Tab] to move from cell to cell**
   You can edit the text in a table by placing the insertion point in a cell and then typing. You can also select the text in a table and then format it using the buttons on the Formatting toolbar. If you want to modify the structure of a table, you can use the Insert and Delete commands on the Table menu to add and remove rows and columns. You can also use the AutoFit command on the Table menu to change the width of table columns and the height of table rows. To select a column, row, or table before performing an action, place the insertion point in the row, column, or table you want to select, and then use the Select command on the Table menu.
9. **Save the document**

QUICK TIP

To apply a different table style to a table once it is created, place the insertion point in the table, click Table Auto-Format on the Table menu, and then modify the selections in the Table Auto-Format dialog box.

TROUBLE

If you pressed [Tab] after the last row, click the Undo button on the Standard toolbar to remove the blank row.

FIGURE D-17: Insert Table dialog box

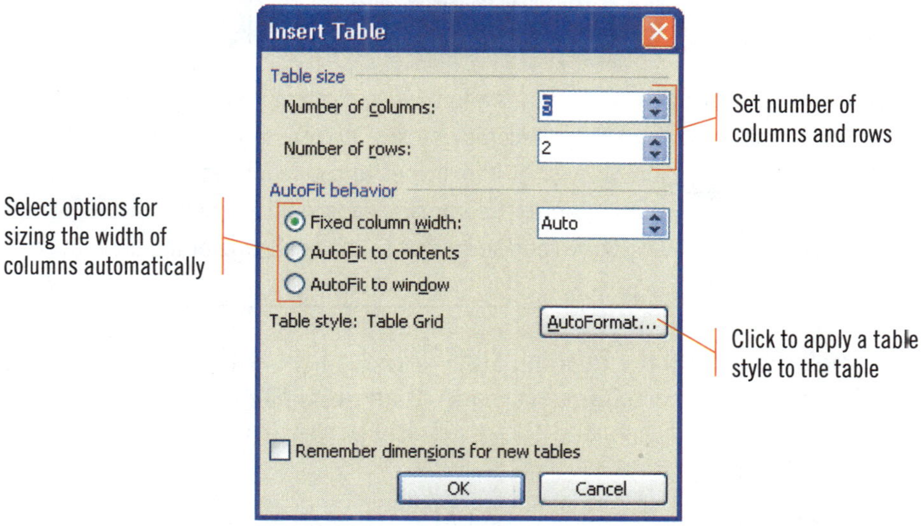

FIGURE D-18: Completed table

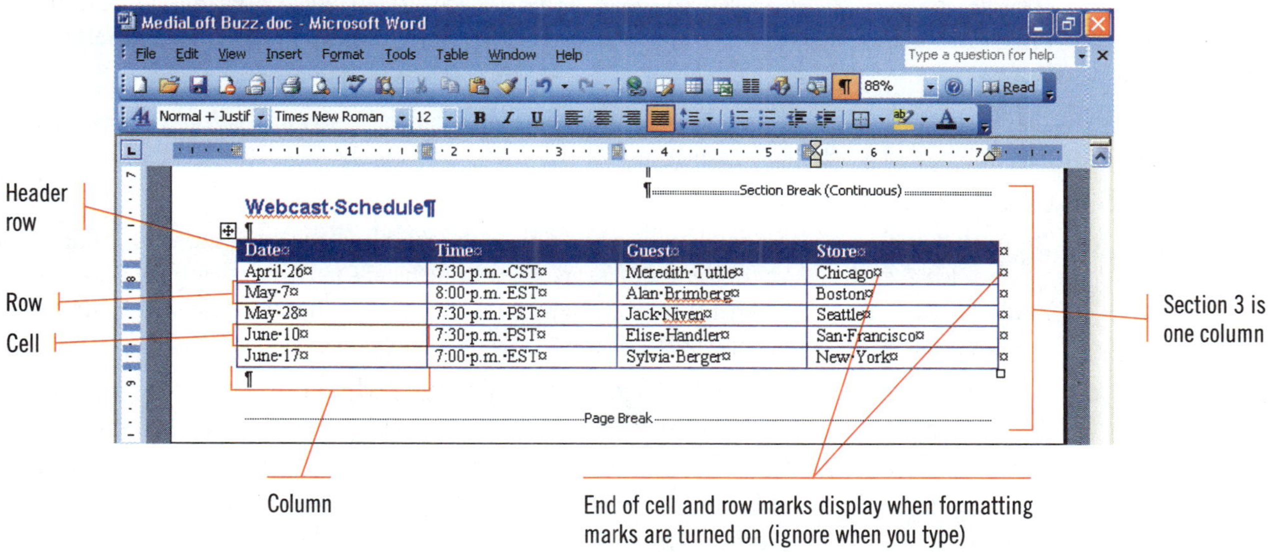

Word 2003

Clues to Use

Moving around in a long document

Rather than scrolling to move to a different place in a long document, you can use the Browse by Object feature, the Go To command, or the Document Map to quickly move the insertion point to a specific location. Browse by Object allows you to browse to the next or previous page, section, line, table, graphic, or other item of the same type in a document. To do this, first click the Select Browse Object button below the vertical scroll bar to open a palette of object types. On this palette, click the button for the type of item by which you want to browse, and then click the Next or Previous buttons to scroll through the items of that type in the document.

To move a specific page, section, or other item in a document, you can click the Go To command on the Edit menu. On the Go To tab in the Find and Replace dialog box, select the type of item in the Go to what list box, type the item number in the text box, and then click Go To to move the insertion point to the item.

If your document is formatted with heading styles, you can also use the Document Map to navigate a document. The Document Map is a separate pane in the document window that displays a list of headings in the document. You click a heading in the Document Map to move the insertion point to that heading in the document. To open and close the Document Map, click Document Map on the View menu or click the Document Map button on the Standard toolbar.

UNIT
D
Word 2003

Inserting WordArt

Illustrating a document with WordArt is a fun way to spice up the layout of a page. **WordArt** is an object that contains specially formatted, decorative text. The text in a WordArt object can be skewed, rotated, stretched, shadowed, patterned, or fit into shapes to create interesting effects. To insert a WordArt object into a document, you use the WordArt command on the Insert menu. You decide to format the Staff News headline as WordArt to add some zest to the final page of the newsletter.

STEPS

1. **Scroll down until the heading Staff News is at the top of your screen, select Staff News (not including the paragraph mark), then press [Delete]**
   The insertion point is at the top of page 4 in the third section of the document. The third section is formatted as a single column.
2. **Click Insert on the menu bar, point to Picture, then click WordArt**
   The WordArt Gallery dialog box opens, as shown in Figure D-19. You use the WordArt Gallery to select a style for the WordArt object.
3. **Click the fourth style in the third row, then click OK**
   The Edit WordArt Text dialog box opens. You type the text you want to format as WordArt in this dialog box. You can also use the Edit WordArt Text dialog box to change the font and font size of the WordArt text.
4. **Type Staff News, then click OK**
   The WordArt object appears at the location of the insertion point. The object is an **inline graphic**, or part of the line of text in which it was inserted.
5. **Click the WordArt object to select it**
   The black squares that appear on the corners and sides of the object are the **sizing handles**. Sizing handles appear when a graphic object is selected. You can drag a sizing handle to change the size of the object. The WordArt toolbar also appears when a WordArt object is selected. You use the buttons on the WordArt toolbar to edit and modify the format of WordArt objects.
6. **Position the pointer over the lower-right sizing handle, when the pointer changes to ↘ drag down and to the right to make the object about 1½" tall and 5½" wide**
   Refer to the vertical and horizontal rulers for guidance as you drag the sizing handle to resize the object. When you release the mouse button, the WordArt object is enlarged, as shown in Figure D-20.
7. **Click the Center button on the Formatting toolbar**
   The WordArt object is centered between the margins.
8. **Click the WordArt Shape button on the WordArt toolbar, then click the Wave 1 shape (the fifth shape in the third row)**
   The shape of the WordArt text changes.
9. **Click outside the WordArt object to deselect it, click the Zoom list arrow on the Standard toolbar, click Two Pages, then save the document**
   The completed pages 3 and 4 are displayed, as shown in Figure D-21.

QUICK TIP

Use the Text Wrapping button on the WordArt toolbar to convert the object to a floating graphic.

TROUBLE

If the newsletter is five pages instead of four, reduce the height of the WordArt object.

FIGURE D-19: WordArt Gallery dialog box

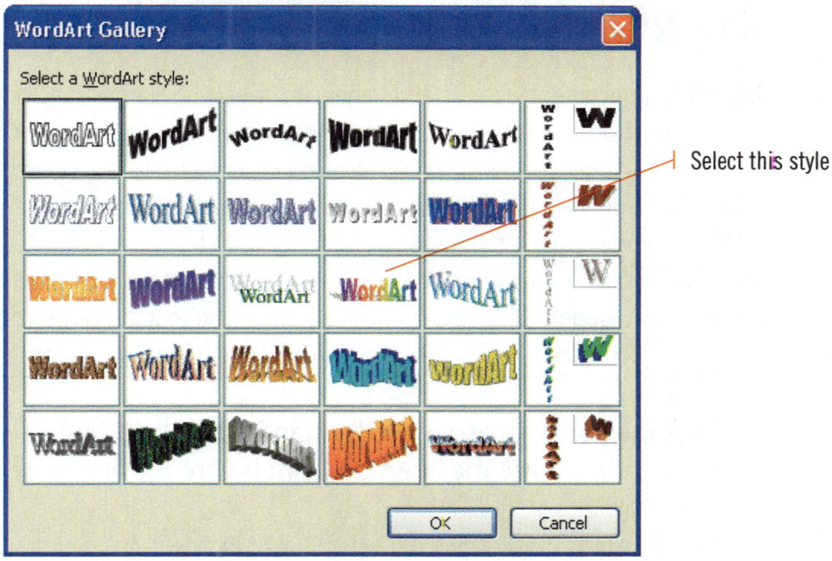

FIGURE D-20: Resized WordArt object

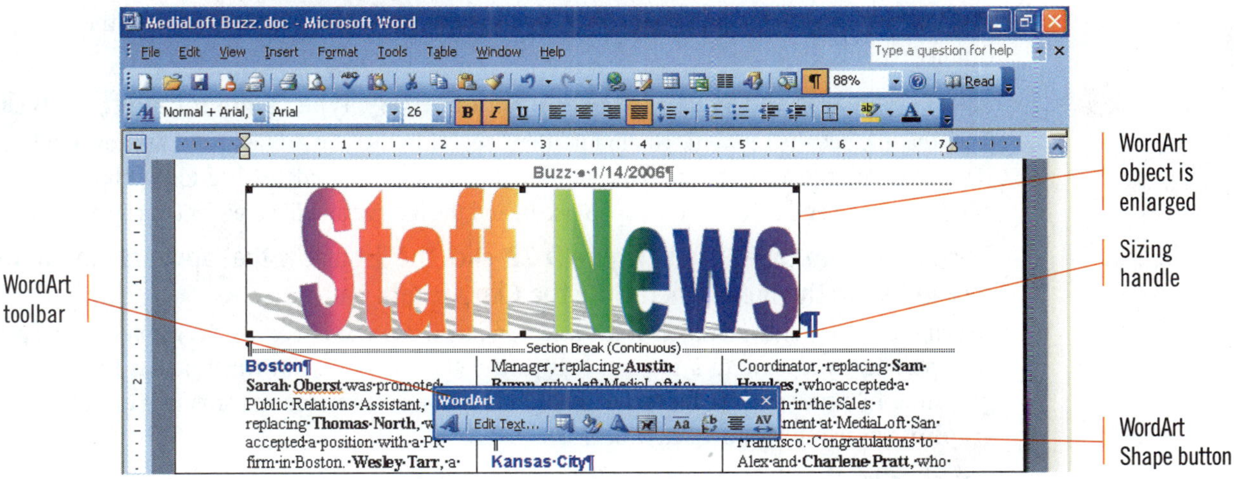

FIGURE D-21: Completed pages 3 and 4

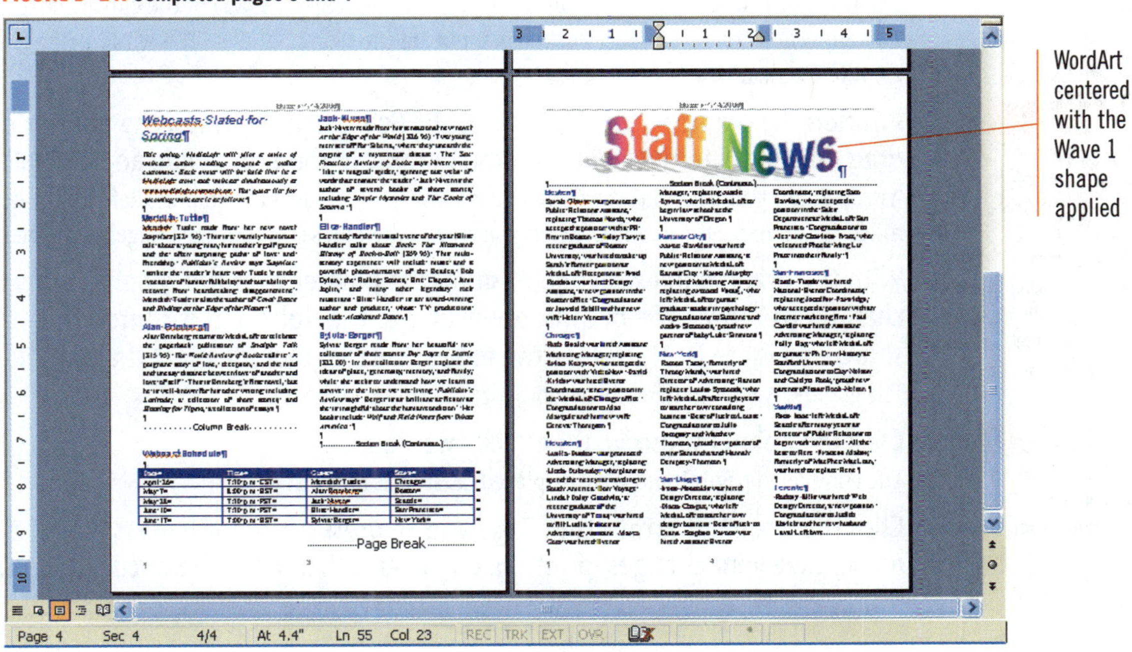

UNIT
D
Word 2003

Inserting Clip Art

Illustrating a document with clip art images can give it visual appeal and help to communicate your ideas. **Clip art** is a collection of graphic images that you can insert into a document. Clip art images are stored in the **Clip Organizer**, a library of the **clips**—media files, including graphics, photographs, sounds, movies, and animations—that come with Word. You can add a clip to a document using the Clip Art command on the Insert menu. Once you insert a clip art image, you can wrap text around it, resize it, and move it to a different location. You illustrate the second page of the newsletter with a clip art image. After you insert the image, you wrap text around it, enlarge it, and then move it so that it is centered between the two columns of text.

STEPS

1. **Click the Zoom list arrow on the Standard toolbar, click Page Width, scroll to the top of page 2, then place the insertion point before the first body paragraph, which begins Did you know...**
   You insert the clip art graphic at the location of the insertion point.
2. **Click Insert on the menu bar, point to Picture, then click Clip Art**
   The Clip Art task pane opens. You can use this task pane to search for clips related to a keyword. If you are working with an active Internet connection, your search results will include clip art from the Microsoft Office Online Web site.
3. **Select the text in the Search for text box if necessary, type communication, then click Go**
   Clips that include the keyword "communication" appear in the Clip Art task pane, as shown in Figure D-22. When you point to a clip, a ScreenTip showing the first few keywords applied to the clip (listed alphabetically), the width and height of the clip in pixels, and the file size and file type for the clip appears.

> **TROUBLE**
> Make sure the All media types check box in the Results should be in list box has a check mark. Select a different clip if the clip shown in Figure D-22 is not available to you.

4. **Point to the clip called out in Figure D-22, click the list arrow that appears next to the clip, click Insert on the menu, then close the Clip Art task pane**
   The clip is inserted at the location of the insertion point. You want to center the graphic on the page. Until you apply text wrapping to a graphic, it is part of the line of text in which it was inserted (an **inline graphic**). To move a graphic independently of text, you must wrap the text around it to make it a **floating graphic**, which can be moved anywhere on a page.
5. **Double-click the clip art image, click the Layout tab in the Format Picture dialog box, click Tight, then click OK**
   The text in the first body paragraph wraps around the irregular shape of the clip art image. The white circles that appear on the square edges of the graphic are the sizing handles. The white sizing handles indicate the graphic is a floating graphic.
6. **Position the pointer over the lower-right sizing handle, when the pointer changes to ↘ drag down and to the right until the graphic is about 2½" wide and 2½" tall**
   As you drag a sizing handle, the dotted lines show the outline of the graphic. Refer to the dotted lines and the rulers as you resize the graphic. When you release the mouse button, the image is enlarged.

> **QUICK TIP**
> To verify the size of a graphic or to set precise measurements, double-click the graphic to open the Format Picture dialog box, then adjust the Height and Width settings on the Size tab.

7. **With the graphic still selected, position the pointer over the graphic, when the pointer changes to ✥ drag the graphic down and to the right so it is centered on the page as shown in Figure D-23, release the mouse button, then deselect the graphic**
   The graphic is now centered between the two columns of text.
8. **Click the Zoom list arrow, then click Two Pages**
   The completed pages 1 and 2 are displayed, as shown in Figure D-24.

> **TROUBLE**
> If page 3 is a blank page or contains text continued from page 2, reduce the size of the graphic on page 2.

9. **Click the Zoom list arrow, click Page Width, press [Ctrl][End], press [Enter] twice, type your name, save your changes, print the document, then close the document and exit Word**

FIGURE D-22: Clip Art task pane

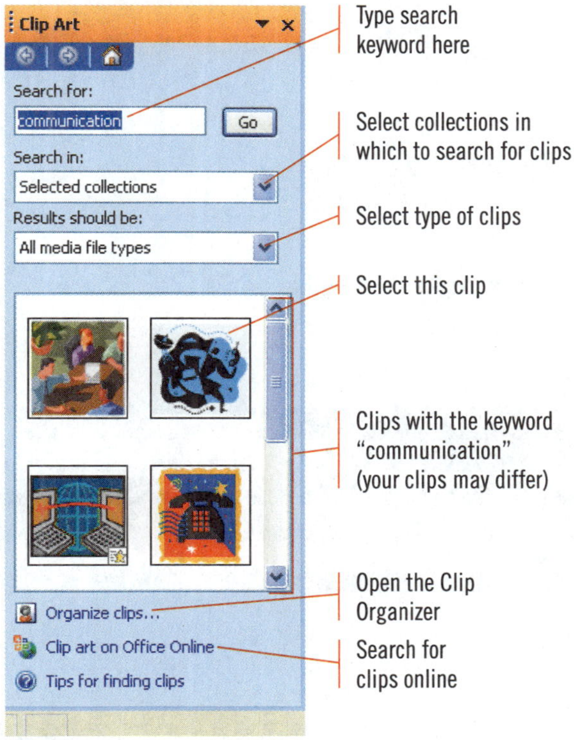

FIGURE D-23: Graphic being moved to a new location

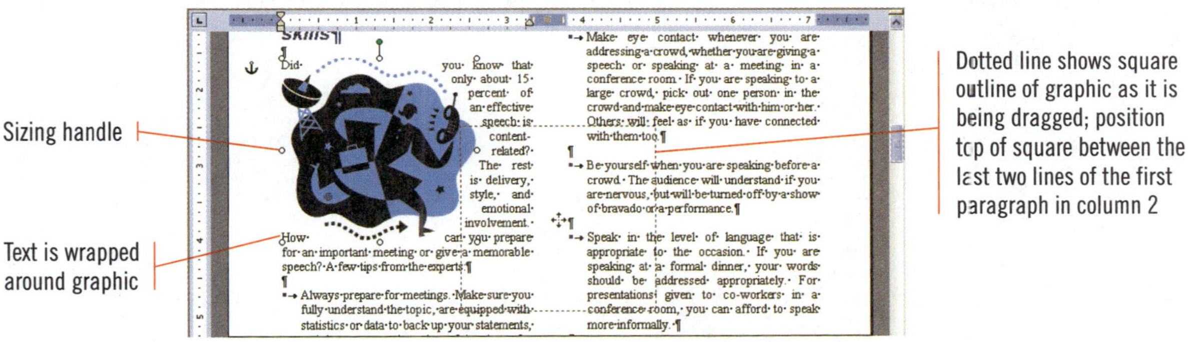

FIGURE D-24: Completed pages 1 and 2 of newsletter

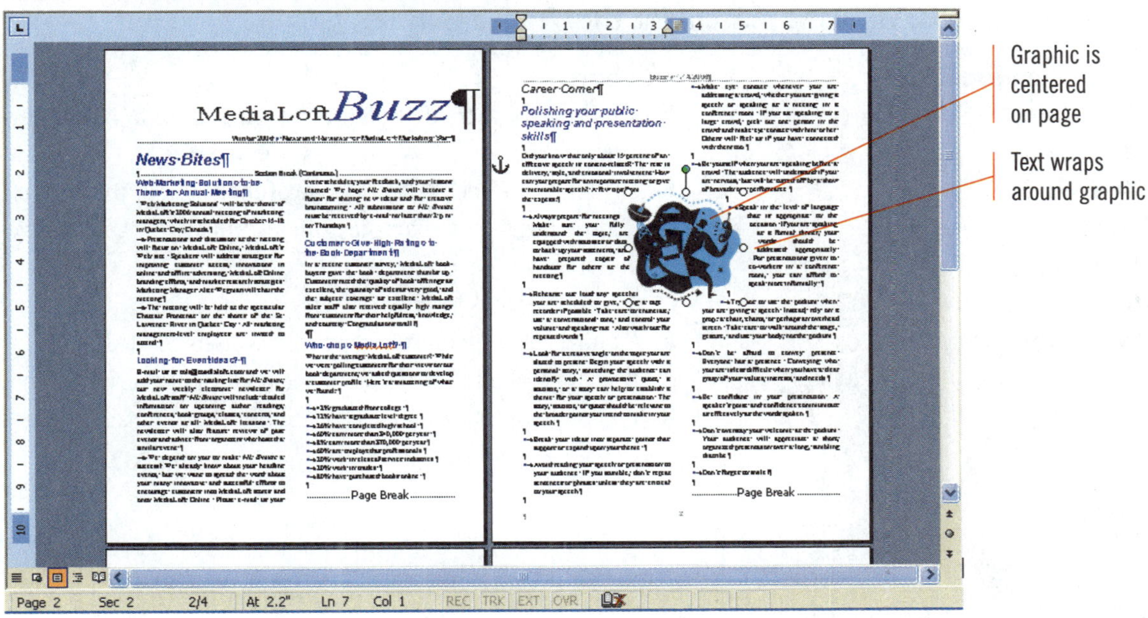

Practice

▼ CONCEPTS REVIEW

Label each element shown in Figure D-25.

FIGURE D-25

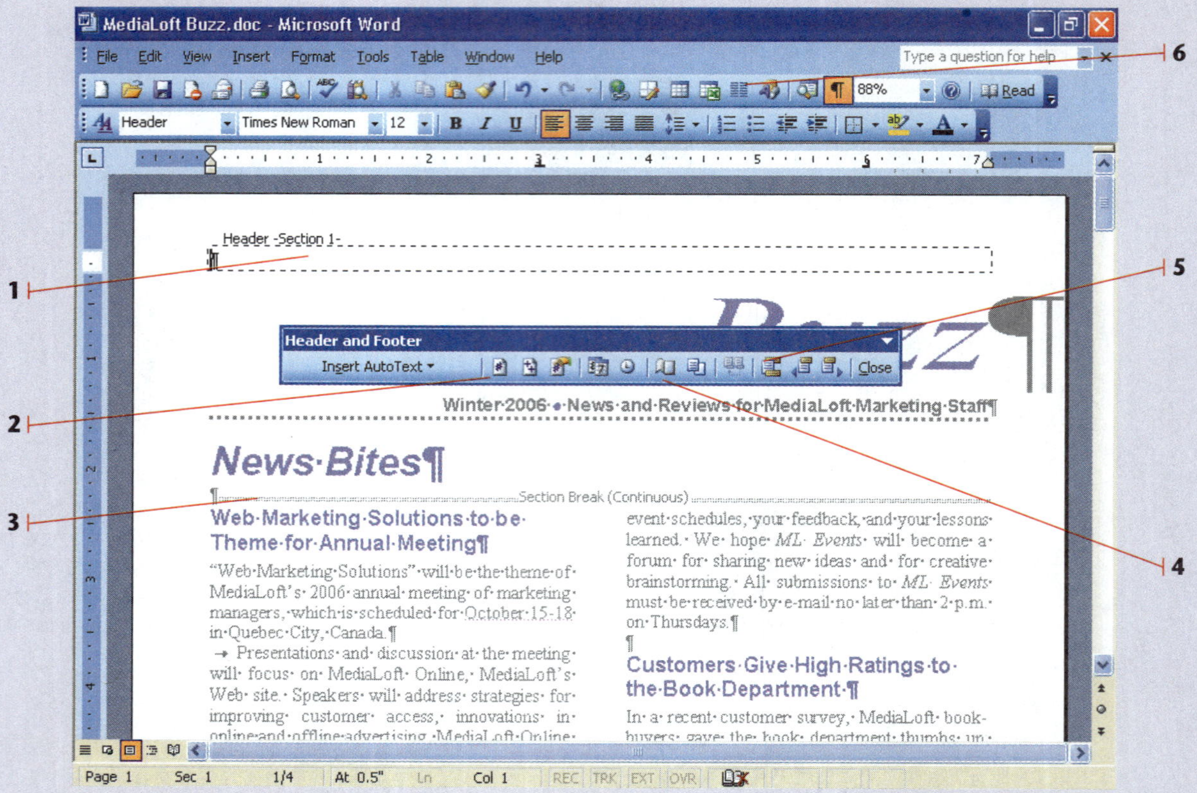

Match each term with the statement that best describes it.

7. **Section break**
8. **Header**
9. **Footer**
10. **Field**
11. **Manual page break**
12. **Margin**
13. **Inline graphic**
14. **Floating graphic**

- **a.** A placeholder for information that changes
- **b.** A formatting mark that divides a document into parts that can be formatted differently
- **c.** The blank area between the edge of the text and the edge of the page
- **d.** A formatting mark that forces the text following the mark to begin at the top of the next page
- **e.** An image that is inserted as part of a line of text
- **f.** An image to which text wrapping has been applied
- **g.** Text or graphics that appear at the bottom of every page in a document
- **h.** Text or graphics that appear at the top of every page in a document

Select the best answer from the list of choices.

15. Which of the following do documents with mirror margins always have?

a. Inside and outside margins
b. Different first page headers and footers
c. Gutters
d. Landscape orientation

16. Which button is used to insert a field into a header or footer?

a. 
b. 
c. 
d. 

17. Which type of break do you insert if you want to force text to begin on the next page?

a. Text wrapping break
b. Manual page break
c. Automatic page break
d. Continuous section break

18. Which type of break do you insert if you want to balance the columns in a section?

a. Text wrapping break
b. Column break
c. Continuous section break
d. Automatic page break

19. What must you do to change an inline graphic to a floating graphic?

a. Move the graphic
b. Resize the graphic
c. Anchor the graphic
d. Apply text wrapping to the graphic

20. Pressing [Ctrl][Enter] does which of the following?

a. Inserts a manual page break
b. Moves the insertion point to the beginning of the document
c. Inserts a continuous section break
d. Inserts an automatic page break

▼ SKILLS REVIEW

1. Set document margins.

a. Start Word, open the file WD D-2.doc from the drive and folder where your Data Files are located, then save it as **Happy Valley Fitness**.
b. Change the top and bottom margins to 1.2" and the left and right margins to 1".
c. Save your changes to the document.

2. Divide a document into sections.

a. Hide the white space in the document by moving the pointer to the top of a page, then clicking the Hide White Space pointer that appears.
b. Scroll down, then insert a continuous section break before the **Facilities** heading.
c. Format the text in section 2 in two columns, then save your changes to the document.

3. Insert page breaks.

a. Insert a manual page break before the heading **Welcome to the Happy Valley Fitness Center!**.
b. Scroll down and insert a manual page break before the heading **Services**.
c. Scroll down and insert a manual page break before the heading **Membership**.
d. Show the white space in the document by moving the pointer over the thick black line that separates the pages, then clicking the Show White Space pointer that appears.
e. Press [Ctrl][Home], then save your changes to the document.

4. Insert page numbers.

a. Insert page numbers in the document. Center the page numbers at the bottom of the page.
b. View the page numbers on each page in Print Preview, close Print Preview, then save your changes to the document.

▼ SKILLS REVIEW (CONTINUED)

5. **Add headers and footers.**
   a. Change the view to Page Width, then open the Header and Footer areas.
   b. Type your name in the Header area, press [Tab] twice, then use the Insert Date button on the Header and Footer toolbar to insert the current date.
   c. On the horizontal ruler, drag the right tab stop from the 6" mark to the 6½" mark so that the date aligns with the right margin of the document.
   d. Move the insertion point to the Footer area.
   e. Double-click the page number to select it, then format the page number in bold italic.
   f. Close headers and footers, preview the header and footer on each page in Print Preview, close Print Preview, then save your changes to the document.
6. **Edit headers and footers.**
   a. Open headers and footers, then apply italic to the text in the header.
   b. Move the insertion point to the Footer area, double-click the page number to select it, then press [Delete].
   c. Click the Align Right button on the Formatting toolbar.
   d. Use the Symbol command on the Insert menu to open the Symbol dialog box.
   e. Insert a black right-pointing triangle symbol (character code: 25BA), then close the Symbol dialog box.
   f. Use the Insert Page Number button on the Header and Footer toolbar to insert a page number.
   g. Use the Page Setup button on the Header and Footer toolbar to open the Page Setup dialog box.
   h. Use the Layout tab to create a different header and footer for the first page of the document.
   i. Scroll to the beginning of the document, type your name in the First Page Header area, then apply italic to your name.
   j. Close headers and footers, preview the header and footer on each page in Print Preview, close Print Preview, then save your changes to the document.
7. **Format columns.**
   a. On page 2, select **Facilities** and the paragraph mark below it, use the Columns button to format the selected text as one column, then center **Facilities** on the page.
   b. Balance the columns on page 2 by inserting a continuous section break at the bottom of the second column.
   c. On page 3, select **Services** and the paragraph mark below it, format the selected text as one column, then center the text.
   d. Balance the columns on page 3.
   e. On page 4, select **Membership** and the paragraph mark below it, format the selected text as one column, then center the text.
   f. Insert a column break before the **Membership Cards** heading, press [Ctrl][Home], then save your changes to the document.
8. **Insert a table.**
   a. Click the Document Map button on the Standard toolbar to open the Document Map.
   b. In the Document Map, click the heading Membership Rates, then close the Document Map. (*Hint*: The Document Map button is a toggle button.)
   c. Select the word Table at the end of the Membership Rates section, press [Delete], then open the Insert Table dialog box.
   d. Create a table with two columns and five rows, open the AutoFormat dialog box, and then apply the Table Classic 3 style to the table, clearing the Last row check box. Close the dialog box.
   e. Press [Tab] to leave the first cell in the header row blank, then type **Rate**.
   f. Press [Tab], then type the following text in the table, pressing [Tab] to move from cell to cell.

Enrollment/Individual	**$100**
Enrollment/Couple	**$150**
Monthly membership/Individual	**$35**
Monthly membership/Couple	**$60**

g. With the insertion point in the table, right-click the table, point to AutoFit on the shortcut menu, then click AutoFit to Contents.
h. With the insertion point in the table, right-click again, point to AutoFit, then click AutoFit to Window.
i. Save your changes to the document.

9. Insert WordArt.

a. Scroll to page 3, place the insertion point before the **Personal Training** heading, then insert a WordArt object.
b. Select any horizontal WordArt style, type **Get Fit!**, then click OK.
c. Click the WordArt object to select it, click the Text Wrapping button on the WordArt toolbar, then apply the Tight text-wrapping style to the object so that it is a floating object.
d. Move the object so that it is centered below the text at the bottom of the page (below the page break mark).
e. Adjust the size and position of the object so that the page looks attractive. (*Hint*: The sizing handles on floating objects are white circles.)
f. Apply a different WordArt shape to the object, preview the page, adjust the size and position if necessary, then save your changes to the document.

10. Insert clip art.

a. On page 1, place the insertion point in the second blank paragraph below **A Rehabilitation and Exercise Facility**. (*Hint*: Place the insertion point to the left of the paragraph mark.)
b. Open the Clip Art task pane. Search for clips related to the keyword **fitness**.
c. Insert the clip shown in Figure D-26. (*Note*: An active Internet connection is needed to select the clip shown in the figure. Select a different clip if this one is not available to you. If you are working offline, you might need to search using a keyword such as sports.)
d. Select the graphic, then drag the lower-right sizing handle down and to the right so that the graphic is about 2.5" wide and 3" tall. Size the graphic so that all the text and the manual page break fit on page 1. (*Hint*: The sizing handles on inline graphics are black squares.)
e. Save your changes to the document. Preview the document, print a copy, then close the document and exit Word.

FIGURE D-26

Word 2003

▼ INDEPENDENT CHALLENGE 1

You are the owner of a small business in Latona, Ontario, called Small World Catering. You have begun work on the text for a brochure advertising your business and are now ready to lay out the pages and prepare the final copy. The brochure will be printed on both sides of an 8½" × 11" sheet of paper, and folded in thirds.

- **a.** Start Word, open the file WD D-3.doc from the drive and folder where your Data Files are located, then save it as **Small World**. Read the document to get a feel for its contents.
- **b.** Change the page orientation to landscape, and change all four margins to .6".
- **c.** Format the document in three columns of equal width.
- **d.** Insert a manual page break before the heading **Catering Services**.
- **e.** On page 1, insert column breaks before the headings **Sample Indian Banquet Menu** and **Sample Tuscan Banquet Menu**.
- **f.** On page 1, insert a continuous section break at the end of the third column to create separate sections on pages one and two.
- **g.** Add lines between the columns on the first page, then center the text in the columns.
- **h.** Create a different header and footer for the first page. Type **Call for custom menus designed to your taste and budget** in the First Page Footer area.
- **i.** Center the text in the footer area, format it in 20-point Comic Sans MS, all caps, with a violet font color, then close headers and footers.
- **j.** On page 2, insert a column break before Your Name. Press [Enter] as many times as necessary to move the contact information to the bottom of the second column. Be sure all five lines of the contact information are in column 2 and do not flow to the next column.
- **k.** Replace Your Name with your name, then center the contact information in the column.
- **l.** Insert a column break at the bottom of the second column. Then, type the text shown in Figure D-27 in the third column. Refer to the figure as you follow the instructions for formatting the text in the third column.
- **m.** Use the Font dialog box to format Small World Catering in 32-point Comic Sans MS, bold, with a violet font color.
- **n.** Format the remaining text in 12-point Comic Sans MS, with a violet font color. Center the text in the third column.
- **o.** Insert the clip art graphic shown in Figure D-27 or another appropriate clip art graphic. Do not wrap text around the graphic.
- **p.** Resize the graphic and add and remove blank paragraphs in the third column of your brochure so that the spacing between elements roughly matches the spacing shown in Figure D-27.

FIGURE D-27

Advanced Challenge Exercise

- Format Small World as a WordArt object using a WordArt style and shape of your choice.
- Format Catering as a WordArt object using a WordArt style and shape of your choice.
- Adjust the size, position, and spacing of the WordArt objects, clip art graphic, and text in the third column so that the brochure is attractive and eye-catching.

- **q.** Save your changes, preview the brochure in Print Preview, then print a copy. If possible, print the two pages of the brochure back to back so that the brochure can be folded in thirds.
- **r.** Close the document and exit Word.

▼ INDEPENDENT CHALLENGE 2

You work in the Campus Safety Department at Hudson State College. You have written the text for an informational flyer about parking regulations on campus and now you need to format the flyer so it is attractive and readable.

- **a.** Start Word, open the file WD D-4.doc from the drive and folder where your Data Files are located, then save it as **Hudson Parking FAQ**. Read the document to get a feel for its contents.
- **b.** Change all four margins to .7".
- **c.** Insert a continuous section break before **1. May I bring a car to school?** (*Hint*: Place the insertion point before May.)
- **d.** Scroll down and insert a next page section break before **Sample Parking Permit**.
- **e.** Format the section 2 text in three columns of equal width with .3" of space between the columns.
- **f.** Hyphenate the document using the automatic hyphenation feature. (*Hint*: If the Hyphenation feature is not installed on your computer, skip this step.)
- **g.** Add a 3-point dotted-line bottom border to the blank paragraph under Hudson State College. (*Hint*: Place the insertion point before the paragraph mark under Hudson State College, then apply a bottom border to the paragraph.)
- **h.** Add your name to the header. Right-align your name and format it in 10-point Arial.
- **i.** Add the following text to the footer, inserting symbols between words as indicated: **Parking and Shuttle Service Office • 54 Buckley Street • Hudson State College • 942-555-2227**.
- **j.** Format the footer text in 9-point Arial Black and center it in the footer. Use a different font if Arial Black is not available to you. If necessary, adjust the font and font size so that the entire address fits on one line.
- **k.** Apply a 3-point dotted-line border above the footer text. Make sure to apply the border to the paragraph.
- **l.** Balance the columns in section 2.
- **m.** Add the clip art graphic shown in Figure D-28 or another appropriate clip art graphic to the upper-right corner of the document, above the border. Make sure the graphic does not obscure the border. (*Hint*: Apply text wrapping to the graphic before positioning it.)

FIGURE D-28

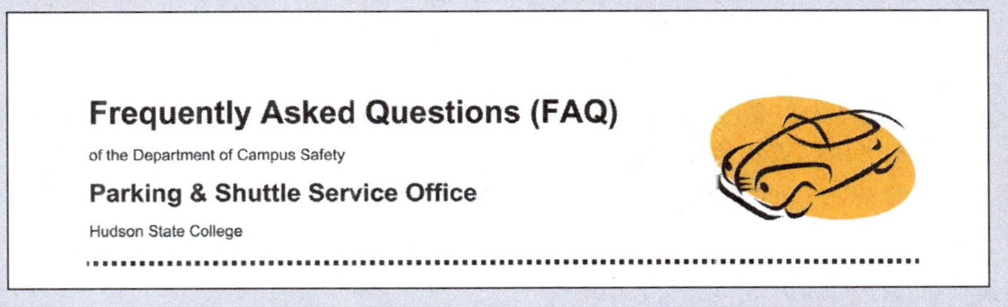

- **n.** Place the insertion point on page 2 (which is section 4). Change the left and right margins in section 4 to 1". Also change the page orientation of section 4 to landscape.
- **o.** Change the vertical alignment of section 4 to Center.
- **p.** Save your changes, preview the flyer in Print Preview, then print a copy. If possible, print the two pages of the flyer back to back.
- **q.** Close the document and exit Word.

▼ INDEPENDENT CHALLENGE 3

A book publisher would like to publish an article you wrote on stormwater pollution in Australia as a chapter in a forthcoming book called *Environmental Issues for the New Millennium*. The publisher has requested that you format your article like a book chapter before submitting it for publication, and has provided you with a style sheet.

- **a.** Start Word, open the file WD D-5.doc from the drive and folder where your Data Files are located, then save it as **Stormwater**.
- **b.** Change the font of the entire document to 11-point Book Antiqua. If this font is not available to you, select a different font suitable for the pages of a book. Change the alignment to justified.
- **c.** Change the paper size to 6" × 9".
- **d.** Create mirror margins. (*Hint*: Use the Multiple Pages list arrow.) Change the top and bottom margins to .8", change the inside margin to .4", change the outside margin to .6", and create a .3" gutter to allow room for the book's binding.
- **e.** Change the Zoom level to Two Pages, then apply the setting to create different headers and footers for odd- and even-numbered pages.
- **f.** Change the Zoom level to Page Width. In the odd-page header, type **Chapter 5**, insert a symbol of your choice, then type **Stormwater Pollution in the Fairy Creek Catchment**.
- **g.** Format the header text in 9-point Book Antiqua italic, then right-align the text.
- **h.** In the even-page header, type your name, insert a symbol of your choice, then insert the current date. (*Hint*: Scroll down or use the Show Next button to move the insertion point to the even-page header.)
- **i.** Change the format of the date to include just the month and the year. (*Hint*: Right-click the date field, then click Edit Field.)
- **j.** Format the header text in 9-point Book Antiqua italic. The even-page header should be left-aligned.
- **k.** Insert page numbers that are centered in the footer. Format the page number in 10-point Book Antiqua. Make sure to insert a page number field in both the odd- and even-page footer areas.
- **l.** Format the page numbers so that the first page of your chapter, which is Chapter 5 in the book, begins on page 53. (*Hint*: Select a page number field, then use the Format Page Number button.)
- **m.** Go to the beginning of the document, press [Enter] 10 times, type **Chapter 5: Stormwater Pollution in the Fairy Creek Catchment**, press [Enter] twice, type your name, then press [Enter] twice.
- **n.** Format the chapter title in 16-point Book Antiqua bold, format your name in 14-point Book Antiqua using small caps, then left-align the title text and your name.

Advanced Challenge Exercise

- Use the Browse by Object feature to move the insertion point to page 4 in the document, scroll down, place the insertion point at the end of the paragraph above the Potential health effects... heading, press [Enter] twice, type **Table 1: Total annual pollutant loads per year in the Fairy Creek Catchment**, format the text as bold, then press [Enter] twice.
- Insert a table with four columns and four rows that is formatted in the Table Professional style.
- Type the text shown in Figure D-29 in the table. Do not be concerned when the text wraps to the next line in a cell.
- Format the text as bold in the header row, then remove the bold formatting from the text in the remaining rows.
- Place the insertion point in the table, point to AutoFit on the Table menu, click Distribute Rows Evenly, point to AutoFit on the Table menu a second time, then click AutoFit to Contents.

FIGURE D-29

Area	Nitrogen	Phosphorus	Suspended solids
Fairy Creek	9.3 tonnes	1.2 tonnes	756.4 tonnes
Durras Arm	6.2 tonnes	.9 tonnes	348.2 tonnes
Cabbage Tree Creek	9.8 tonnes	2.3 tonnes	485.7 tonnes

- **o.** Save your changes, preview the chapter in Print Preview, print the first four pages of the chapter, then close the document and exit Word.

▼ INDEPENDENT CHALLENGE 4

One of the most common opportunities to use the page layout features of Word is when formatting a research paper. The format recommended by the *MLA Handbook for Writers of Research Papers*, a style guide that includes information on preparing, writing, and formatting research papers, is the standard format used by many schools, colleges, and universities. In this independent challenge, you will research the MLA (Modern Language Association) guidelines for formatting a research paper and use the guidelines you find to prepare a sample first page of a research report.

a. Start Word, open the file WD D-6.doc from the drive and folder where your Data Files are located, then save it as **MLA Style**. This document contains the questions you will answer about MLA style guidelines.

b. Use your favorite search engine to search the Web for information on the MLA guidelines for formatting a research report. Use the keywords **MLA Style** and **research paper format** to conduct your search.

c. Look for information on the proper formatting for the following aspects of a research paper: paper size, margins, title page or first page of the report, line spacing, paragraph indentation, page numbers, and works cited.

d. Type your answers to the questions in the MLA Style document, save it, print a copy, then close the document.

e. Using the information you learned, start a new document and create a sample first page of a research report. Use **MLA Format for Research Papers** as the title for your sample report, and make up information about the course and instructor, if necessary. For the body of the report, type several sentences about MLA style. Make sure to format the page exactly as the MLA style dictates.

f. Save the document as **MLA Sample Format** to the drive and folder where your Data Files are located, print a copy, close the document, then exit Word.

▼ VISUAL WORKSHOP

Use the file WD D-7.doc, found on the drive and folder where your Data Files are located, to create the article shown in Figure D-30. (*Hint*: Change all four margins to .6". To locate the flower clip art image, search using the keyword **flower**, and be sure only the Photographs check box in the Results should be in list box in the Clip Art task pane has a check mark. Select a different clip if the clip shown in the figure is not available to you.) Save the document with the filename **Gardener's Corner**, then print a copy.

FIGURE D-30

GARDENER'S CORNER

Putting a Perennial Garden to Bed

By Your Name

A certain sense of peace descends when a perennial garden is put to bed for the season. The plants are safely tucked in against the elements, and the garden is ready to welcome the first signs of life. When the work is done, you can sit back and anticipate the bright blooms of spring. Many gardeners are uncertain of how to close a perennial garden. This week's column demystifies the process.

Clean up

Garden clean up can be a gradual process—plants will deteriorate at different rates, allowing you to do a little bit each week.

1. Edge beds and borders and remove stakes and other plant supports.
2. Dig and divide irises, daylilies, and other early bloomers.
3. Cut back plants when foliage starts to deteriorate.
4. Rake all debris out of the garden and pull any weeds that remain.

Plant perennials

Fall is the perfect time to plant perennials! The warm, sunny days and cool nights provide optimal conditions for new root growth.

1. Dig deeply and enhance soil with organic matter.
2. Use a good starter fertilizer to speed up new root growth.
3. Untangle the roots of new plants before planting them.
4. Water deeply after planting as the weather dictates.

Add compost

Organic matter is the key ingredient to healthy soil. If you take care of the soil, your plants will become strong and disease resistant.

1. Use an iron rake to loosen the top few inches of soil.
2. Spread a one to two inch layer of compost over the entire garden.
3. Refrain from stepping on the area and compacting the soil.

To mulch or not to mulch?

Winter protection for perennial beds can only help plants survive the winter. Here's what works and what doesn't:

1. Always apply mulch after the ground is frozen.
2. Never apply generic hay because is contains billions of weed seeds. Also, whole leaves and bark mulch hold too much moisture.
3. Straw and salt marsh hay are excellent choices for mulch.

For copies of earlier Gardener's Corner columns, call 1-800-555-3827.

Glossary

A

Alignment The position of text in a document relative to the margins.

Application *See* Program.

AutoComplete A feature that automatically suggests text to insert.

AutoCorrect A feature that automatically detects and corrects typing errors, minor spelling errors, and capitalization, and inserts certain typographical symbols as you type.

Automatic page break A page break that is inserted automatically at the bottom of a page.

AutoText A feature that stores frequently used text and graphics so they can be easily inserted into a document.

B

Bold Formatting applied to text to make it thicker and darker.

Border A line that can be added above, below, or to the sides of a paragraph, text, or table cell; a line that divides the columns and rows of a table.

Bullet A small graphic symbol used to identify items in a list.

C

Cell The box formed by the intersection of a table row and table column.

Center Alignment in which an item is centered between the margins.

Character spacing Formatting that changes the width or scale of characters, expands or condenses the amount of space between characters, raises or lowers characters relative to the line of text, and adjusts kerning (the space between standard combinations of letters).

Character style A named set of character format settings that can be applied to text to format it all at once.

Click and Type A feature that allows you to automatically apply the necessary paragraph formatting to a table, graphic, or text when you insert the item in a blank area of a document in Print Layout or Web Layout view.

Click and type pointer A pointer used to move the insertion point and automatically apply the paragraph formatting necessary to insert text at that location in the document.

Clip A media file, such as a graphic, photograph, sound, movie, or animation, that can be inserted into a document.

Clip art A collection of graphic images that can be inserted into documents, presentations, Web pages, spreadsheets, and other Office files.

Clip Organizer A library of the clips that come with Word.

Clipboard A temporary storage area for items that are cut or copied from any Office file and are available for pasting. *See* Office Clipboard and System Clipboard.

Column break A break that forces text following the break to begin at the top of the next column.

Copy To place a copy of an item on the Clipboard without removing it from a document.

Cut To remove an item from a document and place it on the Clipboard.

Cut and paste To move text or graphics using the Cut and Paste commands.

D

Delete To permanently remove an item from a document.

Document The electronic file you create using Word.

Document properties Details about a file, such as author name or the date the file was created, that are used to organize and search for files.

Document window The workspace in the program window that displays the current document.

Drag and drop To move text or a graphic by dragging it to a new location using the mouse.

Drop cap A large dropped initial capital letter that is often used to set off the first paragraph of an article.

F

Field A code that serves as a placeholder for data that changes in a document, such as a page number.

File An electronic collection of information that has a unique name, distinguishing it from other files.

Filename The name given to a document when it is saved.

First line indent A type of indent in which the first line of a paragraph is indented more than the subsequent lines.

Floating graphic A graphic to which text wrapping has been applied, making the graphic independent of text and able to be moved anywhere on a page.

Font The typeface or design of a set of characters (letters, numbers, symbols, and punctuation marks).

Font effect Font formatting that applies a special effect to text, such as a shadow, an outline, small caps, or superscript.

Font size The size of characters, measured in points (pts).

Footer Information, such as text, a page number, or a graphic, that appears at the bottom of every page in a document or a section.

Format Painter A feature used to copy the format settings applied to the selected text to other text you want to format the same way.

Formatting marks Nonprinting characters that appear on screen to indicate the ends of paragraphs, tabs, and other formatting elements.

Formatting toolbar A toolbar that contains buttons for frequently used formatting commands.

Full screen view A view that shows only the document window on screen.

Getting Started task pane A task pane that contains shortcuts for opening documents, for creating new documents, and for accessing information on the Microsoft Web site.

Gutter Extra space left for a binding at the top, left, or inside margin of a document.

Hanging indent A type of indent in which the second and subsequent lines of a paragraph are indented more than the first.

Hard page break *See* Manual page break.

Header Information, such as text, a page number, or a graphic, that appears at the top of every page in a document or a section.

Highlighting Transparent color that can be applied to text to call attention to it.

Horizontal ruler A ruler that appears at the top of the document window in Print Layout, Normal, and Web Layout view.

Hyperlink Text or a graphic that opens a file, Web page, or other item when clicked. Also known as a link.

I-beam pointer The pointer used to move the insertion point and select text.

Indent The space between the edge of a line of text or a paragraph and the margin.

Indent marker A marker on the horizontal ruler that shows the indent settings for the active paragraph.

Inline graphic A graphic that is part of a line of text.

Insertion point The blinking vertical line that shows where text will appear when you type in a document.

Italic Formatting applied to text to make the characters slant to the right.

Justify Alignment in which an item is flush with both the left and right margins.

Keyboard shortcut A combination of keys or a function key that can be pressed to perform a command.

Landscape orientation Page orientation in which the page is wider than it is tall.

Left-align Alignment in which the item is flush with the left margin.

Left indent A type of indent in which the left edge of a paragraph is moved in from the left margin.

Line spacing The amount of space between lines of text.

List style A named set of format settings, such as indents and outline numbering, that can be applied to a list to format it all at once.

Manual page break A page break inserted to force the text following the break to begin at the top of the next page.

Margin The blank area between the edge of the text and the edge of a page.

Menu bar The bar beneath the title bar that contains the names of menus; clicking a menu name opens a menu of program commands.

Mirror margins Margins used in documents with facing pages, where the inside and outside margins are mirror images of each other.

Negative indent A type of indent in which the left edge of a paragraph is moved to the left of the left margin.

Normal view A view that shows a document without margins, headers and footers, or graphics.

Office Assistant An animated character that offers tips and provides access to the program's Help system.

Office Clipboard A temporary storage area shared by all Office programs that can be used to cut, copy and paste multiple items within and between Office programs. The Office Clipboard can hold up to 24 items collected from any Office program. *See* System Clipboard.

Open To use one of the methods for opening a document to retrieve it and display it in the document window.

Outdent *See* Negative indent.

Outline view A view that shows the headings of a document organized as an outline.

Overtype mode A feature that allows you to overwrite existing text as you type.

Paragraph spacing The amount of space between paragraphs.

Paragraph style A named set of paragraph and character format settings that can be applied to a paragraph to format it all at once.

Paste To insert items stored on the Clipboard into a document.

Point The unit of measurement for text characters and the space between paragraphs and characters; 1/72 of an inch.

Portrait orientation Page orientation in which the page is taller than it is wide.

Print Layout view A view that shows a document as it will look on a printed page.

Print Preview A view of a file as it will appear when printed.

Program Task-oriented software (such as Excel or Word) that enables you to perform a certain type of task such as data calculation or word processing.

Reading Layout view A view that shows a document so that it is easy to read and annotate.

Right-align Alignment in which an item is flush with the right margin.

Right indent A type of indent in which the right edge of a paragraph is moved in from the right margin.

Sans serif font A font (such as Arial) whose characters do not include serifs, which are small strokes at the ends of letters.

Save To store a file permanently on a disk or to overwrite the copy of a file that is stored on a disk with the changes made to the file.

Save As Command used to save a file for the first time or to create a new file with a different filename, leaving the original file intact.

ScreenTip A label that appears on the screen to identify a button or to provide information about a feature.

Scroll To use the scroll bars or the arrow keys to display different parts of a document in the document window.

Scroll arrows The arrows at the ends of the scroll bars that are clicked to scroll a document one line at a time.

Scroll bars The bars on the right edge (vertical scroll bar) and bottom edge (horizontal scroll bar) of the document window that are used to display different parts of the document in the document window.

Scroll box The box in the scroll bars that can be dragged to scroll a document.

Section A portion of a document that is separated from the rest of the document by section breaks.

Section break A formatting mark inserted to divide a document into sections.

Select To click or highlight an item in order to perform some action on it.

Serif font A font (such as Times New Roman) whose characters include serifs, which are small strokes at the ends of letters.

Shading A background color or pattern that can be applied to text, tables, or graphics.

Shortcut key *See* Keyboard shortcut.

Sizing handles The black squares or white circles that appear around a graphic when it is selected; used to change the size or shape of a graphic.

Smart tag A purple dotted line that appears under text that Word identifies as a date, name, address, or place.

Smart Tag Actions button The button that appears when you point to a smart tag.

Soft page break *See* Automatic page break.

Standard toolbar A toolbar that contains buttons for frequently used operating and editing commands.

Status bar The bar at the bottom of the Word program window that shows the vertical position, section, and page number of the insertion point, the total number of pages in a document, and the on/off status of several Word features.

Style A named collection of character and paragraph formats that are stored together and can be applied to text to format it quickly.

Subscript A font effect in which text is formatted in a smaller font size and placed below the line of text.

Superscript A font effect in which text is formatted in a smaller font size and placed above the line of text.

Symbols Special characters that can be inserted into a document using the Symbol command.

System Clipboard A clipboard that stores only the last item cut or copied from a document. *See* Clipboard and Office Clipboard.

Tab *See* Tab stop.

Tab leaders Lines that appear in front of tabbed text.

Tab stop A location on the horizontal ruler that indicates where to align text.

Table A grid made up of rows and columns of cells that you can fill with text and graphics.

Table style A named set of table format settings that can be applied to a table to format it all at once.

Task pane An area of the Word program window that contains shortcuts to Word formatting, editing, research, Help, clip art, mail merge, and other features.

Template A formatted document that contains placeholder text you can replace with your own text.

Title bar The bar at the top of the program window that indicates the program name and the name of the current file.

Toggle button A button that turns a feature on and off.

Toolbar A bar that contains buttons that you can click to perform commands.

Type a question for help box The list box at the right end of the menu bar that is used to query the Help system.

Undo To reverse a change by using the Undo button or command.

Vertical alignment The position of text in a document relative to the top and bottom margins.

Vertical ruler A ruler that appears on the left side of the document window in Print Layout view.

View A way of displaying a document in the document window; each view provides features useful for editing and formatting different types of documents.

View buttons Buttons to the left of the horizontal scroll bar that are used to change views.

Web Layout view A view that shows a document as it will look when viewed with a Web browser.

Wizard An interactive set of dialog boxes that guides you through a task.

Word processing program A software program that includes tools for entering, editing, and formatting text and graphics.

Word program window The window that contains the Word program elements, including the document window, toolbars, menu bar, and status bar.

WordArt A drawing object that contains text formatted with special shapes, patterns, and orientations.

Word-wrap A feature that automatically moves the insertion point to the next line as you type.

Index

▶U

▶V

▶W

▶X

▶Z